Innovative Technologies for Dependable OTS-Based Critical Systems

Domenico Cotroneo
Editor

Innovative Technologies for Dependable OTS-Based Critical Systems

Challenges and Achievements
of the CRITICAL STEP Project

 Springer

Editor
Domenico Cotroneo
University of Naples Federico II
Naples
Italy

ISBN 978-88-470-5557-5 ISBN 978-88-470-2772-5 (eBook)
DOI 10.1007/978-88-470-2772-5
Springer Milan Heidelberg New York Dordrecht London

Preface

This book collects part of the research results from the Critical Software Technology for an Evolutionary Partnership (CRITICAL STEP, http://www.critical-step.eu/), which is a Marie-Curie Industry-Academia Partnerships and Pathways (IAPP), belonging to call FP7-PEOPLE-2008-IAPP. The project aimed to establish the basis for long-term strategic research collaboration between partners in the growing and challenging domain of software for large-scale Safety-Critical Systems (SCSs), based on the use of Off-The-Shelf (OTS), software components.

I was honored to coordinate this project with four great partners, very active in the research on dependability technologies for critical systems: SESM and Critical Software, from the industrial side, and CINI University of Naples and University of Coimbra, from the academic one. According to the FP7-PEOPLE-2008-IAPP funding schema, partners shared and combined their knowledge and use the existing synergies/complementarities to set long-term strategic bases to deal with the complexity of the next generation SCSs. The project was implemented via secondments and recruitments of 182 RM in total: 72 RM for recruitment of three experienced researchers and 110 RM for secondments of 13 research fellows from the participating organizations. The researchers involved in the Transfer of Knowledge (ToK), program between Industry and Academy have produced excellent results that this book presents. At the end of this experience, I do believe that the Marie-Curie IAPP project has the real potential of boosting the academic/ industry collaborations and, more in general, the skill of European-wide researchers.

This book is written for engineers and researchers working in the field of dependability. It comprises four parts, i.e., V&V Safety Critical Systems, Fault Injection, Security, and Monitoring and Diagnosing, with a total of 12 contributions, written by researchers belonging to the project. Furthermore, the book provides three introductive papers about the research topics of the project.

Beyond the acknowledgments contained in the chapters of this book, I would like to especially thank the European Commission, which has financed the project and, in particular, Lionel Boillot, the project officer, for his continual support and advice. I would also like to thank Francesca Capobianco for her support in the organizational activities for this book.

Domenico Cotroneo

Contents

Introduction to Software Fault Injection

Domenico Cotroneo and Henrique Madeira

Abstract Software fault injection techniques are beginning to gain a strong recognition in critical domains. Their adoption is already recommended in several safety critical standards, such as automotive, avionics, and aerospace systems. This paper aims to provide an overview on software fault injection, suited both for researchers and practitioners in the field. The work presents the fundamental concepts on Software Fault Injection, and then it discusses existing techniques.

Keywords Fault injection · Fault tolerance · Dependability assessment

1 Introduction

In the context of critical scenarios, intense testing activities are of paramount importance to guarantee that new systems and built-in fault-tolerance mechanisms are behaving as expected. Ensuring the system behaves properly in the presence of a fault is a problem that requires something more than traditional testing. *The process of introducing faults in a system in order to assess its behavior and to measure the efficiency (i.e., coverage and latency) of fault tolerance mechanisms is called fault injection.*

D. Cotroneo (✉)
Dipartimento di Informatica e Sistemistica (DIS), Università degli Studi di Napoli
Federico II, Via Claudio 21, 80125 Naples, Italy
e-mail: cotroneo@unina.it

H. Madeira
Department of Informatics Engineering (DEI), Pólo II, Universidade de Coimbra,
3030-290 Coimbra, Portugal
e-mail: henrique@dei.uc.pt

D. Cotroneo (ed.), *Innovative Technologies for Dependable OTS-Based Critical Systems*,
DOI: 10.1007/978-88-470-2772-5_1, © Springer-Verlag Italia 2013

The evolution of fault injection approaches followed the evolution of digital systems. In the beginning, only simple hardware systems were used in the critical application sectors. Thus, first fault injection approaches consisted of injecting physical faults into the target system hardware (e.g., using radiation, pin-level, power supply disturbances, etc), by assuming simple hardware fault models, such as bit-flip or bit stuck-at. The growing complexity of the hardware turned the use of these physical approaches quite difficult or even impossible, and a new family of fault injection approaches based on the runtime emulation of hardware faults through software (Software-Implemented Fault Injection—SWIFI) become quite popular. With the extension of critical systems in other application domains, such as air traffic control, aerospace, and automotive, we witnessed an increasing complexity of the software part of these systems, which became a non-negligible cause of system failures. An example is the first test flight of the Ariane 5 rocket (June 4th 1996), where the vehicle veered off its flight path and exploded less than one minute after take-off, causing a loss of half-billion dollars. The explosion was caused by a wrong data conversion in the software from 64-bit floating point to 16-bit signed integer representation. The bug resulted from the reuse of a software subsystem, without substantial re-testing, from the Ariane 4 mission, which developers assumed to be compatible with the new system [1]. Another software fault provoked, in August 14th 2003, the blackout of the General Electric energy management system, which left 50 million people in the northeastern America without power and cost around 6 billion dollars of financial loss. The bug affected an alarm and logging software system. The failure of the alarm system led to a cascade of computer and equipment failures and to the blackout [2].

SWIFI tools were used to inject errors both in the program state (e.g., data and address registers, stack and heap memory) and in the program code (e.g., in memory areas where code is stored, before or during program execution). Unfortunately, by means of SWIFI is not possible to accurately emulate the effects of real software faults in a complex software-intensive systems. Just to give an idea on the growth of software complexity in the last three decades, size of NASA flight software [3] used in space missions to Mars in terms of Lines of Code (LoCs) increased exponentially from 5 thousands of LoCs (Viking mission, 1975) to 555 thousands of LoCs (Mars Exploration Rover mission, 2004) [3].

The use of fault injection to emulate the effects of real software faults (i.e., bugs), namely Software Fault Injection (SFI), is relatively recent if compared to the first fault injection approaches. In practice, the injection of software faults consists of the introduction of small changes in the target program code, creating different versions of a program (each version has one injected software fault). The use of SFI has been recently recommended by several safety standards, such as the ISO 26262 standard for automotive safety [4], which prescribes the use of error detection and handling mechanisms in software and their verification through fault injection, and the NASA standard 8719.13B for software safety [5], which recommends fault injection to assess system behavior in the presence of faulty off-the-shelf software. Software Fault Injection is a kind of what-if experimentation, and it may originate during any phase of the software development process including requirement analysis, design, and coding activities. The target is exercised with a given workload, and faults are inserted into specific software components of the target system. The main goal is to observe how the system behaves in the presence of the injected faults, considering that these faults reproduce plausible faults that may affect a given software component of the system during operation. SFI is used in several (typically post-development) scenarios: to validate the effectiveness and to quantify the coverage of software fault tolerance, to assess risk, to perform dependability evaluation [6, 7].

2 Background

2.1 Basic Concepts

Throughout this paper we will use the terminology defined in [8]. A *fault* is the adjudged or hypothesized cause of an incorrect system state, which is referred to as *error*. A *failure* is an event that occurs when an incorrect service is delivered, that is, an error state is perceived by users or external systems. Software Fault injection experiments follow the common schema presented in [9], and shown in Fig. 1. The system under analysis is usually named *target*. There are two entities that stimulate the system, respectively the *load generator* and the *injector*. The former exercises the target with inputs that will be processed during a fault injection experiment, whereas the latter introduces a fault in the system. The set of inputs and faults submitted to the system are respectively referred to as *workload* and *faultload*, which are typically specified by the tester through a *library* by enumerating inputs/faults or by specifying the rules for generating them. A fault is injected by tampering with the state of the system or with the environment in which it executes. Fault injection usually involves the execution of several *experiments* or *runs*, which form a *fault injection campaign*, and only one or few faults from the faultload are injected during each experiment.

The *monitor* entity collects from the target raw data (*readouts* or *measurements*) that are needed to evaluate the effects of injected faults. The choice of readouts depends on the kind of system considered and on the properties that have to be evaluated. They may include the outputs of the target (e.g., messages sent to users or to other systems) and the internal state of the target or its parts (e.g., the contents of a specific area of memory). Readouts are used to assess the outcome of the experiment: for instance, the tester can infer whether the injected fault has been tolerated, or the system has failed. In order to obtain information about the outcome of an experiment, readouts are usually compared to the readouts obtained from fault-free experiments (referred to as *golden runs* or *fault-free runs*). All the described entities are orchestrated by the *controller*, which is also responsible for iterating fault injection experiments forming the fault injection campaign as well as for storing the results of each experiment to be used for subsequent analysis.

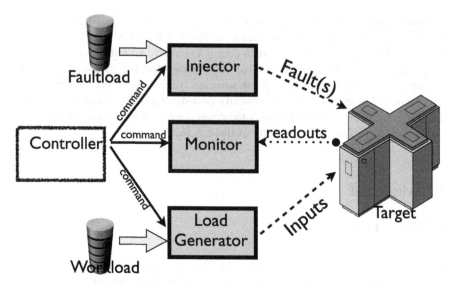

Fig. 1 Conceptual schema of fault injection [9]

Let's now see how to conduct a fault injection experiment. Initially the system is assumed to work in the "Correct" state. As soon as a fault is injected and a workload is applied, two behaviors can be observed. First, the fault is not activated and it remains latent. In this case, after a timeout the experiment runs out and no failure is produced. Second, the fault is activated and it becomes an error. At this stage, an error (i) may propagate, by corrupting other parts of the system state until the system exhibits a failure, (ii) can be latent in the system, and (iii) can be masked in the system due to the presence of redundant entities. On the basis on the collected readouts, the monitor should be able to identify the previous effects as well as the case in which the fault is not activated at all. Unfortunately, only a fraction of fault injection experiments are able to activate faults and to produce a failure; the others are useless since no failure can be observed. This is one of the main reason of why fault injection is felt by industries as a very expensive approach. In order to accelerate the occurrence of failures, a different, and cheaper, form of fault injection can be adopted, namely *error injection*. Here, the *effects* of faults are introduced in place of the actual faults. A well known technique of error injection is the *Software-Implemented Fault Injection* (SWIFI), in which the effect of hardware faults (e.g., CPU or memory faults) are emulated by corrupting the state of the software, instead of physically tampering with hardware devices.

A very important step in a fault injection campaign regards the set of *measures* that are adopted to characterize the behavior of the target system in the presence of faults. Several kinds of measures can be adopted, depending on the fault model and on the kind of target system. More in general, adopted measures in fault injection campaign aim to describe the system from the point of view of its *ability to tolerate faults*. To measure the effectiveness of a fault tolerance mechanism the *coverage factor* has been introduced [10, 11]. It is defined as the *conditional probability* that a fault is correctly handled, given the occurrence of any fault and of any sequence of inputs (i.e., a workload). Deficiencies in fault tolerance result in a coverage factor lesser than 1. They can be due to development faults affecting the design or implementation of fault tolerance algorithms and mechanisms, which cause the lack of *error and fault handling coverage* [12]. Another source of fault tolerance deficiencies is the lack of *fault assumption coverage* [13], that is, incorrect or incomplete assumptions about faults that can occur during operation (e.g., about the behavior of a failed component or the independence between component failures).

The accuracy of results obtained by a Fault Injection campaign is strongly dependent on several key properties of the experiments, namely [10, 14]:

- **Representativeness** refers to the ability of the faultload and the workload to represent the real faults and inputs that the system will experience during operation. Representativeness of faultloads is achieved by defining a realistic fault model, and by accurately reproducing this fault model during an experiment.
- **Non-intrusiveness** requires that the instrumentation adopted in the fault injection process (such as fault insertion and data collection) should not significantly alter the behavior of the actual system. For instance, intrusiveness can be caused by the execution of additional code to corrupt the software state.
- **Repeatability** is the property that guarantees *statistically equivalent* results when a fault injection campaign is executed more than once using the same procedure in the same environment. This property is not trivial to achieve due to the many sources of non-determinism in computer systems, such as thread scheduling and timing of events.
- **Practicability** refers to the effectiveness of fault injection in terms of cost and time. These factors include the time required to implement and setup the fault injection environment, the time to execute the experiments, and the time for the analysis of results. This property requires that experiments are supported by automatic tools, in order to fulfill time and budget constraints.
- **Portability** requires that a fault injection technique or tool is applicable with low effort to different systems, in order to allow their comparison. The portability of a fault injection tool also refers to the ability of the tool to support several fault models and to be extended with new fault models.

2.2 Software Fault Characterization

The injection of software faults requires a precise definition of faults to inject, which in turn requires a clear understanding and characterization of software faults. This is not easy to achieve, since software faults are the due to human mistakes occurring during development, that affect software artifacts in the form of incorrect instructions in the program. Several *fault classification schemas* have been proposed for improving software reliability. Among fault classification schemas, the *Orthogonal Defect Classification* (ODC) [15] is one of the most widely adopted schemas among researchers and practitioners, and has been used in several studies to define fault models for Software Fault Injection. ODC is a framework for classifying software faults with the aim to get measurements and quantitative feedback about the software development process; it generalizes previous classification schemas adopted for OS and DBMS products from IBM [16, 17].

ODC obtains inferences from the analysis of the observed distribution of defects. Differing from reliability growth models, defects are divided among different classes and the per-class distribution along the development process is analyzed. The division among classes is motivated by the finding that there is a cause-effect relationship between the development process phases and the kind of defects found in each phase [17]. ODC proposes a set of *defect types* based on the *defect fix* made by the programmer that corrects the fault (Table 1). The main benefit of this classification is that defect types can be associated with the activities of the different stages of development. For instance, the occurrence of a significant number of Function defects can point out that the development process should be improved in the high-level design phase. Defect types are associated to different process stages (high- and low-level design, coding, documentation, high- and low-level design inspections, code inspections, unit/function/system test), and their distribution measured along stages is exploited to provide feedback on the process. Another benefit of ODC defect types is that they are *orthogonal* (i.e., mutually exclusive), and that they are close to the programmer, since they are based on the *correction* (i.e., *fix*) of the defect: therefore, defects can be easily and unambiguously classified, and measurements lend themselves to quantitative analysis, as confirmed by several pilot projects [15], making ODC also useful for fault injection purposes.

Table 1 ODC defect types

Defect type	Definition
Assignment	Value(s) assigned incorrectly or not assigned at all
Checking	Missing or incorrect validation of parameters or data in conditional statements
Algorithm	Efficiency or correctness problems that affect the task and can be fixed by (re)implementing an algorithm or local data structure without the need for requesting a design change
Timing/ Serialization	Necessary serialization of shared resources is missing, wrong resource has been serialized or wrong serialization technique employed
Interface	Communication problems between users, modules, components or device drivers and software
Function	Affects a sizeable amount of code and refers to capability that is either implemented incorrectly or not implemented at all

3 Application Domains

The main application of fault injection, including Software Fault Injection, is the evaluation and improvement of fault tolerance algorithms and mechanisms, such as assertions and redundant logic that detect an erroneous state, and exception handlers and checkpoint/rollback mechanisms that correct the program state or switch to a degraded mode of service [8]. Fault injection allows to identify issues and to correct the implementation of error detection and recovery mechanisms (*fault removal*), as well as to estimate the effectiveness of fault tolerance that the system will exhibit during operation (*fault forecasting*), in order to obtain confidence that the system will be able to deliver a proper service.

A recent field of application for fault injection is represented by *dependability benchmarking* [18]. A dependability benchmark is a means to characterize and to compare the dependability of a computer component or system in the presence of faults. A key aspect of dependability benchmarking, which makes it different from classical dependability evaluation techniques, is that it represents an *agreement* that is widely accepted both by the computer industry and by the user community. The technical agreement states the measures, the procedure and conditions under which the measures are obtained, and the domain in which these measures are considered valid and meaningful. This agreement requires that the benchmark should specify in detail the procedures and rules to be followed in order to enable users to implement the benchmark for a given system, and to interpret the benchmark results. A general framework for dependability benchmarking has been defined in the context of the DBench European project [19]. This effort was followed by several studies that defined dependability benchmarks for many kind of systems (e.g., OLTP systems, general purpose and real-time operating systems, engine control applications) [18].

There are several emerging domains where SFI is looked as very interesting means. In [20], Software Fault Injection is concerned with the emulation of faults in *software requirements*. Although requirement faults do not directly affect software artifacts, it is recognized that wrong requirements (e.g., incomplete, conflicting, incorrect) have a strong impact on software safety, and that they may cause severe accidents [21]. Software Fault Injection has recently been investigated in the context of *software security*. In this context, SFI emulates *security vulnerabilities* existing in web applications, that is, software defects that may cause unauthorized accesses to confidential data [8]. The injection of vulnerabilities in web applications allows to train security assurance teams that are responsible for code inspection and penetration testing [22], and to evaluate the effectiveness of intrusion detection systems and vulnerability scanners [23]. Finally, Software Fault Injection is currently being investigated in the context of *online failure prediction* in complex software systems. Online failure prediction aims to *anticipate during runtime* the occurrence of failures in the *near term future*, in order to prevent potential accidents and to limit the impact of failures, and can be seen as a *proactive* form of fault tolerance [24]. Prediction is achieved by monitoring and analyzing the current system state in order to spot *symptoms* that a failure is likely to occur soon, such as an anomalous sequence of events or consumption of system resources. Due to the complexity of systems and to the random nature of failures, failure prediction requires the use of *heuristic rules* or *statistical models*, that have to be trained and validated using symptom and failure data. Unfortunately, this kind of data is typically scarce, since failures are rare events and must be collected over a long time. In [25], Software Fault Injection is indicated as a promising approach for accelerating the data collection process by generating realistic failure occurrences, in order to train and to evaluate prediction algorithms.

4 Software Fault Injection Techniques

Many SFI techniques and tools have been developed in more than 20 years. We here illustrate and discuss these efforts, by distinguishing between two fundamental approaches: the injection of faults effects (also referred to as error injection), in which an error is introduced by perturbing the system state, and the injection of actual faults, in which the program code is changed in order to emulate a software fault in the code. The following subsections review Software Fault Injection techniques, respectively: (i) the earliest approaches for "data error injection" that were based on hardware fault injection techniques existing at that time; (ii) approaches for "interface error injection", that aim to test the robustness of components with respect to interactions with other components; (iii) approaches for the injection of actual faults, that introduce small faulty changes in the program code.

4.1 Injection of Data Errors

The early approaches for the injection of fault effects have grown in the context of studies on hardware faults through SWIFI. SWIFI aims at reproducing the effects (i.e., errors) of hardware faults (such as CPU, bus, and memory faults) by perturbing the state of memory or hardware registers through software. SWIFI approaches replace the contents of a memory location or register with a corrupted value, according to the following criteria:

- **What to inject.** The contents of an individual bit, byte, or word in a memory location or register are corrupted. Error types have been defined from the analysis of errors generated by faults at the electrical or gate level. Common error types are the replacement of a bit with a fixed value (*stuck-at-0* and *stuck-at-1* faults) or with its opposite value (*bit flips*).
- **Where to inject.** Errors injected in memory are usually targeted at a subset of locations, due to the large number of memory locations. Injections can be focused

on randomly-selected locations in specific memory areas (e.g., stack, heap, global data) or user-selected locations (e.g., a specific variable in memory). Errors injected in registers can be targeted at those registers that are accessible through software (e.g., data and address registers).

- **When to inject**. The error injection can be *time* or *event* dependent. In the former case, an error is injected after that a given experiment time is elapsed, which is selected by the user or according to a probability distribution. In the latter case, an error is injected when a specific event occurs during execution, such as at the first access or at every access to the target location. Three types of hardware faults can be emulated, respectively *transient* (i.e., occasional), *intermittent* (i.e., recurring several times), and *permanent* faults.

It is worth noting that hardware errors injected by SWIFI tools can be injected both in the program state (e.g., data and address registers, stack and heap memory) and in the program code (e.g., in memory areas where code is stored, before or during program execution). This is an important distinction for Software Fault Injection: corruptions in the program state aim to reflect the *effects* of software faults, i.e., an error caused by the execution of a faulty program, such as a wrong pointer, flag, or control flow, and SWIFI tools can introduce this kind of errors in a straightforward way; instead, corruptions in the program code aim to reflect *actual* software faults in the code, although the adoption of SWIFI tools for this purpose is not trivial. Many tools were proposed for SWIFI. Examples are *FIAT* [26], *ORCHESTRA* [27], NFTAPE [28, 29], *Xception* [30], and GOOFI [31].

4.2 Injection of Interface Errors

The injection of errors at input parameters aims to emulate the effects produced by faults outside the target, including the effects of software faults in external software components, and to evaluate the ability of the target to detect and handle corrupted inputs. In a similar way, the corruption of output values is adopted to emulate the outputs of faulty components, and can be used to assess the impact of faults on the rest of the system.

The corruption of input parameters can reveal deficiencies in the design and implementation of error detection and recovery mechanisms of the target (e.g., input handling code). It is commonly adopted in the context of *robustness testing*, which evaluates "the degree to which a system or component can function correctly in the presence of invalid inputs or stressful environmental conditions" [32]. It should be noted that the objectives of robustness testing and interface error injection are different than functional testing techniques, such as black-box testing: robustness testing aims at assessing the *robust behavior* of a software module in face of invalid inputs (e.g., a process crash is avoided, or a warning signal is produced), and it is not concerned with the *functional correctness* of the target.

Interface error injection can be performed in two ways (Fig. 2). The first approach is based on a *test driver* program that is linked to the target component

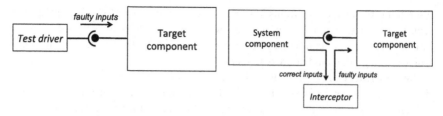

Fig. 2 Approaches for interface error injection

(e.g., a program that uses the API exported by the target), and that exercises it by submitting invalid inputs. This approach resembles unit testing, but in this case robustness, rather than functional correctness, is being evaluated. The second approach consists in intercepting and corrupting the interactions between the target and the rest of the system, i.e., an *interceptor* program is triggered when the target component is invoked, and it modifies the original inputs in order to introduce a corrupted input. In this scenario, the target component is tested in the context of the whole system that integrates the target. This approach resembles SWIFI, since the original data (in this case, interface inputs) flowing through the system is replaced with corrupted data.

In interface error injection experiments, typically only one input parameter and one invocation is corrupted, among the several input parameters and the several invocations of the target API that take place during the experiment. There are three common approaches for generating invalid input values:

- **Fuzzing**: The original value is replaced with a randomly generated value.
- **Bit-flipping**: The corrupted value is generated by inverting the value of one or more bits of the original value.
- **Data-type based injection**: The original value is replaced with an invalid value, which is selected on the basis of the *type* of input parameter being corrupted, where the types are derived from the API exported by the target. This approach defines a pool of invalid values for each data type, which are selected from the analysis of the type domain (e.g., "NULL" in the case of C pointers).

Among many studies on robustness testing, it is worth mentioning the *Ballista* approach [33] for testing and comparing operating systems compliant to the POSIX system call interface [34]. Ballista is a highly scalable approach, as only 20 data types had to be defined to test 233 system calls of the POSIX standard. Data types are used to automatically generate a test driver program for each test case. For each data type, Ballista considers a subset of exceptional values from the data type domain. These values are suggested by the testing literature or selected based on the experience of developers, and represent situations that are likely to be exceptional in some contexts. A robustness testing campaign using Ballista, reported in [33], allowed the comparison of 15 COTS OS. A total of 1,082,541 test cases were automatically executed. Several Abort and Restart failures were observed, along with some Catastrophic failures that affect the system as a whole.

The most prevalent sources of robustness failures were illegal pointer values, numeric overflows, and end-of-file overruns. On the one hand, these results are useful for improving exception handling in OSs; on the other hand, they highlight the importance of robustness testing for complex software, and in particular for COTS components. The Ballista approach was also adopted in subsequent studies on robustness testing of Microsoft Windows OSs and of CORBA ORB implementations [18].

4.3 Injection of Code Changes

The studies discussed in previous subsections emulate software faults by the injection of fault effects (i.e., errors) using SWIFI approaches. An open issue of these approaches is the representativeness of injected errors (e.g., bit-flips), which do not necessarily match errors generated by software faults.

Some experimental evidences of this issue have been provided in [35]. To tackle the issue of representativeness, more recent studies on SFI focused on the injection of faults in the program code (i.e., code changes). This approach is supported by studies on mutation testing, which observed that the injection of code changes can be adopted for emulating real software faults, as injected faults produce errors and failures that are similar to the ones produced by real software faults [36, 37].

The use of SWIFI for injecting code changes (instead of errors) has been studied in [38]. It analyzed whether it is possible to inject faults in a program by applying SWIFI on the code memory area of a process or, equivalently, on the binary executable before running the experiment. To this aim, the study considered a set of programs developed during a programming contest, and that were believed to be correct by the contest judges. The authors identified a set of residual software faults by thoroughly testing these programs. They then tried to emulate these faults by using the Xception SWIFI tool on the PowerPC 601 hardware architecture. This experiment highlighted that SWIFI tools can inject software faults only to a limited extent, and that tools and techniques specifically tailored to Software Fault Injection are required.

The problem of defining a representative fault model, and of accurately injecting faults in the machine (binary) code were investigated in depth in [39], in which the *Generic-Software Fault Injection Technique* (*G-SWFIT*) was proposed. This technique is based on a fault model representative of the most common faults found in the field. The fault model was initially defined based on common C programming bugs from various sources such as programming manuals, best practice tutorials and error reports [40], and later improved in [39]. In [39, 41], it has been shown that programming bugs can be injected through binary code mutations with a good degree of accuracy.

The field data study in [39] looked in detail at the faults in order to achieve a more precise characterization. To this aim, ODC defect types were extended to provide additional details and relate the faults with the *programming language construct* that is either *missing, wrong,* or *extraneous.* This classification is more oriented towards automated fault injection, since it gives an indication on how to manipulate a program in order to introduce a fault (for instance, the construct to be removed in order to inject a *missing* construct fault). The analysis found that the majority of the faults belong to few fault types. Therefore, the study identified a set of fault types to be considered as being representative of faults in the field, based on two criteria: (i) the number of occurrences of the fault type must be at least as high as the average, and (ii) the occurrences should not be restricted to only one or two of the programs. These fault types are also applicable to other procedural programming languages, since they are not tied to specific features of the C language. More recent work enhanced the representativeness of faultloads by improving the selection code locations (i.e., where to inject faults) [42, 43], and by extending fault injection with the ODC Timing/Serialization defect type [44]. Other studies were made to extend this fault model to Java software, such as the one presented in [45].

5 Conclusions

The paper introduced the Software Fault Injection topic, by giving a summary of application domains, techniques and related tools. Some concluding remark are provided in the following. There are peculiarities of discussed fault injection approaches that should be taken into account when selecting an approach to adopt for the system in hand. Error injection is usually adopted for evaluating the robustness of individual components, and to improve error handling of specific parts of the code. The main reason is that the injection of errors allows to perform experiments focused on specific parts of the system, since it can evaluate the effects of errors on a specific component interface or program variable. In fact, error injection does not require to wait that errors are generated and propagated to the specific part of the program state under evaluation. Moreover, since error injection can be applied to individual components, it can be performed at early stages of software verification. The injection of code changes, instead, is aimed at evaluating a fault-tolerant system as a whole, and at performing quantitative evaluations and comparisons between alternative design choices. Code changes are more suitable for these goals since they are based on representative models of software faults and closely emulate the behavior of faulty software. This is an important requirement for quantitative evaluations and comparisons, since they take into account the relative probability of occurrence of faults in order to reflect the behavior that the system will exhibit during operation. This makes the injection of code changes more suitable for the late stages of software verification, when system components have been integrated and developers aim to evaluate the expected fault-tolerance (and derived measures, such as availability) of the system during its operational life. Given these differences, the classes of injection approaches appear to be complementary, rather than alternative.

Acknowledgments Authors would like to thank Dr. Roberto Natella for having supported them in the writing of this paper.

References

1. Weyuker, E.: Testing component-based software: a cautionary tale. IEEE Softw. **15**(5), 54–59 (1998)
2. U.S.-Canada Power System Outage Task Force: Final Report on the August 14, 2003 Blackout in the United States and Canada: Causes and Recommendations. U.S. Energy Department (2004)
3. Dvorak, D.: NASA Study on Flight Software Complexity. NASA Office of Chief Engineer (2009)
4. International Organization for Standardization: Product Development: Software Level. ISO 26262–6 (2012)
5. National Aeronautics and Space Administration: NASA Software Safety Guidebook. NASA-GB-8719.13 (2004)
6. Voas, J., Charron, F., McGraw, G., Miller, K., Friedman, M.: Predicting how badly good software can behave. IEEE Softw. **14**(4), 73–83 (1997)
7. Christmansson, J., Chillarege, R.: Generation of an error set that emulates software faults based on field data. In: Proceedings of Symposium on Fault-Tolerant Computing (1996)
8. Avizienis, A., Laprie, J., Randell, B., Landwehr, C.: Basic concepts and taxonomy of dependable and secure computing. IEEE Trans. Depend. Secure Comput. **1**(1), 11–33 (2004)
9. Hsueh, M., Tsai, T., Iyer, R.: Fault injection techniques and tools. IEEE Comput. **30**(4), 75–82 (1997)
10. Arlat, J., Aguera, M., Amat, L., Crouzet, Y., Fabre, J., Laprie, J., Martins, E., Powell, D.: Fault injection for dependability validation: a methodology and some applications. IEEE Trans. Softw. Eng. **16**(2), 166–182 (1990)
11. Powell, D., Martins, E., Arlat, J., Crouzet, Y.: Estimators for fault tolerance overage evaluation. IEEE Trans. Comput. **44**(2), 261–274 (1995)
12. Bouricius, W., Carter, W., Schneider, P.: Reliability modeling techniques for self-repairing computer systems. In: Proceedings of the 24th ACM National Conference (1969)
13. Powell, D.: Failure mode assumptions and assumption coverage. In: Proceedings of International Symposium on Fault-Tolerant Computing (1992)
14. Bondavalli, A., Ceccarelli, A., Falai, L., Vadursi, M.: Foundations of measurement theory applied to the evaluation of dependability attributes. In: Proceedings of International Conference on Dependable Systems and Networks (2007)
15. Chillarege, R., Bhandari, I., Chaar, J., Halliday, M., Moebus, D., Ray, B., Wong, M.: Orthogonal defect classification—a concept for in-process measurements. IEEE Trans. Softw. Eng. **18**(11), 943–956 (1992)
16. Sullivan, M., Chillarege, R.: Software defects and their impact on system availability: a study of field failures in operating systems. In: Proceedings of International Symposium on Fault-Tolerant Computing (1991)
17. Chillarege, R., Kao, W., Condit, R.: Defect type and its impact on the growth curve. In: Proceedings of 13th International Conference on Software Engineering (1991)
18. Kanoun, K., Spainhower, L.: Dependability Benchmarking for Computer Systems. Wiley-IEEE Computer Society, Hoboken (2008)

19. DBench project: DBench Final Report. http://www.laas.fr/DBench/ (2004)
20. Véras, P., Villani, E., Ambrosio, A., Silva, N., Vieira, M., Madeira, H.: Errors on space software requirements: a field study and application scenarios. In: Proceedings of International Symposium on Software Reliability Engineering (2012)
21. Leveson, N.: Role of software in spacecraft accidents. J. Spacecraft Rockets 41(4), 564–575 (2004)
22. Fonseca, J., Vieira, M., Madeira, H.: Training security assurance teams using vulnerability injection. In: Proceedings of Pacific Rim International Symposium on Dependable Computing (2008)
23. Fonseca, J., Vieira, M., Madeira, H.: Vulnerability& attack injection for web applications. In: Proceedings of International Conference on Dependable Systems and Networks (2009)
24. Salfner, F., Lenk, M., Malek, M.: A survey of online failure prediction methods. ACM Comput. Surv. 42(3), 1–42 (2010)
25. Vieira, M., Madeira, H., Irrera, I., Malek, M.: Fault injection for failure prediction methods validation. In: Proceedings of Workshop on Hot Topics in System Dependability (2009)
26. Barton, J., Czeck, E., Segall, Z., Siewiorek, D.: Fault injection experiments using FIAT. IEEE Trans. Comput. 39(4), 575–582 (1990)
27. Dawson, S., Jahanian, F., Mitton, T., Tung, T.: Testing of Fault-Tolerant and real-time distributed systems via protocol fault injection. In: Proceedings of International Symposium on Fault-Tolerant Computing (1996)
28. Xu, J., Chen, S., Kalbarczyk, Z., Iyer, R.: An experimental study of security vulnerabilities caused by errors. In: Proceedings of International Conference on Dependable Systems and Networks (2001)
29. Bondavalli, A., Chiaradonna, S., Cotroneo, D., Romano, L.: Effective fault treatment for improving the dependability of COTS and legacy-based applications. IEEE Trans. Depend. Secure Comput. 1(4), 223–237 (2004)
30. Carreira, J., Madeira, H., Silva, J.: Xception: a technique for the experimental evaluation of dependability in modern computers. IEEE Trans. Softw. Eng. 24(2), 125–136 (1998)
31. Aidemark, J., Vinter, J., Folkesson, P., Karlsson, J.: GOOFI: generic object-oriented fault injection tool. In: Proceedings of International Conference on Dependable Systems and Networks (2001)
32. IEEE: IEEE Standard Glossary of Software Engineering Terminology. IEEE Std 610.12-1990 (1990)
33. Koopman, P., DeVale, J.: The exception handling effectiveness of POSIX operating systems. IEEE Trans. Softw. Eng. 26(9), 837–848 (2000)
34. IEEE: IEEE Standard for Information Technology—Portable Operating System Interface (POSIX) Part 1. IEEE Std 1003.1b-1993 (1994)
35. Jarboui, T., Arlat, J., Crouzet, Y., Kanoun, K., Marteau, T.: Analysis of the effects of real and injected software faults: Linux as a case study. In: Proceedings of Pacific Rim International Symposium on Dependable Computing (2002)
36. Daran, M., Thévenod-Fosse, P.: Software error analysis: a real case study involving real faults and mutations. ACM Softw. Eng. Notes 21(3), 158–171 (1996)
37. Andrews, J., Briand, L., Labiche, Y.: Is mutation an appropriate tool for testing experiments? In: Proceedings of International Conference on Software Engineering (2005)
38. Madeira, H., Costa, D., Vieira, M.: On the emulation of software faults by software fault injection. In: Proceedings of International Conference on Dependable Systems and Networks (2000)
39. Duraes, J., Madeira, H.: Emulation of software faults: a field data study and a practical approach. IEEE Trans. Softw. Eng. 32(11), 849–867 (2006)
40. Duraes, J., Madeira, H.: Emulation of software faults by educated mutations at machine-code level. In: Proceedings of International Symposium on Software Reliability Engineering (2002)

41. Cotroneo, D., Lanzaro, A., Natella, R., Barbosa, R.: Experimental analysis of binary-level software fault injection in complex software. In: Proceedings of Ninth European Dependable Computing Conference (2012)
42. Natella, R., Cotroneo, D., Duraes, J., Madeira, H.: Representativeness analysis of injected software faults in complex software. In: Proceedings of 2010 IEEE/IFIP International Conference on Dependable Systems and Networks (2010)
43. Natella, R., Cotroneo, D., Duraes, J., Madeira, H.: On fault representativeness of software fault injection. IEEE Trans. Softw. Eng. (2011) (PrePrint). 10.1109/TSE.2011.124
44. Natella, R., Cotroneo, D.: Emulation of transient software faults for dependability assessment: a case study. In: European Dependable Computing Conference (2010)
45. Basso, T., Moraes, R., Sanches, B., Jino, M.: An investigation of java faults operators derived from a field data study on java software faults. In: Workshop de Testes e Tolerância a Falhas (2009)

Introduction to Safety Critical Systems

Roberto Pietrantuono and Stefano Russo

Abstract Today's software-intensive Safety-critical Systems (SCSs) are required to cover a wide range of functionalities, to do it in a safe way, and to be developed under stringent time and cost constraints. That is the challenge which the Critical Step project dealt with. In the following, an overview of the main concepts, challenges, and currently implemented solutions in SCSs development is presented.

Keywords Certification · RAMS · Verification and validation

1 Introduction

A system is referred to as safety-critical when the consequences of its failure can lead to loss of life, or to significant property or environmental damage. Safety-critical Systems (SCSs) are developed in many domains, ranging from transportation (e.g., avionics, railway, automotive) to space and telecommunication systems, from civil and military infrastructure (e.g., nuclear and power plants) to medical and control devices. Depending on the domain, SCSs are developed following guidelines

R. Pietrantuono (✉) · S. Russo
Dipartimento di Informatica e Sistemistica (DIS), Università di Napoli Federico II, via Claudio 21 80125 Naples, Italy
e-mail: roberto.pietrantuono@unina.it

S. Russo
Consorzio Interuniversitario Nazionale per l'Informatica (CINI),
Complesso Universitario Monte Sant'Angelo, Via Cinthia 80126 Naples, Italy
e-mail: stefano.russo@unina.it

D. Cotroneo (ed.), *Innovative Technologies for Dependable OTS-Based Critical Systems*,   17
DOI: 10.1007/978-88-470-2772-5_2, © Springer-Verlag Italia 2013

provided by certification standards, whose typical aim is to give recommendations to developers regarding all the development process activities.

Software in such systems has by now a prevalent role. Systems are required to accomplish more and more tasks, and thus software becomes considerably large and complex to satisfy these requirements. Moreover, even though software is only a part of the entire system, its impact on overall safety has an increasingly significant weight. The numerous reported accidents due to software falls [1] suggest that its reliability is one of the weakest links of system reliability [2]. As a consequence, cost related to software development and assessment activities is among the *highest and least controllable* ones of the entire system development cycle.- Thus, researchers and practitioners in this field are more and more convinced that *software is the problem*.

Although software in SCS is developed by using the most consolidated practices in software engineering, no methodology, technique, or strategy is currently able to assure the absence of software failures. More worryingly, it remains extremely hard, and expensive, to obtain precise and reliable measures of the quality of a software product from the safety point of view. Most of difficulties depend on the intrinsic characteristics of software as compared to other physical systems, such as its "non-linearity" and discontinuity. Its unique features make it difficult to develop *effective* safety assessment methodologies in analogy with other fields of engineering. This produced, in the last decades, a proliferation of techniques to tackle software assessment issues. However, results are still far from being as satisfactory as for system or mechanical engineering.

Since in a SCS development process software development is strictly intertwined with system development, many of the used techniques have been derived directly from system-level techniques; but tailoring them to software is not so immediate and has not always produced the expected results. As a matter of fact, implementing such techniques for software often requires very costly solutions to achieve adequate performance.

Techniques in this area typically address a set of quality attributes commonly used also in other engineering fields, and referred to as RAMS (Reliability, Availability, Maintainability, Safety). The way to achieve acceptable RAMS levels for software, and then to assess the product quality with respect to them, has generated software-tailored techniques acting in every phase of the development lifecycle. Examples are: SFMECA (Software Failure Modes, Effect, and Criticality Analysis), SFTA (Software Fault Tree Analysis), ETA (Event Tree Analysis), SCCFA (Software Common Cause and Failure Analysis), HSIA (Hardware-Software Interaction Analysis) at upper level; wider techniques are then used at lower level in order to enforce and provide feedback to RAMS analysis [3–5]. They cover all the phases of the development process: design principles and techniques (e.g., reuse, modularity, partitioning, or supporting techniques as simulations, mathematical modelling), coding standards and convention, software verification and validation (V&V) techniques (e.g., testing and analysis), assessment techniques (e.g., measurements-based RAMS assessment), fault tolerance mechanisms. The key issues in actually implementing these techniques regard their cost-effectiveness in relation to the quality to assure; in the case of software, this presents unique and hard-to-tackle challenges, both in the "cost" and in the "quality assurance" aspect.

In the following, we briefly survey: what is required to developers in order to produce dependable SCSs; what are the current state-of-the-practice in industry; what is the contribution that the Critical Step Project provides.

2 What is Required to Do: Certification Standards

Software certification is a key aspect of critical systems development and assessment, and its influence on development practices and relation to systems cost is relevant. It is a matter of fact that certification of software is crucial for many companies developing mission- and safety-critical systems. As a result of software-related disasters, professionals and authorities are convinced that certification is nowadays inevitable. But at present, there is no common agreement on what practices are more suitable to provide evidences, safety cases or insurance on which to base software certification (and consequently system certification). Several organizations (such as FAA, NRC, EUROCONTROL, CENELEC, IEC, ISO) produced, in the past, standards for developing critical systems in different domains, e.g., avionics, railway, automotive, nuclear, healthcare. These standards are conceived to provide recommendations about activities in the software development lifecycle (SDLC). For this reason, they are viewed as *process-oriented* standards, working under the assumption that high and controlled quality in software development activities along all the process implies a high product quality. Evidences are required on every produced artifact during the development in order to claim the certification of the final product.

A process-oriented certification process involves four main entities: the standard(s), an applicant, an authority and an assessment body that has to be independent of the applicant. The certification process typically implies interactions between the applicant and assessor, so as to drive the SDLC. Applicant has to provide evidences (sometimes referred to as "certification package") that the standard recommendations have been properly implemented. The assessment body evaluates the certification package and the software product (if it is available at that specific stage) in order to prove that they comply to the standards. The authority releases the certification to the applicant on the basis of the assessment body evaluation, or it can ask for further evidences.

In practice, it is not trivial to apply recommendations and to produce evidences for several reasons; for instance: (i) standard guidelines do not prescribe a precise set of techniques, but they are recommendations; (ii) applying a technique may yield very different results depending on the way and the extent it is applied to the specific software under assessment; (iii) it may happen that applying a technique thoroughly requires unacceptable cost, and thus the applicant needs to find the most cost-effective way to apply it and produce the required evidences.

A lot of certification standards are in effect. We can group them on the basis of the industrial domain in which they are applied, such as nuclear, avionic, automotive. Examples are: DO-178B and DO-178C, in the Avionic/Aeronautics Domain; CENELEC EN 50126, EN 50128 and EN 50129 in the railway domain; ISO 26262 in the Automotive Domain; IEC 61508 for the industrial domain; ECSS standards for the Space Domain. Despite this wide variety of standards, they have many aspects in common. All of them require activities (and related documentation) for quality assurance along all the SDLC phases, from planning to deployment. In most of cases, software is not thought as a standalone part of the system, it does not stand on its own; thus, such activities start from system-level analysis, and then are linked to software: in a typical standard-compliant process, the following steps and related activities are outlined (e.g., [5]):

- from system-level activities, the following artifacts are given as input to the software development process: system requirements specification, system safety requirements specification and system architecture description: safety requirements are derived from the risk analysis (i.e., the activity of identifying risks, estimating their severity and occurrence, and mitigation strategies);
- from these artifacts, safety functions allocated to software are identified; safety functions are assigned an integrity, or assurance, level to satisfy (the name varies with the standard), representing the risk associated with that function (scales vary according to the standard);
- safety functions allocated to software are used in the software requirements specification phase, and in the software architecture specification (which is based on system architecture information); software requirements are then apportioned to software components in the architecture;
- from these artifacts, software is designed, implemented and verified/tested according to a selected SDLC, and according to tools, for which usage further rules are specified depending on the standard, in order to guarantee that they do not introduce faults;
- software is finally validated, and handed over to system engineers;
- the operational life of the system and its maintenance is also regulated.

Besides these phases, other aspects that are addressed by almost every standard are recommendations for integration of Commercial Off The Shelf (COTS) software, reusability recommendations (also of legacy software); fault tolerance recommendations; requirements traceability recommendations; use of tools recommendations.

3 From Theory to Practice: Current Solutions and Open Challenges

Although certification standards provide a valuable support, one of the major problems is that the guidelines they suggest are quite general, since their purpose is not to define what techniques a company must use, or what is their impact on company's cost. For instance, cost and effectiveness issues are often neglected in such guidance documents. As a consequence, there is a gap between what they suggest and strategies, techniques, and tools that can actually be adopted by a company. For many of the proposed practices, there are contradictory studies about their actual effectiveness. This uncertainty poses serious difficulties to companies, which on one hand are constrained to meet predefined certification goals, whereas, on the other hand, are required to deliver systems at competitive cost and time.

Standards' annexes list a number of techniques recommended for each phase of the SDLC. Among the many available techniques, in this Section we survey only the most used ones, in order to have an idea about the type of activities carried out in practice for each phase.

In the early stages, when safety requirements need to be defined at system and software level, and allocated to software components, techniques for RAMS analysis first come into play. RAMS analysis starts at the very beginning of the system development, but it interacts with system (and software) development along all the development activities, providing useful information to them and, at the same time, getting feedbacks from them. As development goes on, RAMS analysis becomes more and more accurate, since it obtains more information from results of the activities.

As for the software development activities, the best software engineering state-of-the-practice techniques and principles are adopted, from requirements to maintenance phase. However, even being the best in this field, the relative immaturity of software engineering make it challenging to provide highly safe software.

3.1 SW RAMS Analysis Techniques

SFMEA
Software FMEA (Failure Modes and Effect Analysis) and FMECA (Failure Modes, Effect and Criticality Analysis) are widely used to analyze failure modes and effect for software components. SFMEA/SFMECA aims at identifying software-related design deficiencies; it determines the effect of hardware failures and human errors on software operation, and the effect on the system of a (software) component failing in a specific failure mode [3].

SFMEA/SFMECA is based on the more established FMEA/FMECA [6] for hardware, and has a similar structure. It includes an initial set up of a list of failure modes; failure modes are meant as the possible incorrect behavior of the software, and include: computational failures, algorithmic failures, synchronization failures, data handling failures, interface failures [4]. Then it analyzes the possible causes and consequences (in terms of local component-level effects and final effects); from its output, several indications for the overall development are derived, such as: recommendations for mitigating the identified software failures at design level; guidance for criticality level assignment to the components (at lower levels of the

SDLC); suggestions to allocate V&V activities on the most critical software components. It also produces knowledge about possible software failures useful for successive developments.

Despite the similarity with hardware FMEA, there are relevant differences between SFMEA and FMEA making its application considerably trickier [7]. The most relevant ones are: (i) in FMEA, system is considered free from failed components, whereas in SFMEA system is considered as containing software faults, that may lead to failures if triggered; (ii) failure modes are totally different, and hard-to-define for SFMEA; (iii) in SFMEA, measures taken to prevent or mitigate the consequences of a failure are different: they can, for example, show that a fault leading to the failure mode will be necessarily detected by the tests performed on the component, or demonstrate that there is no credible cause leading to this failure mode due to the software design and coding rules applied.

The main challenges in SFMEA/SFMECA come from failure modes definition. In [7] authors point out that the term failure mode is different for hardware and software. For hardware components it is straightforward and can be based on operational experience of the same and similar components; for software such history-based information is much less reliable and uniquely identifiable. Moreover, the frequency of occurrence is much harder to define for a software-based system, and their probability distribution over time is much less characterizable. Triggering and propagation depend on the operational profile and on complex interactions between software at different layers (e.g., OS, middleware, other applications); sometimes it even appear to be non-deterministic [8]. This makes SFMEA/SFMECA trickier to apply than the corresponding hardware counterpart.

SFTA

The output of SFMEA can be used in combination with another widely used technique, namely the Software Fault Tree Analysis (SFTA). Also in this case, SFTA comes from system-level FTA [9]. FTA aims at analyzing events or combination of events that can make the system fail (i.e., that can lead to a hazard). Starting from an event representing the immediate cause of a hazard (named 'top event'), the analysis is carried out along a tree path, in which events combination is described with logical operators (AND, OR, etc). The analysis stops when basic events are reached, representing elementary causes whose further decomposition is not of interest. Probabilistic analysis are performed by assigning probabilities to basic events, and computing the top event probability. Basic FT works provided that there are no dependent events. There are many extensions to basic FT, to perform more complex analysis than the simple combinatorial one allowed by basic FT, e.g., when dependencies are involved.

Fault Tree Analysis is mainly meant for hardware systems, but it is used also for software failures analysis. When used in conjunction with SFMEA/SFMECA, the identified software failure modes are useful to construct the software fault tree. As for SFMEA/SFMECA, there are interactions between SFTA and development activities; output of SFTA may help to identify critical software components, to identify the mitigation means able to inhibit the occurrence of the top event failure, to analyze software design with respect to the top event failure occurrence and take design decisions (e.g., partitioning components), to help V&V (for instance, if used at source code level, it helps to understand the relation between faults and identified critical failures, in turn useful for test case writing and techniques selection) and testing resource allocation.

The problems of SFTA are the following: it is not suitable for state-based analyses, whit dependencies among events; it does not scale well, since trees can become very large and complex; it has the same problems of SFMEA about the ambiguity of software failures and software faults. The latter is not an inherent problem of the techniques, but it is about the nature of software itself which is very difficult to characterize.

SCCFA

SCCFA (Software Common Cause and Failure Analysis) derives from CCA (Common Cause Analysis). The purpose of CCA is to identify any accident sequences in which two or more events could occur as the result of one common event [6]. Examples in computer systems are common physical location (e.g., if a system is in one single room, shortcomings in the air-conditioning or external events such as fire or earthquakes are common mode failures), common design processes (e.g., error in the common specification of diverse components), common errors in the maintenance procedure.

SCCFA aims at identifying these causes, relatively to software failures, and at providing recommendations to mitigate them. It can be used in conjunction with SFMEA/SFMECA and SFTA that can help in identifying dependencies among groups of components, which is essential in SCCFA. The basic steps of CCA/SSCFA include [6, 10]: (i) identification of critical components group to be evaluated (by identifying the physical/functional links in the system, functional dependencies and interfaces); (ii) within the groups, check for commonalities such as physical location, a common design process that could introduce a generic design defect; (iii) within each identified commonality, checking for credible failure modes (SFMEA/SFMECA can help); (iv) identifying causes or trigger events that could lead to the failure modes; (v) based on the above, draw conclusions and make recommendations for corrective actions. Corrective actions include requirements redesign, invoking emergency procedures, and function degradation. SSCFA can be seen as a complement to the previous ones, since it uncovers system failures caused by *common* software failures. However, these failures are very difficult to uncover, especially at requirement/design stage, and it requires expensive manual reviews/inspection activities and highly skilled and experienced personnel.

Other techniques that are worth to mention for supporting RAMS analysis are, the Hardware-Software Interaction Analysis (*HSIA*) [11], aiming at examining the hardware/software interface of a design to ensure that hardware failure modes are taken into account in the software requirements, the State Machine Hazard Analysis (SMHA), used to determine software safety requirements directly from the system design, to identify safety-critical software functions, and to help in the design of failure detection and recovery procedures and fail-safe requirements [1].

3.2 Software Engineering Techniques in the SDLC

RAMS analysis supports the SDLC activities and receives feedback from them. Standards recommend a set of techniques and practices for each of the SDLC phase. Companies try to comply with the standard and at the same time to reduce the cost, by selecting techniques that they believe more suitable for their product/process.

We briefly review the most commonly used ones in practice. In the early stage, despite the advantages of formal languages, the software requirements specification is mostly based on natural language. It is the easiest way to specify the user needs, to communicate with stakeholders, as well as among developers, and to document the software product at this stage. Of course, the main problem of natural language is ambiguity; thus, often natural language is supported by structured notations, by multiple level of specification, or by semi-formal modeling techniques (e.g., requirement diagram, use cases). Whenever possible, formal methods are adopted; they are more often used on smaller critical systems (e.g., automotive or control systems domain), or on most critical parts of the system (RAMS analysis can help in identifying them). The practical problem of formal methods is the cost for specification, especially in large systems, and the cost deriving from the required skills: moreover, since interaction with stakeholder is more and more common also in these domains, it may happen that requirements need to be specified also in some form of natural language, besides their formal specification. One more very common recommendation that is by now adopted by many companies is the support to a full traceability, from requirements to code and to the corresponding test cases.

At design stage, there are principles commonly accepted by many companies, such as modularity, information hiding/encapsulation, iterative refinement, temporal/spatial partitioning, low decoupling and high cohesion, reuse. This is often part of process flows definition in companies, at least theoretically. Instead, some of the most expensive design strategies among which producers typically are called to choose to optimize their cost-quality trade-offs are related to architectural choices to prevent, remove or tolerate faults: hardware-software redundancy, N-version programming, safety bag, recovery block, backward/forward recovery, reconfiguration, defensive programming, design by contract, design for change, formal methods. In many of these cases, there is the support either of modeling (semi-formal or formal) and/or of simulation. More recently, model-driven engineering is gaining ground in this field.

As for coding, standards may recommend specific restrictions on the coding process, such as the adoption of particular techniques, code style, or programming language, tied to a specific safety level. For instance, some kinds of programming techniques, such as recursion, may be prescribed for the highest safety levels. Some functionalities covering a critical role may require the adoption of a language that does not permit dynamic memory allocation. Companies may have their own coding standard, specifying restrictions adhering to the certification standard, such as avoidance of uninitialized variables, low cyclomatic complexity, limited use of pointers, use of naming conventions, correct indentation.

After implementation, **the most expensive phase** takes place: **Verification & Validation (V&V)** [12]. On this point, companies really strive to find the best cost-quality point. A lot of techniques exist, and are permitted by standards. Big families are testing and analysis techniques: the former are used typically after the implementation, while the latter are more used from requirements specification to coding (especially static manual analysis). As for testing, we may distinguish three main groups: functional testing, non-functional testing, structural testing. Typical functional testing techniques are uniform random testing and partition-based testing. Others, e.g., operational testing, are less used. Functional testing is by far the most adopted techniques family, and often times also the only adopted one at system-level, despite the criticality of systems. At lower level (e.g., unit testing) structural testing is adopted, also known as white-box testing. Techniques in this category are distinguished according to the coverage criterion: statement coverage, branch coverage, condition coverage, MC/DC coverage. Standard may prescribe coverage adequacy according to one of these criteria (e.g., DO-178B requires MC/DC full coverage [13]). Non-functional testing includes techniques to test quality requirements (in SCSs dependability requirements), such as performance testing, stress/load testing, robustness testing. These are in some cases required by standards (for high level of safety); for instance, performance testing is suggested by CENELEC EN 50128 for railway [5], whereas robustness testing is required by DO-178B for avionics [13]. Performance testing aims at evaluating non-functional performance requirements fulfillment (such as constraints on response times). Stress testing evaluates the application's ability to react to unexpected loads. Robustness testing generates test cases aiming to evaluate the system behavior under exceptional conditions. Thus, it deliberately forces the system with unexpected inputs and observes its ability to manage such values. Robustness testing is often used in conjunction with functional testing techniques especially in critical systems, since its purpose is the opposite of functional testing (it has to verify that the system does not do what is not required).

As for analysis techniques, the most common ones are code/design inspection. They are static manual analysis techniques, and are the principal means by which artifacts consistency and correctness at different stage is verified, from requirements completeness to design, down to the code. Code analysis is also often supported by automatic analysis tools for determining, for instance, metrics of interest of the produced code, such as cyclomatic complexity, size metrics, Halstead's science metrics, coupling metrics, and others.

Finally, in the cases in which formal methods are used at upper level (prescribed at some highest critical levels of some standards), formal verification techniques are adopted at this stage. They include all the verification techniques that automatically verify the software's correctness against its specification: model checking, symbolic execution through pre and post condition, formal proof.

As for maintenance, a common supporting strategy is keeping records of data produced during software development process and during operation. Such data are then analyzed to facilitate software process improvement starting from relevant data from about individual projects and persons. Also, if traceability is implemented, the impact analysis is used at this stage, in order to identify the effect of a change in the product before implementing it.

4 Contribution of the Critical Step Project

The *Critical Step* project favored the development and exchange of know-how in topics of interest in the field of SCSs. With reference to the topics mentioned above, involved researchers, other than knowing about the world of SCSs, of their domains, and of the related certification standards, gained key competences covering very important parts of the SCS development cycle, namely the software dependability analysis and evaluation. The focus has been posed on two complementary perspectives, whose themes have been, during the project, subject of several knowledge exchanges and joint work: V&V issues on the one hand, and RAMS analysis process and methods on the other hand.

These topics have been dealt with in the context of certification standards, which have been the common ground on top of which knowledge has been developed and shared. Several standards have been surveyed in their basic replaces, with particular reference to the V&V phase and RAMS analysis.

More specifically, V&V has been studied mainly with respect to non-functional requirements. Works on robustness testing in the field of critical systems have been jointly conducted, with the aim of reporting experiences about the usage of techniques for robustness evaluation in middleware software infrastructure in critical contexts (e.g., publish/subscribe and web services). Further testing techniques, such as fault-injection, have been also used to risk assessment and robustness evaluation, being both valuable outputs for RAMS analysis. From the RAMS perspective, researchers acquired familiarity with the whole process of RAMS analysis at software level, with its interaction with system-level RAMS and with SDLC phases, especially with testing. The main supported and gainful techniques in real industrial contexts have been taken into account.

Overall, besides single joint works, the project developed background and guidance to address software-specific challenges at RAMS and V&V level, on how one can benefit from the other, and on potential opportunities to improve the software product cost-quality balance.

References

1. Leveson, N.G.: The role of software in spacecraft accidents. AIAA J. Spacecraft Rockets **41**, 564–575 (2004)

2. Calzarossa, M.C., Tucci, S.: Performance evaluation of complex systems: techniques and tools. In: Calzarossa, M.C., Tucci, S. (eds.) performance 2002 tutorial lectures. Lecture Notes in Computer Science, vol. 2459, pp. 208–235. Springer, Berlin (2002)
3. European Organization for the Safety of Air Navigation: Review of Techniques to Support the EATMP Safety Assessment Methodology I (2004)
4. European Cooperation on Space Standardization (ECSS): ECSS-Q-HB-80-03 Draft (2012)
5. CENELEC: EN 50128:2011—Railway applications—Communication, signalling and processing systems—Software for railway control and protection systems (2011)
6. Amberkar, S., Czerny, B.J., D'Ambrosio, J.G., Demerly, J.D., Murray, B.T.: A Comprehensive Hazard Analysis Technique for Safety-Critical Automotive Systems. SAE Technical Paper Series (2001)
7. Pentti, H., Atte, H.: Failure Mode and Effects Analysis of software-based automation systems. VTT Industrial Systems 190 (2002)
8. Grottke, M., Trivedi, K.S.: Fighting bugs: remove, retry, replicate, and rejuvenate. IEEE Comput. **40**(2), 107–109 (2007)
9. Vesely, W.: Fault Tree Handbook with Aerospace Applications. NASA office of safety and mission assurance, Version 1.1 (2002)
10. Stephens, R.A., Talso, W.: System safety analysis handbook: a source book for safety practitioners. In: Stephans, R., Talso, W. (eds.) System Safety Society, 2nd edn. Albuquerque, NM (1997)
11. Von Hoegen, M.: Product assurance requirements for first/Planck scientific instruments. PT-RQ-04410, Number 1 (1997)
12. Pezze', M., Young, M.: Software Testing and Analysis: Process, Principles and Techniques. Wiley, New York (2007)
13. RTCA and EUROCAE: Software consideration in airborne systems and equipment certification (1992)

Introduction to Software Security Concepts

Marco Vieira and Nuno Antunes

Abstract The main problem faced by system administrators nowadays is the protection of data against unauthorized access or corruption due to malicious actions. In fact, due to the impressive growth of the Internet, software security has become one vital concern in any information infrastructure. Unfortunately, software security is still commonly misunderstood. This chapter presents key concepts on security, also providing the basis for understanding existing challenges on developing and deploying secure software systems.

Keywords Security · Software security · Security testing · Software vulnerabilities · Security benchmarking · Vulnerability injection · Attack injection · Secure software development

1 Introduction

Security, "the practice of building software to be secure and function properly under intentional malicious attack" [13], is an integrative concept that includes four key properties [1]: confidentiality (absence of unauthorized disclosure of a service or piece of information), authenticity (guarantees that a service or piece of information is authentic), integrity (protection of a service or piece of information against illicit and/or undetected modification), and availability (protection against possible denials of service caused maliciously). To achieve these properties

M. Vieira (✉) · N. Antunes
Department of Informatics Engineering, University of Coimbra,
DEI, Pólo II—Universidade de Coimbra, 3030-290 Coimbra, Portugal
e-mail: mvieira@dei.uc.pt

D. Cotroneo (ed.), *Innovative Technologies for Dependable OTS-Based Critical Systems*, 29
DOI: 10.1007/978-88-470-2772-5_3, © Springer-Verlag Italia 2013

several security mechanisms have been developed in the past, targeting especially subsystems such as operating systems, database management systems, and web servers. These mechanisms can be classified as follows [1]:

- **Secure channels and envelops:** mechanisms that provide communication in a secure way. The information is transmitted thought the network using secure channels or encapsulated in envelops.
- **Authentication:** mechanisms that assure that the data accessed by the users is authentic.
- **Protection and authorization:** mechanisms that protect resources and data from unauthorized access and guarantee that users only do what they are authorized to do.
- **Auditing and intrusion detection:** these mechanisms allow a posteriori analysis of the accesses to resources and data, allowing the detection of unauthorized accesses or anomalous usage.

In practice, the goal of security is to protect systems and data from intrusion. The risk of intrusion is related to the system vulnerabilities and the potential security attacks. The **system vulnerabilities** are an internal factor related to the set of security mechanisms available (or not available) in the system, the correct configuration of those mechanisms, and the hidden flaws on the system implementation. Many types of vulnerabilities are known and also taxonomies to classify them [22]. Vulnerability prevention consists on guarantying that the software has the minimum vulnerabilities possible. On the other hand, as the effectiveness of the security mechanisms depend on their correct configuration, the system administrator must correctly configure the security mechanisms by following administration best practices. Vulnerability removal consists on reducing the vulnerabilities found in the system. The administrator must pay attention to the new security patches release by software vendors and install those patches as soon as possible. Furthermore, any configuration problems detected on the security mechanisms must be immediately corrected.

Security attacks are an external factor that mainly depends on the intentionality and capability of humans to maliciously break into the system tacking advantage of vulnerabilities. In fact, the success of a security attack depends on the vulnerabilities of the system and attacks are harmless in a system without vulnerabilities. On the other hand, vulnerabilities are harmless if the system is not subject of security attacks. The prevention against security attacks includes all the measures needed to minimize or eliminate the potential attacks against the system. Attack removal is related to the adoption of measures to stop attacks that have occurred before.

Secure Software behaves correctly in the presence of a malicious utilization (attack), even though software failures may also happen when the software is used correctly [12]. Thus, many times software development and testing concerns only with what happens when software fails and not with the intentions. This is where the difference between software safety and software security lies: in the presence of an intelligent adversary with the intention of damaging the system.

In the last two decades, the World Wide Web radically changed the way people communicate and do business. Even critical infrastructures like water supply, power supply, banking, insurance, stock market, retail, communications, defense, etc., nowadays rely on networks, on the web and on the applications that run in these distributed environments. The problem is that, as the importance of the assets stored and managed by web applications increases, so does the natural interest of malicious minds in exploiting this new streak. In fact, web applications are so widely exposed that any existing security vulnerability will most probably be uncovered and exploited by hackers. Hence, the security of web applications is a major concern and is receiving more and more attention from the research community. However, in spite of this growing awareness of security aspects at web application level, there is an increase in the number of reported attacks that exploit web application vulnerabilities [3, 21]. In fact, hackers have moved their focus beyond network attacks to the exploitation of vulnerabilities in the code of web applications. This poorly programmed code represents the current major risk in software security as they are the target of attacks that explore applications' inputs with specially tampered values. These values take advantage of existing vulnerabilities, representing a considerable danger to the application's owner (e.g., by giving to an attacker privileges to read, modify or destroy reserved resources).

To prevent vulnerabilities developers must apply best coding practices, perform security reviews, execute penetration testing, use code vulnerability detectors, etc. Still, many times developers focus on the implementation of functionalities and on satisfying the costumer's requirements and disregard security aspects. Also, most developers are not security specialists and the common time-to-market constraints limit an in-depth search for vulnerabilities. Another problem is that, traditional security mechanisms like network firewalls, intrusion detection systems (IDS), and encryption, are not able to mitigate web application attacks because they are performed through ports that are used for regular web traffic [20] and even application layer firewalls cannot protect the applications as that requires a deep understanding of the business context [18]. In this scenario, a large effort should be put on improving the state of the art in the security of software systems.

This chapter surveys key concepts, techniques and tools for developing and deploying secure software, namely:

- **Security Testing.** Techniques and tools for detecting vulnerabilities have the greatest importance to help developers producing more secure code. Penetration testing and static code analysis are the two techniques most used by web service developers to detect security vulnerabilities in their code [22]. Section 2 overviews the key concepts on security testing.
- **Vulnerability and Attack Injection.** The goal of vulnerability injection is to provide the means to introduce realistic vulnerabilities in applications code. This methodology is extremely useful in different contexts, including: (1) for training security teams; (2) to evaluate security teams in a controlled environment; (3) to estimate the total number of vulnerabilities still present in the code; and (4) as a

building block for an attack injection tool. **Attack injection** is a methodology to automatically attack applications, which can be a valuable tool for testing various counter measure mechanisms, like IDS, Firewalls, Vulnerability Scanners, etc. Section 3 overviews the key concepts on vulnerability and attack injection.

- **Security Benchmarking.** Security evaluation methodologies available nowadays have several limitations. Either they are too complex, too costly, or applicable only to particular parts of a system. This way, comparing different alternatives in terms of security is a difficult assignment faced by many system administrators. Security benchmarking allows assessing and comparing the security of systems and/or components, allowing making informed decisions while designing, developing, and deploying complex software systems. Section 4 presents the main concepts on security benchmarking.

- **Secure Software Development.** Avoiding software vulnerabilities depends on the best practices and tools applied during the implementation, testing and deployment phases of the software development cycle. However, many times those practices are disregarded, as developers are frequently not specialized in security and face hard time-to-deploy constraints. Realizing the benefits of secure coding and the limitations of existing processes requires rethinking the way we build software. Section 5 provides an introduction to key security aspects that should be kept in mind when developing software, putting into the context of the software process the techniques presented before.

2 Security Testing

To identify security issues, developers must focus not only on testing the functionalities of the application but also on searching for dangerous security vulnerabilities that are present in the code and that can be maliciously exploited [12]. This includes applying best coding practices, performing security inspections, execute penetration tests, static code analysis, etc. [22]. However, many times developers do not have the required security training and/or the hard time-to-market constraints make them to focus on satisfying the user's functional requirements, disregarding security aspects. In this scenario, automated tools have a very important role on helping the developers to produce less vulnerable code.

Different techniques for the detection of vulnerabilities have been proposed in the past [22], but in practice these techniques can be divided in two main groups: **White-box** analysis, which consists of examining the code of the application without executing it (this can be done in one of two ways: manually during code inspections and reviews or automatically by using automated analysis tools); and **Black-box** testing, which refers to the analysis of the program execution from an external point-of-view (in short, it consists of exercising the software and comparing the execution outcome with the expected result). Black-box testing is probably the most used technique for verification and validation of software.

The main limitation of black-box approaches is that vulnerability detection is limited by the output of the application. On the other hand, white-box analysis does not take into account the runtime view of the code. **Gray-box** approaches combine black-box and white-box techniques in order to overcome their limitations. A preliminary analysis of the code can be used to find possible vulnerable points or to establish the attacks to perform in a later phase. Another option is to use code instrumentation to obtain more information about the internal status of the application.

Chapter 12 (**Security Testing in SOAs: Techniques and Tools**) of this book discusses existing techniques and tools to perform security testing in web applications and services. Additionally, the chapter discusses the new security challenges raised by the Service Oriented Architecture (SOA) concept, also proposing research directions on required techniques and tools.

3 Vulnerability and Attack Injection

The use of fault injection techniques to assess security is a particular case of software fault injection (discussed in detail in a previous chapter), focused on the software faults that represent security vulnerabilities or may cause the system to fail in avoiding a security problem. Security vulnerabilities are in fact a particular case of software faults, which require adapted injection approaches. In [6] the vulnerabilities of six web applications were analyzed using field data based on a set of 655 security fixes. Results show that only a small subset of 12 generic software faults is responsible for all the security problems. In fact, there are considerable differences by comparing the distribution of the fault types related to security with studies of common software faults.

Neves et al. proposed a tool (AJECT) focused on discovering vulnerabilities on network servers, specifically on IMAP servers [17]. In their work the fault space is the binomial (attack, vulnerability) creating an intrusion that may cause an error and, possibly, a failure of the target system. To attack the target system they used predefined test classes of attacks and some sort of fuzzing.

A procedure inspired on the fault injection technique (that has been used for decades in the dependability area) targeting security vulnerabilities is proposed in [6]. In this work, the "security vulnerability" plus the "attack" represent the space of the "faults" that can be injected in a web application; and the "intrusion" is the "error" [5, 7]. To emulate with accuracy real world web vulnerabilities this work relies on the results obtained in a field study on real security vulnerabilities, which were used to develop a novel Vulnerability Injection tool.

Conceptually, attack injection is based on the injection of realistic vulnerabilities that are automatically attacked, and finally the result of the attack is evaluated. As proposed in [7], a tool able to perform vulnerability and attack injection is a key instrument that can be used in several relevant scenarios, namely: building a realistic attack injector, train security teams, evaluate security teams, and estimate the total number of vulnerabilities still present in the code, among others.

4 Security Benchmarking

Several security evaluation methods have been proposed in the past [4, 10, 19, 24]. The Orange Book [19] and the Common Criteria for Information Technology Security Evaluation [10] define a set of generic rules that allow developers to specify the security attributes of their products and evaluators to verify if products actually meet their claims. Another example is the red team strategy [24], which consists of a group of experts trying to hack its own computer systems to evaluate security.

The work presented in [11] addresses the problem of determining, in a thorough and consistent way, the reliability and accuracy of anomaly detectors. This work addresses some key aspects that must be taken into consideration when benchmarking the performance of anomaly detection in the cyber-domain.

The set of security configuration benchmarks created by the Center for Internet Security (CIS) is a very interesting initiative [2]. CIS is a non-profit organization formed by several well-known academic, commercial, and governmental entities that has created a series of security configuration documents for several commercial and open source systems. These documents focus on the practical aspects of the configuration of these systems and state the concrete values each configuration option should have in order to enhance overall security of real installations. Although CIS refers to these documents as benchmarks they mainly reflect best practices and are not explicitly designed for systems assessment or comparison.

Vieira and Madeira proposed a practical way to characterize the security mechanisms in database systems [23]. In this approach database management systems (DBMS) are classified according to a set of security classes ranging from Class 0 to Class 5 (from the worst to the best). Systems are classified in a given class according to the security requirements satisfied.

In [15] the authors analyze the security best practices behind the many configuration options available in several well-known DBMS. These security best practices are then generalized and used to define a set of configuration tests that can be used to compare different database installations. A benchmark that allows database administrators to assess and compare database configurations is presented in [14]. The benchmark provides a trust-based security metric, named minimum untrustworthiness, that expresses the minimum level of distrust the DBA should have in a given configuration regarding its ability to prevent attacks.

The use of trust-based metrics as an alternative to security measurement is discussed in [16]. Araújo and Vieira also proposed a trustworthiness benchmark based on the systematic collection of evidences (collected using static analysis techniques) that can be used to select one among several web applications, from a security point-of-view.

5 Security in the Software Process

A software development process is composed of multiple phases [8]. To improve the situation in software security it is important not only to understand the existing approaches and tools but also to adequately integrate them in the development process, i.e., to use such approaches and tools in the points of the process where they can make the difference. Different authors divide the software process in different ways, but usually software development includes the following phases (which can be repeated in an iterative manner): initialization, design, implementation, testing, deployment and decommissioning. Figure 1 shows a simplified representation.

The process starts with requirements gathering (including security requirements), followed by specification and design, implementation (coding), testing and deployment. Decommission takes place when the product is not useful/ used anymore. Although code security concerns should be addressed during the entire software product development lifecycle, as highlighted by [13] especial focus should be put in three key phases [9]: implementation, testing, and deployment. The next points summarize the main challenges and put in the context of these three phases the concepts, techniques and tools introduced in the previous sections:

- **Implementation:** during coding we must use best practices that avoid the most critical vulnerabilities in the specific application domain. Examples of practices include input and output validation, the escaping of malicious characters, and the use of parameterized commands [22]. Vulnerability and attack injection techniques have in this phase a very important job in the evaluation of the best security testing tools to use. Also, for the success of this phase, it is essential to adequately train the development teams. For instance, experience shows that the main reason for the vulnerabilities existing in web application's code is related to training and education. First, there is a lack of courses/topics regarding secure design, secure coding, and security testing, in most computer science degrees [9].

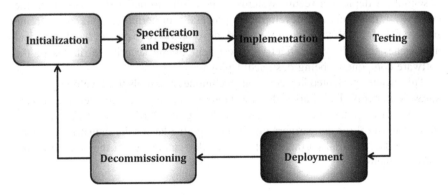

Fig. 1 Simplified version of a software product lifecycle

Second, security is not usually among the developers' main skills as it is considered a boring and uninteresting topic (from the development point-of-view), and not as a way to develop new and exciting functionalities.

- **Testing.** As introduced in Sect. 2, there are many security testing techniques available for the identification of vulnerabilities during the testing phase [22]. To mitigate vulnerabilities, it is necessary to have well-trained teams read that adequately apply those techniques during the development of the application. The problem is that software quality assurance teams typically lack the knowledge required to effectively detect security problems. It is necessary to devise approaches to quickly and effectively train security assurance teams in the context of web applications development, by combining vulnerability injection with relevant guidance information about the most common security vulnerabilities. Also, benchmarking techniques should be applied to assess, compare, and select the most adequate security testing tools for each concrete scenario.

- **Deployment.** At runtime, it is possible to include in the environment different attack detection mechanisms, such as Intrusion Detection Systems (IDS) and Web Application Firewalls (WAF), among others. These mechanisms can operate at different levels and use different detection approaches. The main problems preventing their use are related to the performance overheads and to the false positives that disrupt the normal behavior of the system. In this phase, security benchmarking plays a fundamental role in helping to select the best alternatives (in terms of servers, security mechanisms, etc.) to use, according to specific security requirements. Also, vulnerability and attack injection techniques represent in this phase an efficient way to evaluate the effectiveness of attack detections mechanism to be installed.

6 Conclusions

Essential for deploying secure systems is the ability to understand aspects in the context of the software development process. Furthermore, it is of extreme importance for software designers and developers to have at hand practical approaches that allow an effective assessment of the security attributes of the software components being designed/deployed.

This chapter presented key concepts, techniques and tools for developing secure software systems. The chapter did not intend to provide a comprehensive survey, but to focus on the aspects researched during the CRITICAL STEP project, making it useful for the partners involved, in particular for the industrial partners, and for other external partners that face similar challenges in the context of the software industry.

References

1. Cachin, C., Camenisch, J., Deswarte, Y., Dobson, J., Horne, D., Kursawe, K., Laprie, J.-C., Lebraud, J.-C., Long, D., McCutcheon, T., Muller, J., Petzold, F., Pfitzmann, B., Powell, D., Randell, B., Schunter, M., Shoup, V., Veríssimo, P., Trouessin, G., Stroud, Robert J., Waidner, M., Welch, I.S.: MAFTIA: reference model and use cases (2000)
2. Center for Internet Security. http://www.cisecurity.org/
3. Christey, S., Martin, R.A.: Vulnerability type distributions in CVE. V1. 0. 10, 04 (2006)
4. Commission of the European Communities: The IT security evaluation manual (ITSEM) (1993)
5. Echtle, K., Leu, M.: The EFA fault injector for fault-tolerant distributed system testing. In: Workshop on Fault-Tolerant Parallel and Distributed Systems. IEEE Computer Society Press, Amherst (1992)
6. Fonseca, J., Vieira, M., Madeira, H.: Testing and comparing web vulnerability scanning tools for SQL injection and XSS attacks. In: 13th Pacific Rim International Symposium on Dependable Computing (PRDC 2007) (2007)
7. Fonseca, J., Vieira, M., Madeira, H.: Vulnerability & attack injection for web applications. In: IEEE/IFIP International Conference on Dependable Systems & Networks, 2009, DSN '09 (2009)
8. Ghezzi, C., Jazayeri, M., Mandrioli, D.: Fundamentals of software engineering. Prentice Hall PTR, Upper Saddle River (2002)
9. Howard, M., Leblanc, D.E.: Writing Secure Code. Microsoft Press, Redmond (2002)
10. Infrastructure, P.K., Profile, T.P.: Common criteria for information technology security evaluation. National Security Agency (2002)
11. Maxion, R.A., Tan, K.M.C.: Benchmarking anomaly-based detection systems. In: Proceedings International Conference on Dependable Systems and Networks, 2000, DSN 2000 (2000)
12. McGraw, G., Potter, B.: Software security testing. IEEE Secur. Priv. 2(5), 81–85 (2004)
13. McGraw, G.: Software security: building security in. Addison-Wesley Professional, Boston (2006)
14. Neto, A.A., Vieira, M.: A trust-based benchmark for DBMS configurations. In: 15th IEEE Pacific Rim International Symposium on Dependable Computing, PRDC '09, pp. 143–150 (2009)
15. Neto, A.A., Vieira, M.: Towards assessing the security of DBMS configurations. In: IEEE International Conference on Dependable Systems and Networks with FTCS and DCC, DSN 2008, pp. 90–95 (2008)
16. Neto, A.A., Vieira, M.: Benchmarking untrustworthiness. Int. J. Dependable Trustworthy Inf Syst 1(2), 32–54 (2010)
17. Neves, N., Antunes, J., Correia, M., Verissimo, P.: Using attack injection to discover new vulnerabilities. In: International Conference on Dependable Systems and Networks, DSN 2006 (2006)
18. OWASP Foundation: OWASP application security FAQ version 3. http://www.owasp.org/index.php/OWASP_Application_Security_FAQ
19. Qiu, L., Zhang, Y., Wang, F., Kyung, M., Mahajan, H.R.: Trusted computer system evaluation criteria. In: National Computer Security Center (1985)
20. Singhal, A., Winograd, T., Scarfone, K.: Guide to secure web services: recommendations of the national institute of standards and technology. Report, National Institute of Standards and Technology, US Department of Commerce (2007)
21. Stock, A., Williams, J., Wichers, D.: OWASP top 10 (2007)

22. Stuttard, D., Pinto, M.: The web application hacker's handbook: discovering and exploiting security flaws. Wiley, Chichester (2007)
23. Vieira, M., Madeira, H.: Towards a security benchmark for database management systems. In: International Conference on Dependable Systems and Networks, DSN 2005 (2005)
24. Sandia National Laboratories: Information operations red team and assessments^{TM}. http://www.sandia.gov/iorta/

Part I
V&V in Safety Critical System

This section contains three papers presenting research activities on the investigation of peculiar issues related to the process of Verification and Validation (V&V) in Safety Critical Systems. The first paper presents a study on how V&V activities are described by the widely-known standards regulating the development of Safety Critical Systems. In particular, it highlights the differences among these standards on the definitions and the recommended techniques for conducting V&V activities. The remaining papers describe a tool for performing Robustness Testing of middleware solutions adopted in Safety Critical Systems: the second paper focuses on Web Services, while the third one on Publish/Subscribe Services.

Christian Esposito

Safety-Critical Standards for Verification and Validation

Christian Esposito, Ricardo Barbosa and Nuno Silva

Abstract Verification and Validation represent key activities to be properly conducted during the development of safety-critical systems. Due to their importance, international organizations have issued regulations to disciple how these activities have to be performed in order to achieve systems of high quality. In particular, each of them indicates a definition of what safety means, proper qualitative and quantitative properties for evaluating the quality of the system under development, and a set of methodologies to be used for assessing the fulfillment of the mentioned properties. These standards are today an essential tool for ensuring the required safety levels in many domains that require extremely high dependability. This paper summarizes the analysis on a set of well-known safety standards in different domains of critical systems with the intend of highlighting similarities and differences among them, pointing out common areas of interest and reporting on which features the newest (and upcoming) standards are focusing.

Keywords Safety · Verification and validation · Standards

C. Esposito (✉)
Consorzio Interuniversitario Nazionale per l'Informatica (CINI),
Complesso Universitario M.S. Angelo, via Cinthia, 80126 Naples, Italy
e-mail: christian.esposito@unina.it

R. Barbosa · N. Silva
ASD-T Aeronautics, Space, Defense and Transportation, Critical Software,
Parque Industrial de Taveiro, Lt 48, 4470-605 Coimbra, Portugal
e-mail: rbarbosa@criticalsoftware.com

N. Silva
e-mail: nsilva@criticalsoftware.com

D. Cotroneo (ed.), *Innovative Technologies for Dependable OTS-Based Critical Systems*, 41
DOI: 10.1007/978-88-470-2772-5_4, © Springer-Verlag Italia 2013

1 Introduction (NS)

Systems can be defined as safety-critical if the consequences of a failure could lead to loss of life, significant property damage, or damage to the environment. Due to such severe consequences of a failure occurring in these systems, it is mandatory to adopt a proper development process with activities that aim at achieving and preserving the safety requirements imposed upon these systems. Such activities are known in literature as Verification and Validation (V&V) process. With few words, we can define *Verification* as the process to check if we are building the system right. More specifically, the system under development is tested so to ensure that it fully meets its functional requirements, described as a set of inputs to which corresponds a certain behavior and outputs. Such tests are typically conducted, for example, by looking at the output responses to various combinations of inputs, and the goal is to look for eventual bugs within the system code, so that proper debugging methods allows the programmer to correct them. On the other hand, *Validation* is briefly definable as a series of activities to test if we are building the right system. More specifically, it aims at ensuring that the system performs as it is supposed to do (without unintended functions), and measuring its quality, i.e., it meets key features, such as performance, safety or security. In other words, verification is guaranteeing that the system has been devised according to the requirements and design specifications, while validation ensures that the product actually meets the user needs [1].

During the last decades, several specifications have been proposed by international organizations to standardize the series of activities that compose a V&V process. Some exhibit a generic multi-domain nature, such as IEC 61508, but other ones are tailored to specific application domains, e.g., aeronautic or space. The scope of this paper is to highlight the key characteristics and the V&V process proposed by some key standards, and to identify the methods recommended by such different standards to perform V&V activities. Specifically, we have considered and studied the standards listed in Table 1, and analyzed their similarities and differences so to point out common areas of interest, and features in which they diverge. Last, we also present a preview of future evolution for some of the mentioned standards (i.e., DO-178C, or the new ISO/IEC 29119 Software Testing standard).

2 V&V Overview

Verification and Validation are the most common software engineering disciplines that help building quality into software. V&V is a set of analysis and testing activities that are executed across the systems life cycle and that complement the quality building efforts of the development activities. These disciplines are important, especially if planned in parallel with the software/system development since they provide invaluable benefits:

- they help uncovering errors early, providing the development teams ways to correct them and avoid propagation of the effects;
- they support the evaluation of important system properties such as performance and allow early adjustment of the properties;
- they evaluate the products against system requirements;
- they provide management consistent and comprehensive status about the quality and progress of the development;
- they provide guarantees and evidences to reach high quality and qualification/certification of the systems.

The V&V disciplines are an essential part of the systems dependability and evaluation efforts, and are today considered in all the safety-critical standards that have the main objective of guaranteeing software/systems development and certification. In general, the V&V activities that can be planned for a system can cover all the artifacts that are produced and include

- Concept/System verification;
- Requirements verification;
- Architecture and Design verification;
- Implementation (code) verification;
- Testing/Validation artefacts verification;
- Unit/Integration testing;
- Validation/System testing.

The verification discipline applies methods and techniques that range from artifacts analysis, traceabilities, interface analysis, simulations, etc. The validation discipline is more dependent on tools and testing methods, such as unit/integration tests, validation tests, robustness and stress tests, etc. These tools, methods and techniques must always be properly planned and implemented. They are important disciplines for the development life cycle and this is why they are key in the safety-critical standards that usually request their usage to guarantee the safety and dependability of the systems, either by providing detailed evidences of all the verification activities or by providing evidences of the proper implementation of the requirements and the functions of the system, as well as coverages.

3 State of the Art

In the current research literature, it is possible to find other research papers that focus on certain safety-related standards and propose some kinds of comparisons among them. We have studied a large amount of these papers, and classified them based on their scope:

1. Papers aiming at overviewing the activities and methods recommended by one, or even more, standard. A concrete example is represented by [2], which presents the main aspects of the IEC 61508 standard.

2. Papers illustrating practical experiences in applying safety-related standards, such as [3] that talks about 25 assessments conducted using IEC 61508 or IEC 61511.

3. Papers presenting the evolution from one version to an other one of a given standard, such as [4] that discusses some features of the 2000 version of IEC 61508 standard and indicates the main changes incorporated into its new edition, published in 2010.

4. Papers proposing methods and tools to be used within the context of safety-related standards to improve their application and achievable results. Examples are [5], which introduces a conceptual model for evidences used to reason about software safety, and [6], which proposes a workflow for verification and validation of models and generated code.

5. Papers analyzing and then, criticizing some of the main features of one, or even more, standard. A practical examples is [7], which provides suggestions for improvements to the IEC 61508 standard.

6. Papers comparing safety-related standards belonging only to one particular application domain, such as [8] that discusses the application of IEC 61508 and IEC 60880 in the domain of nuclear plants.

7. Papers comparing safety-related standards of more than one domain. Such papers may be focused on the overall regulation, such as [9] that explores the differences and similarities between DO-178B (aeronautics domain) and MIL-STD-498 (defence domain), and [10] that provides a comparison of ISO 26262 (autonomic domain) and DO-178B (aeronautics domain), or even focused on a particular aspect of the standards, such as [11] that investigates the application of formal methods in several different standards.

Clearly, our work is out of the scope of the first four mentioned classes, so we moved our attention to the remaining ones. Focusing on standards belonging to the same application domain would not provide us a clear picture of the current practice and methods for V&V process in safety-critical systems; therefore, we had to enlarge our analysis bringing in representative standards for the main domains of such systems. Therefore, the only papers that are related to our work belong to the last class of the previous classification. In particular, our work goes beyond [9–11], since in the first two cases we have analyzed a larger set of standards, and in the last case we have focused our attention to a broader group of methods in our comparison. The only work that is closer to ours is the brief overview of safety-related standards provided by [12], since it analyze a large number of standards with respect to several different aspects, as we do. However, despite having some comparison metrics in common, we introduce other ones, such as use of fault-injection or description of the risk and hazard assessment, that [12] does not consider in its overview.

4 Overview of Industrial Standards

For our comparison, we have analyzed the standards listed in Table 1, which have been extensively adopted in the industry, precisely ten taken from six different application domains and two exhibiting a generic nature and applicable to any possible safety-critical system. Generally speaking, safety-related standards have two aspects: (1) requirements for the process for developing highly reliable software, encompassing specification, design and verification; and (2) requirements for safety management, including the way that the possibility of software failure is allowed for in the system safety analysis. These aspects can be covered in a single standard, as in eight of the selected standards, but in other cases, two or more standards are needed to cover the required scope. Specifically, three of them comprise a couple of documents, one on the V&V process, such as EN 50126, and one on the generic development process of safety-critical systems, such as EN 50128, while one, i.e., the series of standards from European Cooperation on Space Standardization (ECSS), covers the full spectrum of System Development Process (SDP) and is composed of 21 different standards, each on a particular aspect and/or method applicable within SDP.

5 Comparison

In this section, we compare the above mentioned standard with respect to the following metrics; more details in Tables I-IV of [13]:

1. Reliability, Availability, Maintainability and Safety (RAMS) Analysis—inclusion of a methodology for performing proper RAMS analysis;
2. Safety Integrity Levels—measure of the degree of criticality for each component within the system, obtained by considering the consequences of failures, and indication of the method used for assigning such levels;
3. Risk and Hazard Analysis—recommendations on which method adopt for these activities;
4. Verification and Validation—definition of these activities and their implementation;
5. Fault Injection, Testing, Formal Methods, Failure Mode and Effect Analysis (FMEA)/Failure Mode, Effects, and Criticality Analysis (FMECA) and Fault Tree Analysis (FTA)—role of these methods within the context of the V&V process envisioned by the selected standards.

RAMS Analysis Only a minority of the studied standards define a proper methodology for these analyses, specifically ISO 26262, EN 50126 and ECSS series of standards. Other ones suggest only on how performing hazard and risk analysis, which covers only a part of RAMS analysis. IEC 62304 does not contains indications for RAMS analysis, but refers to ISO 14971.

Table 1 Main standards in the different application domains

Standard	Application domain	Scope
IEEE 1012-2004	Generic	A complete methodology for V&V process for software being developed, maintained, or reused
IEC 61508	Generic	Functional safety for electrical/ electronic/ programmable electronic (E/E/PS) safety-related systems, and methods to guarantee it
ISO 26262	Automotive domain	Adaptation of IEC 61508 for the automotive industry
EN 50126[b] and EN 50128[a]	Railways	(A) Process for managing dependability, and for demonstrating that requirements have been met. (B) Procedures and technical requirements for the development of software
IEC 60880	Nuclear plants	Software aspects for I&C systems performing category a functions
DO-178B	Aeronautics domain	Aspects of airworthiness certification that pertain to the production of software for airborne systems
Euro-CONTROL - SAM	Aeronautics domain	Best practices for safety assessment of air navigation systems and guidance for their application
Defence Standard 00 − 56[b] and 00 − 55[a]	Defence domain	(A) Safety programme requirements. (B) Requirements for the development of safety related software, covering specification, design, coding, test and integration
$MIL - STD - 882D^b$ and $MIL - STD - 498^a$	Defence domain	(A) Requirements for implementing a safety program, so to identify hazards and prevent mishaps. (B) Activities required for software development
ECSS series of standards	Space domain	Management, engineering and product assurance in space projects and applications
NASA-STD-8719.13B	Space domain	Software safety activities, data, and documentation necessary for the acquisition or development of software in a safety-critical system
ESA ISVV Guide	Space domain	Cost effective and reproducible independent software verification and validation (ISVV) process, and best practices for the different verification and validation activities
IEC 62304	Medical domain	Framework of life cycle processes with activities and tasks necessary for the safe design and maintenance of medical device software

[a] Requirements for development process
[b] Requirements for safety management

Safety Integrity Levels With the exception of IEC 60880 that has no reference to the safety integrity level concept, all the other standards include their own definition for Safety Integrity Levels. IEEE 1012-2004 defines four levels of software integrity, and examples of classification schemes are given based on the concepts of consequences and mitigation potential or on risk, but there is no assignment method indicated since software integrity levels should result from agreements among the acquirer, supplier, developer, and independent assurance authorities (such lack in the assignment scheme is present also in DO-178B and EN 50126). Also IEC 61508, as well as IEC 62304, specifies 4 levels, called Safety Integrity Levels (SIL), but on the contrary to IEEE 1012-2004 it contains a detailed description of the methods to be used in the Hazard and risk assessment for SIL assignment. Defence Standard 00-55 defines such levels in a more formal manner, making it a measure of the required likelihood that a system achieves its safety requirements, and requiring the construction of formal arguments and statistical validation testing to provide a direct measure of the safety integrity level.

Risk Analysis Neither MIL-STD-882D or MIL-STD-498 indicate how to perform risk analysis, IEEE 1012-2004 and DO-178B only specify when to perform it, and EN 50126 gives few details on how to perform it. But, all the other standards provide guidelines and a set of methods to support performing such analysis. If from one side, in IEC 61508 there is a great deal of subjectivity in conducting this analysis, NASA-STD-8719.13B and ECSS series of standards describe rigorously its implementation. On one side, NASA-STD-8719.13B identifies in FMEA and FTA the systematic top down deductive approaches to risk analysis. On the other one, ECSS series of standards puts as core of the risk analysis data from all project domains (managerial, programmatic, technical). As mentioned, IEC 62304 refers to ISO 14971 for the definition of risk analysis, intended as the first part of an overall risk management process. In particular, there are several annex that provides guidelines for manufacturers throughout the risk assessment process: Annex C contains questions that can be used to identify medical device characteristics that could impact on safety, and Annex D presents risk concepts applied to medical devices.

Hazard Analysis The standards that do not present indications on how to conduct the risk analysis also do not provide details on the implementation of the hazard analysis. In general, standard recommendations with respect to hazard analysis are less vague than risk analysis:

1. ISO 26262 states that hazards shall be systematically determined, with techniques such as brainstorming, checklists, FMEA and field studies;
2. EuroCONTROL SAM contains a detailed list of methods to be used: (1) systematic application of a set of keywords to each function; (2) Brainstorming sessions; and (3) analysis of hazard database, accident/incident reports, and lessons learned;
3. ECSS series of standards indicates that failure causes as identified through FMECA and other analyses, while hazard consequences can be determined with qualitative methods, such as brainstorming, or even with more quantitative methods such as Fault Injection;
4. NASA-STD-8719.13B specifies that hazards and their causes are identified by using lessons learned, mishap data, analysis from similar systems, and engineering judgment; in addition to generic checklist with some generic hazards, which represents a good starting place.

Therefore, we can conclude that when detailed, the first methods for hazard analysis are qualitative methods such as brainstorming and analysis of historical data. Then, if more accuracy is needed, quantitative methods are applied, where FMEA/FMECA is the preferred one. A surprising claim we have found in the definition of hazard analysis within the context of the IEC 61508: "It may be quantitative or qualitative. However, the standard recognizes that, because software failure is systematic and not random, qualitative methods must be used only in the case of software". By definition, systematic failures are produced by human errors during system development and operation, and it is indeed true that the majority of bugs in software components belong to this category. However, studies within the context of software reliability have also identified an other kind of software bugs, named as Mandelbug [14], whose causes, activation and/or error propagation result so complex that its behavior appears random. This topic is still controversial, and there is a strong debate around it, as [15] presents the reluctance of a part of researchers and industrial practitioners to acknowledge uncertainty in failure occurrence. In our opinion, the reason of this claim in IEC 61508 is due to the fact that it was theorized at a time when software were quite simple and do not contain the source of non-determinism that we can find nowadays, such as concurrent programming or heavy use of IO routines. As previously said before, IEC 62304 refers to ISO 14971 for describing hazard analysis for medical devices: Annex E is especially useful, as it contains examples of hazards, foreseeable sequences of events and hazardous situations.

Verification In our analysis of indications within the context of verification, we have focused our attention towards two aspects: definition of the objectives, and implementation of verification. The standards agree with our definition of verification given in the introduction: Was the system built right? In fact, verification stands in IEEE 1012-2004 for providing objective evidence that software conform to requirements, or in IEC 61508 for conforming that the requirements have been fulfilled. However, most of the standards, even if with different words, specify a more detailed definition of verification, which provides also generic indications on how to perform verification: evaluation of the results of a process to ensure correctness and consistency with respect to the inputs and requirements provided to that process (DO-178B).

Less agreement we have found when describing on how to perform verification: (i) there is MIL-STD-882D that provides no indication of a clear verification phase, only a series of activities at the end of coding for assessing the quality of the implemented software, i.e., unit testing (suggested also by IEEE 1012-2004); (ii) EuroCONTROL SAM recommends to review and analyze the results of the given process, but also checklists could be identified to support these methods; (iii) ECSS series of standards proposes a well structured and documented process by suggesting tests, analysis, review of design and inspection; (iv) other standards, such as ESA ISVV Guide, IEC 60880, IEC 62304 and EN 50128 (just to cite the main ones) contain long lists of methods to be used by discussing their characteristics and providing advices on when and how using them, and upon which items.

Validation As done for verification, we have considered in our analysis both objectives and implementation of validation, and we have notice divergence from the definition we provided in the introduction. Apart from MIL-STD-498 that does not provide any reference definition, some standards, such as IEEE 1012-2004, define the objectives of validation as providing evidence that the software and its associated products satisfy system requirements, solve the right problem, and satisfy intended use and user needs, which is a similar definition to the one presented in the paper. On the other hand, other standards adopt a completely different formalization: (i) ISO 26262: Provision of evidences on the absence of erroneous activation for safety mechanisms, and of compliance to the safety goals; (ii) DO-178B: Determination that the requirements are the correct requirements and that they are complete; (iii) EuroCONTROL SAM: Confirmation that the safety objectives are (and remain) correct and complete, and ensuring that all critical assumptions are credible, appropriately justified and documented. Last, IEC 62304 does not cover validation, which is addressed by ISO 14971.

Also on the methods for implementing validation there is no agreement. Apart from some standards that do not indicate any specific method or implementation approach to use, such as DO-178B, and MIL-STD-498, standards typically provide a list of methods to be used, as follows some practical examples:

- IEEE 1012-2004 suggests integration testing;
- IEC 61508 indicates functional testing under environmental conditions, interference surge immunity testing, static and dynamic analysis;
- ISO 26262 recommends (i) reproducible tests with specific procedure and pass/fail criteria; (ii) analysis (e.g., FMEA, FTA, ETA, simulation); (iii) long-term tests; (iv) user tests under real-life conditions; (v) reviews;
- EN 50128 mentions (i) probabilistic testing, (ii) performance testing, (iii) functional and black-box testing, and (iv) modeling;
- EuroCONTROL SAM considers (i) checklists to guide validation process, (ii) operational or engineering judgement, (iii) tests through specific analysis, (iv) modeling or simulation, (v) review and analysis of the Safety Evidences to ensure their completeness and correctness.

There are methods listed as usable for validation in one standard that we find listed for verification in another one. A practical example is Unit testing, which is mentioned by IEEE 1012-2004 as a verification mean, and by IEC 60880 as a validation mean; FMEA or FTA as a validation mean in ISO 26262 but as a verification mean in ESA ISVV Guide; or functional and block-box testing as a validation mean in EN 50128, but a verification mean in ESA ISVV Guide.

Fault Injection Not all the selected standards suggest the use of fault-injection methods, despite representing a powerful technique for the evaluation of non-functional properties, such as fault-tolerance, of a software artifact [16], and it has been successfully used in several different application domains and kinds of hardware and software systems by academic researchers. Only four standards, out of the twelve analyzed ones, recommend its use:

- IEC 61508 consider it mandatory for validating fault-tolerance mechanisms;
- ISO 26262 enlists it as one of the methods for validation;

- ECSS series of standards uses to assess mechanisms for detecting, isolating and treating failures;
- NASA-STD-8719.13B considers it as highly recommended tests for safety-critical components;
- ISO 14971 states that fault injection techniques can be used by manufacturers to verify some hardware- and software-based risk controls individually and to determine, at any point in the testing cycle, the number of significant faults remaining in the system.

Testing It is widely used in all the analyzed standards: used in all the phases as in IEC 61508, in the RAMS analysis as in EN 50126, or in the V&V process as in IEC 60880 (only for verification), IEC 62304 or ECSS series of standards. The difference among the standards is what kind of testing methods are suggested: (i) IEEE 1012-2004 specifies software testing, software integration testing, software qualification testing, system integration testing, and system qualification testing; (ii) EN 50128 suggest the use of stress testing, interface testing, probabilistic testing, and integration testing; (iii) NASA-STD-8719.13B contains a rich indication of the testing methods to be used, among which the main ones are the followings: (i) black and white box testing; (ii) unit testing; (iii) incremental integration testing; (iv) functional testing; (v) system testing; (vi) regression testing; (vii) acceptance testing; (viii) load and stress testing; (ix) performance testing; (x) security testing; (xi) alpha and beta testing.

Formal Methods Only IEEE-1012-2004 and MIL-STD-882D/498 do not indicate explicitly the use of formal methods, while the other ones use them for (i) avoiding mistakes during requirement specification and inserting faults during design and development (IEC 61508), (ii) proving the correctness of the system against a formal specification of its behaviour (ISO 26262), (iii) performing hazard and risk analysis (Defence Standard 00-55). Directly, IEC 62304 does not indicate the use of formal methods, but ISO 14971 suggests it for the estimation of the quantitative probability of a risk.

FMEA/FMECA Only four standards do not suggest the use of FMEA, all the other ones make use of FMEA, and also FMECA when applicable, for identifying hazards, and providing evidence of the violation of safety goals. As said before, there is no reference in IEC 62304 to FMEA7FMECA, but in ISO 14971 they are user for risk analysis.

FTA In the standards that indicate FMEA/FMECA application in the safety assessment process, also FTA is present. In some standards it is considered as alternative to FMEA/FMECA, since same results are obtainable (e.g., IEC 61508 or NASA-STD-8719.13B), in an other one, i.e., Defence Standard 00-55, FTA is used after performing FMEA/FMECA, taking as inputs the results of the latter one.

Discussion Despite the several points in common among the different standards, i.e., mostly all of them mention verification and validation activities, testing as core method for safety assessment and need of performing a risk and hazard analysis, there are serious differences that do not make them interchangeable, and do not make it feasible to have a unique standard able to substitute all the existing ones. It is our belief that such differences strongly depend on the specific application domain where the standard should be applied. This is motivated by the need, and spent efforts, of standardization bodies to do not have only generic standards, such as IEC 61508; but to extend them to fit the characteristics and needs of each application domain, such as in case of ISO 26262 and IEC 60880. The latter ones, even if derived from the same standard, exhibit differences among each others: ISO 26262 presents Safety Integrity Levels while IEC 60880 does not; IEC 60880 does not specify a given safety life cycle, while ISO 26262 does; or ISO 26262 suggests fault-injection while IEC 60880 does not. Another evidence of this can be seen in the consideration of hardware components in standards. The general approach is to consider their requirements when software needs to be integrated with hardware, while ISO 26262 disciplines development of both software and hardware components, and their successive integration. This is motivated by the observation that in automotive domain, safety-critical systems are represented by embedded systems where only in the recent years the amount of software is strongly growing [17], and that traditionally the hardware side was the predominant one.

6 Future Standards

The recent years have brought development and evolution in a few important standardization bodies. These activities reflect the efforts to update existing standards according to the practical experience as well as evolutions in terms of implementation and technologies that safety-critical systems suffer. The objective of these standards evolutions is to make the processes more efficient, applicable to reality and lead to safe and dependable systems.

A few of the standards (or frameworks) that have recently evolved include

- ISO 26262: the new standard for embedded applications development for the automotive industry;
- ECSS series of standards: based on the evolution of technologies and industrial experience for the European space domain;
- DO-178C: the evolution of the DO-178B, the standards for airborne systems certification;
- IEC-29119: the new upcoming software testing standard.

Two important examples are DO-178C and ISO/IEC-29119. What changes can industry and certification authorities expect from the new standards?

DO-178C—Software Considerations in Airborne Systems and Equipment Certification The DO-178C includes a large effort from industry and certification authorities and intends to fill the existing gaps and difficulties (from applying DO-178B) and to follow-up with modern processes, technologies and tools. In fact, the consideration of recent software tools and technologies is a key addition to the new standard, but the overall revision of the DO-178B standard cannot be ignored. The main intent behind the revision of the body of DO-178B was to make it more focused and concrete and avoid current ambiguities. For example, when talking about the necessity of modified condition/decision coverage (MC/DC) testing for level A software and requirements with multiple conditions, even at lower levels of criticality. Another issue is related with the need for bidirectional traceability between software artifacts. This issue will be clearly stated and some actual practices will be eliminated in the new standard. DO-178C will be addressing software modelling and the ability to use it to replace/avoid some of the verification techniques required in DO-178B, addressing object-oriented software and the conditions under which it can be used, addressing formal methods to complement dynamic testing, and clarifying software tools and avionics tool qualification.

IEC-29119—New Testing standard This standard can be included in the following chain: ISO-15288⇒ISO-12207⇒IEEE-1012⇒IEC-29119. It will replace a set of older standards such as IEEE-829, IEEE-1008, BS-7925-1 and BS-7925-2, thus making the software testing a more consistent and uniform set of activities. The aim of ISO/IEC 29119 "Software Testing" is to become the definitive standard that includes definitions, vocabulary, processes, documentation and techniques for the software testing lifecycle. The standard includes organizational test strategies and test policies, project and phase test strategies and plans, test case analysis, design, execution, reporting and more. It is supposed to support testing on any software development or maintenance project, and will allow both industry and tool developers to be able to reuse and plan in a much more consistent way the testing activities.

7 Conclusions

This chapter presented a survey of some of the most important safety-critical standards with special focus on Verification and Validation activities. Specifically, we have introduced a series of comparison metrics upon which we have based our discussion, focusing on the proposed development and safety assurance process, suggested approach for V&V process, indicative implementation of risk and hazard analysis, and usage of several verification techniques such as fault injection, testing, formal methods, FMEA/FMECA and FTA. It is clear that domains and industries tend to develop and apply their own standards, thus making the number of existing standards quite large, although the processes, methods and techniques are not totally different. Some of the similarities and differences have been highlighted and discussed, only helping to understand that the certification requirements from domain to domain or from industry to industry do not change that much. In fact, the standards evolutions are allowing the industries to have even more common processes and techniques, while the experiences are being shared and spread, and the new technologies are being adopted and thus bring in new challenges for certification and demand updates to the standards.

References

1. Wallace, D., Fujii, R.: Software verification and validation: an overview. IEEE Softw. **6**(3), 10–17 (1989)
2. Brown, S.: Overview of IEC 61508—Design of electrical/electronic/programmable electronic safety-related systems. Comput. Control Eng. J. (2010)
3. Lloyd, M., Reeve, P.: IEC 61508 and IEC 61511 assessments some lessons learned. In: Proceedings of 4th IET International Conference on Systems Safety 2009 Incorporating the SaRS Annual Conference (2009)
4. Bell, R.: Introduction and revision of IEC 61508. Adv. Syst. Saf. (2011)
5. Panesar-Walawege, R., Sabetzadeh, M., Briand, L., Coq, T.: Characterizing the chain of evidence for software safety cases: a conceptual model based on the IEC 61508 standard. In: Proceedings of 3rd International Conference on Software Testing, Verification and Validation, April 2010
6. Conrad, M.: Testing-based translation validation of generated code in the context of IEC 61508. Formal Methods Syst. Des. **35**(3), 389–401 (2009)
7. Hokstad, P., Corneliussen, K.: Loss of safety assessment and the IEC 61508 standard. Reliab. Eng. Syst. Saf. **83**(1), 111–120 (2004)
8. Baufreton, P., Blanquart, J.P., Boulanger, J.L., Delseny, H., Derrien, J.C., Gassino, J., Ladier, G., Ledinot, E., Leeman, M., Quéré, P., Ricque, B.: Comparison between IEC 60880 and IEC 61508 for certification purposes in the nuclear domain. In: Computer Safety, Reliability, and Security—Lecture Notes in Computer Science 6351/2010 (2010)
9. Johnson, L.: DO-178B, Software considerations in airborne systems and equipment certification. http://www.dcs.gla.ac.uk/johnson/teaching/safety/reports/schad.html
10. Gerlach, M., Hilbrich, R., Weißleder, S.: Can cars fly?. from avionics to automotive comparability of domain specific safety standards. In: Proceedings of the Embedded World Conference, Mar 2011
11. Bell, R.: Introduction and revision of IEC 61508. In: Proceedings of the 1993 Software Engineering Standards Symposium (SESS'93) Aug/Sept 1993
12. Baufreton, P., Blanquart, J.P., Boulanger, J.L., Delseny, H., Derrien, J.C., Gassino, J., Ladier, G., Ledinot, E., Leeman, M., Quéré, P., Ricque, B.: Multi-domain comparison of safety standards. In: Proceedings of the Embedded Real Time Software and Systems Conference, May 2010
13. Esposito, C., Cotroneo, D., Silva, N.: Preliminary investigation on safety-related standards. Technical Report—Mobilab. www.mobilab.unina.it/techreports.html. Sept 2011
14. Grottke, M., Trivedi, K.: A classification of software faults. In: Supplemental Proceedings of Sixteenth International IEEE Symposium on Software Reliability Engineering (2005)
15. Bloomfield, R., Littlewood, B., Wright, D.: Confidence: its role in dependability cases for risk assessment. In: Proceedings of 37th Annual IEEE/IFIP International Conference on Dependable Systems and Networks (DSN 07) June 2007
16. Arlat, J., et al.: Fault injection for dependability validation: a methodology and some applications. IEEE Trans. Softw. Eng. **16**(2), 166–182 (1990)
17. Broy, M.: Challenges in automotive software engineering. In: Proceedings of the 28th International Conference on Software Engineering, May 2006

Robustness Testing of Web Services

Aniello Napolitano, Gabriella Carrozza, Nuno Laranjeiro and Marco Vieira

Abstract Web services are widely used as software components that must provide a robust interface to client applications. Robustness testing is an approach particularly suitable for detecting robustness issues in web services. In fact, several research works have been conducted in the past leading to the proposal of different robustness testing techniques for such environments. However, although of utmost importance, most techniques do not consider the needs of complex systems and services as the ones being developed by the software industry for business and safety critical scenarios. The chapter makes a brief overview on the web service robustness approaches, as well as providing the actual solution available both in scientific literature and on the market for automatically carried put the tests. Stemming from this analysis, the authors show the limitation of those tools in being exploited in the industrial environment, and they describe a new tool capable of addressing the industrial needs.

Keywords Software dependability · Automatic robustness testing · Complex web services · ATC applications

A. Napolitano (✉) · G. Carrozza
SESM s.c.a.r.l, Via Circumvalazione Esterna di Napoli, 80014 Giugliano, Italy
e-mail: anapolitano@sesm.it

G. Carrozza
e-mail: gcarrozza@sesm.it

N. Laranjeiro · M. Vieira
Department of Informatics Engineering, DEI, Pólo II—Universidade de Coimbra,
3030-290 Coimbra, Portugal
e-mail: cnl@dei.uc.pt

M. Vieira
e-mail: mvieira@dei.uc.pt

D. Cotroneo (ed.), *Innovative Technologies for Dependable OTS-Based Critical Systems*,   55
DOI: 10.1007/978-88-470-2772-5_5, © Springer-Verlag Italia 2013

1 Introduction

Web Services (WS) are a key technology in Service Oriented Architecture (SOA) environments, which are increasingly being used in critical applications. A web service is a software component that exposes a given functionality that can be assessed by service consumers in an interoperable manner.

In web services environments the Simple Object Access Protocol (SOAP) [1] is used for exchanging XML-based messages between the consumer and the provider over the network (using, for example, HTTP or HTTPS protocols). In each interaction the consumer (client) sends a SOAP request message to the provider (the server). After processing the request, the server sends a response message to the client with the results. A web service may include several operations (in practice, each operation is a method with one or several input parameters) and is described using WSDL (Web-Services Definition Language) [2], which is an XML-based language used to generate server and client code. A broker enables applications to find web services.

Web services are usually developed against aggressive schedule constraints. Thus, they are frequently deployed before being properly tested and carrying residual defects. Software faults (i.e., program defects or bugs) related to input validation (i.e., interface faults) are particularly relevant in web services as these have to provide a robust interface to client applications, even in the presence of invalid inputs (e.g., invalid SOAP messages).

Robustness testing allows the characterization of the behavior of a system or component in presence of erroneous input conditions [3–5], which may occur due to bugs in the client applications, corruptions caused by silent communication failures, or even security attacks. These may expose real applications to severe problems, including critical vulnerabilities that can be maliciously exploited with serious consequences, such as denial-of-service (DoS), or data loss. This way, robustness testing represents a key approach for the development of robust web services.

Several approaches have been proposed for the evaluation of the robustness of web services (e.g., [6–8]). Typically, these approaches consist of a set of robustness tests (i.e., invalid web services call parameters) that is applied to disclose both programming and design problems. The robustness of the web services tested is characterized according to the observed failure modes. The problem is that existing tools are quite simple and do not consider the real needs faced by software development industry. Some of those limitations are: not recognizing customized and complex parameters, not considering parameters that are XML formatted, not taking into account the service internal state, and not analyzing automatically the results of tests.

In this chapter we provide an overview of robustness testing and discuss the architecture of a robustness testing tool (designated WSRTesting), which was specifically built to target industry needs. The tool was developed at SESM Scarl that is able to conduct robustness tests on complex web services. This tool is based on the work presented in [6] and has been enhanced with features that allow fulfilling real testing needs, turning it into a powerful instrument that goes beyond mere experimental scenarios.

To demonstrate its effectiveness we have used the proposed tool in the context of an Air Traffic Control (ATC) application. Results show that the tool can be successfully used for detecting robustness problems in real scenarios and that it overcomes the limitations of other existing tools. This suggests that companies can successfully use robustness testing during the development of highly complex service based applications.

The structure of the chapter is as follows. The next section presents background on web services robustness testing. Section 3 briefly discusses the testing needs faced by software industry. Section 4 presents an overview of the robustness testing approach implemented by WSRTesting and Sect. 5 presents robustness testing tools that implement the approach, with emphasis on the architecture and functionality of WSRTesting. In Sect. 5 we present an experimental evaluation carried out to evaluate the tool's capabilities. Finally, Sect. 6 concludes the chapter.

2 Background on Robustness Testing

The goal of robustness testing is to characterize the behavior of a system in presence of erroneous input conditions. Although it is not directly related to benchmarking (as there is no standard procedure meant to compare different systems/components concerning robustness), authors usually refer to robustness testing as robustness benchmarking. This way, as proposed by [3], a robustness benchmark is essentially a suite of robustness tests or stimuli. A robustness benchmark stimulates the system in a way that triggers internal errors, and in that way exposes both programming and design errors in the error detection or recovery mechanisms. Systems can be differentiated according to the number of errors uncovered.

Ballista is a tool that combines software testing and fault injection techniques [4]. The main goal is to test software components for robustness, focusing specially on operating systems. Tests are made using combinations of exceptional and acceptable input values of parameters of kernel system calls. The parameter values are extracted randomly from a database of predefined tests and a set of values of a certain data type is associated to each parameter. The robustness of the target OS is classified according to the CRASH scale that distinguishes the following failure modes: Catastrophic (OS becomes corrupted or the machine crashes or reboots), Restart (application hangs and must be terminated by force), Abort (abnormal termination of the application), Silent (no error is indicated by the OS on an operation that cannot be performed), and Hindering (the error code returned is not correct).

MAFALDA (Microkernel Assessment by Fault injection AnaLysis and Design Aid) is a tool that allows the characterization of the behavior of microkernels in the presence of faults [5]. MAFALDA supports fault injection both into the parameters of system calls and into the memory segments implementing the target micro-kernel. However, in what concerns to robustness testing, only the fault injection into the parameters of system calls is relevant.

One of the first examples of robustness testing applied to web services is [7]. This paper proposes a technique to test web services using parameter mutation analysis. The web services description file (defined using WSDL) is parsed initially and mutation operators are applied to it, resulting in several mutated documents that will be used to test the service. In spite of the effort set on this approach, the parameter mutation operators are very limited and consist basically on switching, adding, deleting elements, or setting complex types to null.

In [8] a similar approach is presented. Although it represents a more complete study, the coupling that is done to the XML (eXtensible Markup Language) technology invalidates any kind of test generalization (i.e., it does not apply to other technologies since it is tightly coupled to XML).

Another approach to assess the behavior of web services in the presence of tampered SOAP messages was proposed in [6]. It consists of a set of robustness tests based on invalid call parameters. The services are classified using an adaptation of the CRASH robustness scale, proposed by Koopman and DeVale for operating systems [4].

3 Approach for Robustness Testing of Web Services

In general, a robustness benchmark for web services includes the following components: workload (represents the work that the service must perform during the benchmark run); robustness tests (set of invalid call parameters that is applied to expose robustness problems); and failure modes classification (characterize the behavior of the web service while executing the workload in the presence of the robustness tests). The testing procedure is typically based in the following generic set of steps:

1. **Tests preparation**: analysis of the interface of the WS under testing (e.g., using the WSDL description [2]) in order to gather information about the relevant operations, call parameters and data types.
2. **Tests execution**: execution of robustness tests, generated based on the specific characteristics of the interface of the web service. The goal is to trigger faulty behaviors, and in that way disclose robustness problems.
3. **Web service characterization**: analysis of the results of the robustness tests, including failure modes identification.

Before generating and executing the robustness tests one needs to obtain some definitions about the web service operations, parameters, data types and domains. The web service interface is described as a WSDL file that can be processed to obtain the list of operations, parameters (including return values) and associated data types. However, the valid values for each parameter (i.e., the domain of the parameter) cannot be deduced from the WSDL description. Thus, the tester has typically to provide information on the valid domains for each parameter.

A workload (set of valid web service calls) is needed to exercise each operation of the web service under testing. As it is not possible to propose a generic workload that fits all web services, a specific workload should be generated for the web service under testing. Two options are normally considered for the generation of the workload: user defined workloads and random workloads.

The set of robustness tests performed is automatically generated by applying a set of predefined rules (see examples in [6]) to the parameters of each operation of the web service. An important aspect is that rules focus difficult input validation aspects, such as: null and empty values, valid values with special characteristics, invalid values with special characteristics, maximum and minimum valid values in the domain, values exceeding the maximum and minimum valid values in the domain, and values that cause data type overflow.

The robustness of the web services is classified according to a given robustness scale. An example is wsCRASH [6], an adapted version of the CRASH scale [4], that distinguishes the following failure modes: Catastrophic (the application server used to run the web service under testing becomes corrupted or the machine crashes or reboots), Restart (the web service execution hangs and must be terminated by force), Abort (abnormal termination of the web service execution), Silent (no error is indicated by the application server), and Hindering (the error code returned is not correct or the response is delayed).

4 The Driving Factor: Industry Needs

In the industrial context, Web Services have mainly been exploited to enable the interoperability among heterogeneous subsystems, or even among entire, widely distributed, complex systems. Indeed, they allow integrating independent systems, also coming from different vendors and developed in different moments. Thanks to these attractive features, also the industrials, operating in military and strategic contexts have been starting in the exploitation of this technology for mission critical applications, such as *Vessel Traffic Management System* (*VTMS*), *Combat and Management System* (*CMS*) for aircraft carriers and *Airport Traffic Management* (*ATM*) system.

As an instance, the new information infrastructure, namely *SWIM* (*System Wide Information Management*) [9, 10], defined in *SESAR* (*Single European Sky ATM Research*) European program for sharing data information in seamless manner among ATM stakeholders and ground handler, relies heavy on Web Service technology. In particular, some Web Services are utilized for performing the handover operation related to the aircrafts responsibility between air sectors, or for exchanging flights information during their cruises among ACC centers, as well as surveillance data and weather forecasts.

Anyway, the introduction of the Web Services in this particular filed has given rise to new issues and challenges that have not still been faced or taken into account, when this technology was exploited in simple applications. In fact, the activities for assessing and measuring the dependability level either of availability or the security faults providing from this kind of technology have been neglected. On contrary, in the military, but also in civil applications impacting in mission critical scenarios, such as the ATM, the aforementioned features stand for important parameters to be assessed in order to pre-emptively identify the presence of failures. Thanks to this gained information, suitable countermeasures can be successively built around the system target for avoiding serious effects to the system functionalities.

Moreover, due to the strict dependability requirements imposed by critical scenarios, Web Service technology needs to be assessed along with the target systems in which it operates. In dependability field, robustness assessment allows identifying, through easy tests, the presence of failures affecting the applications under testing and understanding their effects on the target system behavior. In the case of Web Services, and due to their actual role in the system, the presence of a failure can have waterfall effects on the target system, affecting all the consumer applications that rely on the incoming data.

Therefore, robustness assessment needs to be performed during the validation phase of a system, and it, in the best case, should be executed on single subsystems first and on the integrated systems later. It's worth noting that this testing activity, as all the other kind of test phases, is time consuming in the both planning and execution stage, as well as it often needs to involve several skilled testers for performing the tests campaign in order to on the one hand reduce the time to market and on the other hand provide a reliable product. Again, the classic tradeoff between cost or time-to-market and product reliability is still the main issue to be coped with.

To face time to market constraints, companies need technical solutions for automating the tests campaigns and getting results as soon as possible. As for as robustness testing concerns, this is not the only strict requirement to be met from any available tool, bur further needs, coming from the actual industrial applications, have to be covered.

In practice, web service development and tester teams for robustness testing still urge the development of tools capable of providing the following capabilities:

- Recognize customized and complex WS parameters from the description provided in the WSDL file. Typically, parameters are not just base types, like *String, int, float, and* so on, rather they are customized and complex, defined by developers according to the functional application requirements and described into the WS descriptor (i.e. WSDL file).
- Manage WS parameters that are XML-formatted. These inputs are usually exploited for exchanging complex and structured data among WS. In this case, information is a cloud of nested fields, either complex or base type. To perform

robustness tests, a XML base version of the input needs to be built and each field has to be properly filled according to robustness testing rules.

- Create a testing workflow depending on the service invocation semantics. This is to avoid robustness tests from providing meaningless results due to the invocation of patterns that would never occur. For example, let us take into account a WS issuing two functions: *createObject(...)* and *readObject(...)*. The latter accepts as arguments the unique identifier of the *Object* (*ID_Obj*), and some attributes XML-formatted (referred as *ClusterObj*). In this case, performing robustness tests without considering the logic dependency between *ClusterObj* and *ID_Obj* would provide an *ID_Obj not recognized* response, thus preventing to assess the WS behavior when *ClusterObject* is stressed. In other words, many robustness tests require sequences of operations (i.e., a testing workflow) to be successfully performed.
- Manage tests results automatically. The achieved results should be automatically analyzed in order to provide a summary of the tests that have not passed. This is especially relevant when dealing with several hundreds of functions to test, and thousands of related arguments, as well as in the case of several XML formatted inputs, for which many fields have to be investigated.

To the best author's knowledge, after a detailed analysis of existing available solutions/tools for performing robustness testing, it is possible to conclude that neither academic nor commercial solutions have been so far developed to completely cover the above industrial needs.

5 Web Service Robustness Testing Tools

Robustness testing on web service needs to address specific requirements, which have been previously described. Nowadays, some solutions and tools are already available on both the market and developed as prototype in scientific literature for performing web service robustness testing, but none of them allow to meet the aforementioned industrial needs. SoapUI® is one of most famous tools suite for web service testing. It is downloadable both in open source and pro license and allows accomplishing functional and load test, as well as security tests. SoapUI automatically recognizes the operation advertised from the web services, through the wsdl parsing, and for each operation, distinguishes the inputs types, e.g. *string*, *int*, and so on, as well as providing out the xml template of the SOAP request. Stemming from the template, the tester can manually fill the fields of the SOAP request with the values to be exploited for the tests; multiple tests require to the tester the filling out of several templates with different input values. Once all the requests have been adjusted, the SoapUI takes in charge to sequentially submit the request to the web server and automatically stores the responses. No automatic analysis and classification of the responses are performed by the tools. As an instance, Fig. 1 depicts a template achieved by SoapUI parsing the wsdl reachable

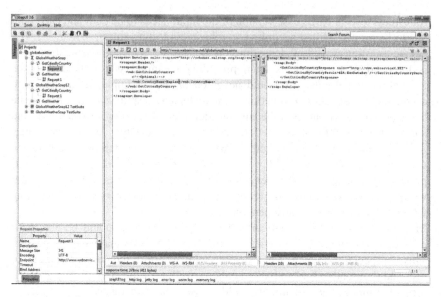

Fig. 1 SoapUI® GUI for web service testing

at the address given in [11]. It's worth noting that the tools doesn't provide proper capabilities for making robustness testing, but the tester must manually set the robustness values to be utilized according with his knowledge on this test field. Anyway, once the setup stage is performed and saved within a project, the tool allows to quickly and continuously testing the web service during its life cycle. That is, a huge setup stage, making use of skilled tester, is returned with a repeatability and automation of the tests running. This approach can sound good when simple web service operations, with few fields, have to be tested. On contrary, this becomes unfeasible when the web service operations accept in input either several inputs or single one with nested fields, such as the case of xml input.

Wsrbench is a further tool, available on line at Fig. 1, properly addressed to perform robustness testing on the web service. Wsrbench provides a web-based interface that allows users to perform configurations and visualize the results of tests. Note that, anyone can use the tool as it is free and very easy to use. Only a very simple registration and posterior authentication is required.

After registration and authentication three key options are available for users: Configuration; Add WSDL; and My Tests. The *Configuration* option allows several configuration aspects to be defined, such as the user's email, number of finished tests to show on screen, etc. The *Add WSDL* option allows users to add the WSDL file describing a web service to be tested for robustness. After submitting the WSDL file the user can visualize the set of operations and parameters provided by the service. This is represented in Fig. 2.

As shown in Fig. 2, for each testable operation the user may define the valid values for each parameter (i.e., the domain of the parameter). When these are not

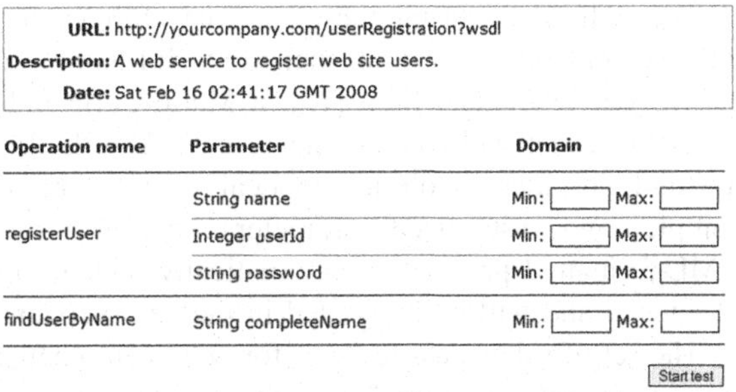

Fig. 2 Web service parameters domain definition by wsrbench

	URL: http://yourcompany.com/userRegistration?wsdl
	Description: A web service to register web site users.
	Date: Sat Feb 16 02:41:17 GMT 2008

Operation name	Parameter	Domain		
registerUser	String name	Min: [ ]	Max: [ ]	
	Integer userId	Min: [ ]	Max: [ ]	
	String password	Min: [ ]	Max: [ ]	
findUserByName	String completeName	Min: [ ]	Max: [ ]	

Start test

defined, the tool considers that the parameter domain is the domain of the corresponding data type. After defining the domain of the parameters the tests can start (by clicking the *Start Test* button). The user will be informed by email when the tests conclude and the results can be analyzed later on.

The *My Tests* option allows the user to visualize the tests previously performed along with information on currently ongoing tests. Detailed results for the concluded tests are available and are presented as shown in Fig. 3. More details are provided in [12]. Anyway, wsrbench tool addresses the industrial needs better that SoapUI, since it allows automatically generating the SOAP requests, filling with correct robustness values the fields, and recognizing and classifying the achieved responses according with a suitable scale, namely wsCRASH scale. Recognize customized and complex WS parameters from the description provided in the WSDL file, along with the management of WS parameters XML-formatted aren't still capabilities covered from the wsrbench tool.

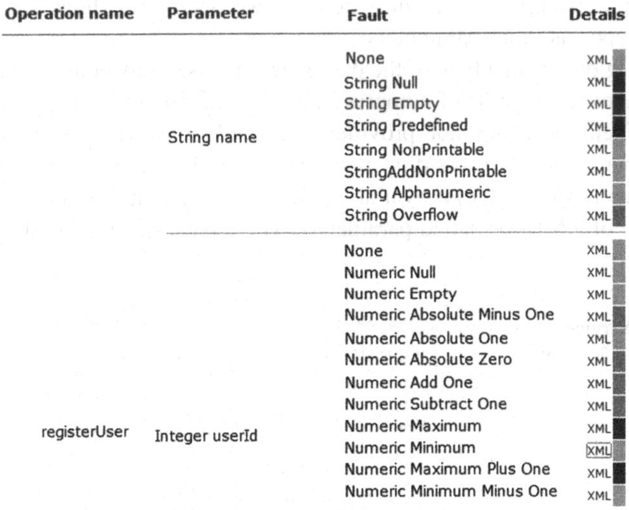

Operation name	Parameter	Fault	Details
		None	XML
		String Null	XML
		String Empty	XML
	String name	String Predefined	XML
		String NonPrintable	XML
		StringAddNonPrintable	XML
		String Alphanumeric	XML
		String Overflow	XML
		None	XML
		Numeric Null	XML
		Numeric Empty	XML
		Numeric Absolute Minus One	XML
		Numeric Absolute One	XML
		Numeric Absolute Zero	XML
		Numeric Add One	XML
		Numeric Subtract One	XML
registerUser	Integer userId	Numeric Maximum	XML
		Numeric Minimum	XML
		Numeric Maximum Plus One	XML
		Numeric Minimum Minus One	XML

Fig. 3 Detailed test results for a web service by wsrbench

The will of covering these new capabilities has driven the authors in the development of a new tool, named WSRTesting, during the scientific activities carried out in Critical Step [13], a Marie-Curie Industry-Academia Partnerships and Pathways (IAPP) belonging to call FP7-PEOPLE-2008-IAPP. In particular, the tool provides a solution to deal with the recognition and management of complex and customized parameters, as well as with the possibility of testing XML-formatted parameters automatically. Other capabilities are currently being developed and will be integrated in the next version of the tool.

The set of robustness tests performed is automatically generated by applying a pool of predefined rules [6] to the parameters of each web service operation. However, adding to the rules proposed in [6], also *enumerative* type is recognized for robustness tests and managed as a *string* type.

Tests are conducted on each operation following two phases. In the first one, the operation is invoked without considering invalid parameters, in order to understand the typical behavior expected from the WS. In the second phase, several tests are run with invalid call parameters (i.e. robustness tests), where each test focuses on a given parameters of the operation and includes many injection periods. In each injection period several faults (from a single type) are applied to the parameter under test.

WSRTesting provides an interface that allows users to configure the tests and analyze the achieved results. As it is provided as a standalone web application, it can be quickly integrated in any application server.

Via the main page users can add the WSDL file describing a WS to be tested for robustness. After the submission and parsing of a WSDL descriptor, a description of all the available operations provided by the service is showed. The tool is able to recognize all the operations and to provide, for each operation, the description of the parameters in terms of their *name* and associated data *type*. Figure 4 provides a simple example of this, in which the two operations showed have *double* and *string* types as input parameters.

Depending on the data type of the parameter, the user may define the admissible range of values (in the case of numeric *type*) or its maximum length (in the case of *strings*). When these are not provided, the tool considers the default values associated with the corresponding data *type*. For the *string* type an additional capability (i.e., load *xsd* file) is available. This allows loading an *xsd* file describing the structure of XML-formatted parameters. The inputs, specified in the XML file,

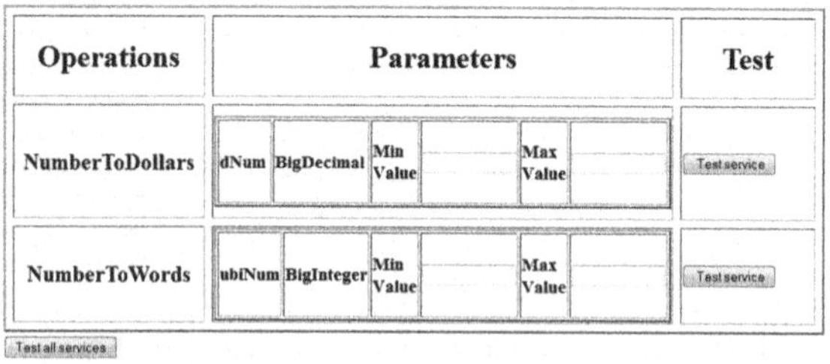

Fig. 4 Web Service parameter definition by WSRTesting

Operations	Parameters					Test
NumberToDollars	dNum	BigDecimal	Min Value		Max Value		Test service
NumberToWords	ubtNum	BigInteger	Min Value		Max Value		Test service

Test all services

Fig. 5 Detailed tests results for a web service by WSRTesting

Name	dNum
Type	BigDecimal
Value	
Request/response	XML
Name	dNum
Type	BigDecimal
Value	-1
Request/response	XML

are then tested according to the data type. Nested files (i.e., XML-formatted inputs inside other XML-formatted input) are recursively processed in the same manner.

Once all configurations are performed, the robustness tests can be executed on a single operation (by clicking *Test service* button) or on all web service operations (i.e. *Test all service* button). The details of the conducted tests results are provided as showed in Fig. 5. The results of the robustness tests applied to each parameter are as follows. The first row for each operation represents the regular request that is performed without considering any invalid input (i.e., no faults are injected). The *"XML"* link opens a popup where more details are provided. These include the request sent and the received response. In this way, the user can see the result of the test and identify the presence (or absence) of robustness issues.

For the sake of completeness, the high level architecture of the WSRTesting tool is presented in Fig. 6. The tool was developed according to the *MVC* (Model View Controller) design pattern implementation, where the logic of the application (*Model*) is separated from the user interface (*View*) under the handling of a *Controller*. The application *Model* performs the operations chain presented in Fig. 6, where the solid lines stand for the normal sequence and the dashed lines are optional paths that are executed when using *xsd* files. A further details on the tools are given in [14].

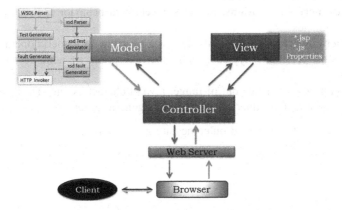

Fig. 6 High-level architecture of WSRTesting tool

Table 1 Achieved outcomes by WSRTesting tool

Publisher	Operation	Parameter	Abort failures				
			DB	Arith.	Null Ref.	Other	XML
Webservicex.net [15]	GetSunSetRiseTime (int, int, int, int)	timeZone		2			
		day		2			
		month		2			
		year		2			
Webservicex.net	VerifyAddress (String, String, String)	city		1	1		
		state		1			
		zip		1			
terraservice.net [16]	ConvertLonLatToNearestPlace (double, double)	Lon	4				
		Lat	4				
	ConvertLonLatPt ToUtmPt (double, double)	Lon		2			
		Lat		2			
	ConvertPlaceToLonLatPt (String, String, String)	City	6				
		State	6				
		Country	6				
Webservicex.net	Book (String, Int)	Symbol				8	
		NumberOfRecords		2		10	
	LastExecution (String, Int)	Symbol				6	
		NumberOfRecords		2			
	TopLists (Int, String, String)	NumberOfRecords		3		6	
		filter		6			
		sort		6			

An intensive tests campaign has been carried out for assessing the tool functionalities. In particular, WSRTesting has been utilized for testing several online web services in order to pinpoint their possible failures. The major detected abort failures observed during the tests have been:

- **Null references**: related to null pointers that reflect none or poor input validation in the service provider.
- **Database access operations**: includes exceptional behavior caused by invalid SQL commands.
- **Arithmetic operations**: typically data type overflow in numeric operations.
- **Conversion problems**: typically class cast exceptions or numeric conversion problems.
- **Other causes**: arguments out of range, invalid characters, etc. These were not very frequent and are thus classified in this generic group.

The details of the achieved outcomes are given in Table 1.

6 Conclusions

This chapter drives the readers in getting awareness of the actual problem in performing robustness testing and how, nowadays, this aspect is crucial for industrials with respect to technologies like the Web Service. Stemming from general and well known guidelines for fulfilling robustness testing, the chapter describes how those guidelines need to be specified for Web Service technologies, which are more and more exploited from the industrial also in mission and critical applications, such as combat management systems, air traffic control, command and controls, and so on. In this context, the industrials ask tools capable of assessing the robustness of web service in order to understand the reliability of the developed systems, which rely on this technology. To this aim, the chapter describes the actual tools and solutions available for performing web service robustness testing, and it compares these with the needs required from the industrial world. The analysis shows that none of the examined tools cover has a limitation and they don't meet all the industrial needs. To overcome this gap, a new tool, namely WSRTesting is presented, which goes one step beyond including advanced testing features, such as the ability to test XML formatted Strings, using their XML Schema definitions. The achieved results indicate that the tool is able to overcome the limitations present in other existing tools, making it a powerful tool to test complex service applications.

References

1. Gudgin, M., Hadley, M., Mendelsohn, N., Moreau, J.-J., Nielsen, H.F., Karmarkar, A., Lafon, Y.: SOAP Version 1.2 Part 1: Messaging Framework (Second Edition). Web Services Activity: XML Protocol Working Group (2007)
2. Curbera, F., Duftler, M., Khalaf, R., Nagy, W., Mukhi, N., Weerawarana, S.: Unraveling the Web services web: an introduction to SOAP, WSDL, and UDDI. IEEE Internet Comput. 6, 86–93 (2002)
3. Mukherjee, A., Siewiorek, D.P.: Measuring software dependability by robustness benchmarking. Trans. Softw. Eng. 23, 366–376 (1997)
4. Koopman, P., DeVale, J.: Comparing the robustness of POSIX operating systems. In: Twenty-Ninth Annual International Symposium on Fault-Tolerant Computing (1999)
5. Rodríguez, M., Salles, F., Fabre, J.-C., Arlat, J.: MAFALDA: microkernel assessment by fault injection and design aid. In: The Third European Dependable Computing Conference on Dependable Computing. Springer (1999)
6. Vieira, M., Laranjeiro, N., Madeira, H.: Benchmarking the robustness of web services. In: 13th IEEE Pacific Rim Dependable Computing Conference (PRDC 2007). IEEE Computer Society, Melbourne, Australia (2007)
7. Siblini, R., Mansour, N.: Testing web services. In: The 3rd ACS/IEEE International Conference on Computer Systems and Applications (2005)
8. Offutt, J., Xu, W., Luo, J.: Testing web services by XML perturbation. In: 16th IEEE International Symposium on Software Reliability Engineering (2005)

9. Carrozza, G., Crescenzo, D., Napolitano, A., Strano, A.: Data distribution technologies in wide area systems: lessons learned from the SWIM-SUIT project experience. Netw. Protoc. Algorithms **2**(3), 100–115 (2010)
10. System Wide Information Management Supported by Innovative Technologies. http://www.swim-suit.aero/swimsuit
11. http://www.webservicex.net/globalweather.asmx?WSDL
12. Wsrbench—Web Services Robustness Benchmarking. http://wsrbench.dei.uc.pt
13. http://www.critical-step.eu/
14. Napolitano, A., Carrozza, G., Laranjeiro, N., Vieira, M.: WSRTesting: hands-on solution to improve web services robustness testing. In: 5th Latin-American Symposium on Dependable Computing (2011)
15. http://www.webservicex.net/ws/default.aspx
16. TerraService. http://terraservice.net/TerraService.asmx?WSDL

JFIT: An Automatic Tool for Assessing Robustness of DDS-Compliant Middleware

Antonio Bovenzi, Aniello Napolitano, Christian Esposito
and Gabriella Carrozza

Abstract The use of publish/subscribe middleware within the context of critical systems has raised the issue of assessing the provided degree of reliability and fault tolerance. Literature is rich of frameworks for the performance evaluation of publish/subscribe services. However, it lacks efficient solutions for an effective robustness evaluation of these middleware. For this purpose, this paper proposes a tool to automatically evaluate the robustness of DDS-compliant solutions. In addition, experiments have been conducted on an actual implementation of the DDS standard, by means of injecting a set of invalid and/or exceptional inputs through its API and analyzing the observed behaviors. The tool has helped revealing two types of middleware misbehaviors, which according to the CRASH scale, were classified as *Silent* and *Restart*.

Keywords Robustness testing · Publish/subscribe · DDS middleware

A. Bovenzi (✉)
Dipartimento di Informatica e Sistemistica (DIS),
Universitá degli Studi di Napoli Federico II, Via Claudio 21, Naples, Italy
e-mail: antonio.bovenzi@unina.it

A. Napolitano · G. Carrozza
SESM S.c.a.r.l, Via Circumvallazione Esterna di Napoli 80014 Giugliano, Italy
e-mail: anapolitano@sesm.it

G. Carrozza
e-mail: gcarrozza@sesm.it

C. Esposito
Consorzio Interuniversitario Nazionale per l'Informatica (CINI), Complesso
Universitario M.S. Angelo, via Cinthia, 80126 Naples, Italy
e-mail: christian.esposito@unina.it

D. Cotroneo (ed.), *Innovative Technologies for Dependable OTS-Based Critical Systems*,   69
DOI: 10.1007/978-88-470-2772-5_6, © Springer-Verlag Italia 2013

1 Introduction

Middleware solutions based on the event-based architectures and the publish/
subscribe interaction model have faced a considerable success as a way to provide
a scalable and efficient asynchronous communication [1]. The typical application
domains of these middleware solutions mainly focused on on-line gaming or
media content distribution. However, in the recent years we have witnessed the
growing adoption of publish/subscribe middleware also within the context of
critical systems [2]. This is due to the fact that mission critical systems are
undergoing an important evolution by adopting federated architectures. Such
architectures are known as *Large-scale Complex Critical Infrastructures*
(LCCI) [3], and aim at the integration of several existing, mostly legacy, systems
and their cooperation to take more efficient control decisions. Such evolution is not
only the outcome of an investigation of certain academic research centers, but it is
about to be applied in concrete industrial systems such as the novel framework for
Air Traffic Management (ATM) funded by EUROCONTROL in the context of the
Single European Sky ATM Research (SESAR) project[1] to establish a seamless
interoperability among heterogeneous ATM stakeholders and entities.

The adoption of publish/subscribe middleware in critical systems imposes the
satisfaction of additional non-functional requirements that were not the focus of
the research community on publish/subscribe middleware. In fact, apart from
scalability and performance, whose evaluation was seamless studied by
researchers, critical systems require that the communication infrastructure offers
highly reliability and fault tolerance, i.e., message deliveries have to be guaranteed
despite failures may occur. Several surveys, such as [2], have shown that several
approaches are available for realizing a reliable event notification and each is
characterized by a certain degree of provided reliability and fault tolerance.
Therefore, industrial practitioners are facing the demanding need of having a
proper evaluation method to assess the different available publish/subscribe middleware products so to select the solution that best fits the imposed reliability
requirements. In addition, the design of critical systems is strictly regulated by
proper safety standards, such as IEC61508 [4] and DO178B [5], that require a
rigorous verification and validation (V&V) of each parts constituting the overall
system. Among the several objectives of a V&V process, it is crucial to provide
evidences that there is no violation of non-functional requirements imposed on the
adopted communication infrastructure, which can be obtained by a proper evaluation method.

In this paper we present an evaluation approach for assessing publish/subscribe
middleware. We have focused on the assessment of Robustness of such communication infrastructures, i.e., "the degree to which a system or component can
function correctly in the presence of invalid inputs or stressful environmental
conditions" [6], as commonly required by many standards. Specifically, we have

---

[1] http://www.eurocontrol.int/content/sesar-and-research

focused on invalid inputs, leaving for future work the test of stressful environmental conditions. We have drawn on the available literature on *Robustness testing* [7] by injecting exceptional and/or invalid inputs in the middleware API and checking that the observed behavior of the middleware is compliant with the specifications. We have designed a tool to perform robustness testing experiments, collect the observed behavior and to finally perform an automatically failure classification. We have selected a publish/subscribe middleware compliant to the OMG *Data Dissemination Service* (DDS) specification [8], which has been chosen as reference technology within the SESAR program. Hence, we have experimented the proposed tool using a real case study coming from ATM domain, which is exploited in an industrial prototype, namely SWIM-BOX$^{(R)}$, developed by SELEX-SI^2 in the framework of SESAR research. However, our tool can be easily adapted to any possible publish/subscribe solution. In this paper, we present an evolution of our work with respect to what previously presented in [9]: the tool has been enriched with a repository that allows automatic storage and analysis of test outcomes, and a richer experimental campaign has been performed with a total of about 1500 experiments.

The structure of the paper is as follows. Section 2 provides an introduction to publish/subscribe services and an overview of the related work on robustness testing. Section 3 describes the approach to assess robustness of DDS middleware; while, Sect. 4 provides the implementation details of the proposed tool. Section 5 presents the experimental results, showing that the proposed tool has automatically detected robustness issues in the DDS middleware under study. Conclusions and future work are in Sect. 6.

2 Background and Related Work

The *OMG Data-Distribution Service* (DDS) [8] is a specification for publish/subscribe services issued by the OMG with the scope of providing (i) a common application-level interface for achieving interoperability, (ii) real-time communications, i.e., by offering predictable messages deliverable, and (iii) high performance. It realizes a data-centric communication, where the information exchanges refer to values of an imaginary global data object, in opposition to the traditional address-centric, where information exchanges refer to certain destinations univocally identified by a network address. OMG DDS defines a publish/subscribe service where objects of the global data space are identified by topics and keys.

An exhaustive discussion about approaches and methodologies for robustness testing can be found in [7]. Hereinafter, a brief discussion of most popular approach to Robustness Testing is provided. Through the last years, research on robustness testing at interface level has produced several tools, such as Fuzz [10]

---

^{2} A Finmeccanica company. http://www.selex-si.com/

and Ballista [11], mainly based on the idea of producing several test cases with random values. Ballista is probably the most popular robustness tool, and its focus is especially on the assessment of the robustness of Operating Systems (OS). Microkernel Assessment by Fault injection AnaLysis and Design Aid (MAF-ALDA) [12] is another popular tool allowing the characterization of the behavior of microkernels in the presence of faults. MAFALDA also supports fault injection at lower level than API, by allowing the corruption of memory segments implementing the target microkernel. Recently it has been extended in [13] in order to allow the characterization of CORBA-based middleware.

To the best of our knowledge, the only publish/subscribe service technology analyzed is the Java Message System (JMS) [14]. Authors have tested the middleware functionalities with exceptional parameters, unexpected and/or malicious messages coming from remote applications. In this work we have adopted a similar approach to test DDS-complaint middleware robustness by focusing on invalid and exceptional inputs.

3 Robustness Testing of DDS Middleware

Robustness testing mainly aims at uncovering software dependability pitfalls due to residual faults. In this work we focus on invalid inputs to stimulate the DDS middleware API to check if the observe behavior is compliant with the specification. Furthermore, robustness testing campaigns provide to developers useful insights to build and undertake ad-hoc countermeasures.

As widely addressed in the literature [14, 15], there are many robustness testing strategies aiming at gaining specific outcomes in terms of system behavior against different inputs. These depend on several factors:

- the target software: invalid inputs can be injected at application, middleware and operating system level;
- the point of injection: the methods selected to perform the injection of invalid input parameters;
- the nature of the input to send to the system: the subset of representative values/ types that are injected.

Clearly, the subset of API to be tested and the invalid values to be injected depend on the system complexity and/or on the testing resources, in terms of time and budget constrains.

In this work robustness tests are performed at application level, since it is reasonable that OSs have been tested better than custom applications one. In particular, we develop a novel tool, named JFIT, to stimulate DDS middleware API with invalid or exceptional inputs. It is noteworthy that the following approach only requires that middleware APIs are known a-priori, and considers all the software layers below as a black-box. Hence, it allows to realize robustness testing campaigns even if the source code of the middleware is not available.

Table 1 Functions core

dds.dcps.DomainParticipantImpl.create_topic	dds.LivelinessQosPolicyKind.from_int
dds.dcps.DomainParticipantImpl.get_default_subscriber_qos	dds.OwnershipQosPolicyKind.from_int
dds.dcps.DomainParticipantImpl.get_default_topic_qos	dds.ParticipantBuiltinTopicDataTypeSupport.register_type
dds.dcps.FooDataReaderImpl.take	dds.PresentationQosPolicyAccessScopeKind.from_int
dds.dcps.FooTypeSupportImpl.Alloc	dds.PublicationBuiltinTopicDataTypeSupport.register_type
dds.dcps.FooTypeSupportImpl.registerType	dds.ReliabilityQosPolicyKind.from_int
dds.dcps.StatusConditionImpl.set_enabled_statuses	dds.SchedulingClassQosPolicyKind.from_int
dds.dcps.SubscriberImpl.create_datareader	dds.SchedulingPriorityQosPolicyKind.from_int
dds.dcps.SubscriberImpl.get_default_datareader_qos	dds.SubscriptionBuiltinTopicDataTypeSupport.register_type
dds.DestinationOrderQosPolicyKind.from_int	dds.TopicBuiltinTopicDataTypeSupport.register_type
dds.DomainParticipantFactory.create_participant	dds.WaitSet._wait
dds.DomainParticipantFactory.get_default_participant_qos	dds.WaitSet.attach_condition
dds.DurabilityQosPolicyKind.from_int	

The design of a robustness testing campaign asks for the definition and the setting of several parameters that have to be tailored for the specific system under test [14, 15]. Namely, we identify (i) the workload, (ii) the fault model and (iii) the failure modes characterizing the DDS middleware implementation representing our injection and evaluation target. These parameters can influence testing outcomes significantly, if set unproperly.

Workload

Workload selection is never trivial when designing testing campaigns; it should be representative of usual system usage conditions in order to well reproduce its real working conditions. As discussed in [16], *real workloads, realistic workloads,* and *synthetic workloads* can be used to this aim. In the very specific case of robustness testing, standard benchmarks represent a viable and simple way to test all the middleware functionalities assuring a large degree of representativeness, since they widely stimulate the platform API. However, no vendor-independent benchmark has been found for DDS middleware. For this reason we cannot be confident that a vendor specific benchmark would cover all DDS functionalities. To overcome this lack, we have conducted a function coverage analysis as suggested in [11] in order to generate the list of the most used functions for a DDS middleware. We have compared three different applications relying on DDS middleware for data dissemination:

- *Ping-pong*: a simple application in which a publisher sends a continuous data flow toward one o more subscribers, which resend back the received data.
- *Touchstone*: a vendor specific benchmark proposed for DDS performance assessment. It defines different scenarios in which the DDS middleware may work, i.e., one or more topics and different QoS settings.
- *SWIM-BOXSWIM-BOX$^{(R)}$*: an industrial prototype that relies on the DDS middleware for building a seamless communication bus in order to disseminate different ATM type of data, such as surveillance, flight, and aeronautical data.

The performed analysis aimed at defining a set of DDS functions, referred as *Functions Core* and listed in Table 1, used by all the mentioned applications: it revealed the Touchstone benchmark to be the best choice since able to address all the listed functions in a very generic, non application specific, way.

Fault model

The invalid and exceptional inputs, i.e., the actual faults to be injected have to be chosen according to a Fault model [16]: in our scenario, faults are mutation rules to apply to the inputs parameters of the API functions. The injected faults depend on the input parameter type according to the values given in Table 2. A simple but effective way to define rules is to focus on limits and exceptional values. Indeed, these values are typically the source of robustness problems [14]. In particular, we considered the following limit values:

- null and empty values (e.g. set a parameter as null or empty);
- maximum and minimum values in the domain;
- values that may cause data type overflow.

Table 2 Mutation rules and considered exceptional or invalid inputs

Parameter type	Mutation rule
String	Replaced by null value
	Replaced by empty string
	Replaced by predefined string
	Replaced by string with nonprintable characters
	Add nonprintable characters to the string
	Replaced by non-alphanumeric string
	Replaced by large string
Numeric	Replaced by null value
	Replaced by empty value
	Replaced by −1
	Replaced by 1
	Replaced by 0
	Add one
	Subtract 1
	Replaced by maximum valid number for the type
	Replaced by minimum number valid for the type
	Replaced by maximum valid number for the type plus one
	Replaced by minimum number valid for the type minus one
	Replaced by maximum value valid for the parameter
	Replaced by minimum value valid for the parameter
	Replaced by maximum valid value for the parameter plus one
	Replaced by minimum valid value for the parameter minus one
Collection	Replaced by null value
	Remove an element from the collection
	Add element to the collection
	Duplicate elements of the collection
	Remove all elements from the collection except the first one
	Remove all elements from the collection
Boolean	Replaced by null value
	Replaced by empty value
	Replaced by predefined value
	Add characters to overflow max size
Object	Replaced by null value
	Replaced by a correct target class empty object
	Replaced by an objectified primitive datatype (boolean, byte, short, etc)
Byte	Replaced by null value

As for the issue "where and how to inject faults", our tests consist of two distinct phases, named *PI* and *PII*, stemming from what [14] suggests as injection strategy definition. In PI, a series of injections are performed by considering only one invalid parameter at time into the given function. For instance, if the target input parameter is numeric, e.g., integer, all possible integer mutations are sequentially performed, in different and independent tests, without modifying the values of other input parameters. Obviously, the return value is stored for successive analysis. *PII*, instead, consists of normal execution, i.e., without injecting any fault.

This phase is necessary for registering the correct behaviour of the middleware when valid inputs are provided. Then, the behavior in *PII* is compared with the behavior observed in *PI* so to infer tiny deviation; it is clear that *PII* is performed if *PI* ends correctly, i.e., without system hang or crash; otherwise the system is manually recovered (e.g., by means of reboot). After the execution of each *PII* phase, the DDS middleware is restarted in order to avoid error accumulation.

Failure modes

Test outcomes are classified according to the criticality of the failure behavior. The classification has been accomplished by means of the CRASH scale also adopted in [11, 14].

4 JFIT Architecture

JFIT architecture stems from the preliminary one already described [9], in which a first draft of the tool is given. Actual JFIT version allows automatically injecting external faults to DDS API functions, without altering the DDS source code, as well as analyzing in semi-automatic way the achieved tests outcomes. Moreover, JFIT is able to run the tests campaigns both in local and networking configuration in order to encompass all the actual DDS usage scenarios (e.g., dissemination of flight data plan). For the sake of clarifying the design choice and the JFIT features, an exhaustive overview of the tool architecture is provided in the following sections.

4.1 Overview of JFIT Architecture

Fault injector pattern [17] is nowadays the most useful approach exploited for injecting faults. This pattern addresses the recurring phases relative to the suitable fault injection activities, that is: (i) target system activation and monitoring, (ii) experiment coordination, and (iii) storage and analysis of collected data. The implementation of this pattern allows reducing development time and preserving tool efficiency, extensibility, reusability, maintainability and portability. JFIT tool follows this patter extending it to best satisfy robustness testing needs. In doing so, the following components has been identified in the JFIT architecture:

1. **Injection Library**. According to the discussed mutation rules, it stores the *Fault Library*, namely the exceptional or invalid values that have to replace the original inputs in the method call. Moreover, the Injection Library keeps the *Method List*, namely the signature of methods to be tested (in our case, the methods of the function core). Finally, it stores the *Trigger List*, which consists of the timing rules for injecting the faults in the target methods. This injection

Library is actually implemented through a *xml* file to assure high flexibility and extensibility;

2. **Experiment Repository**. It is a well-structured database following an OnLine Analytical Processing (OLAP) approach, which stores experimental outputs in order to simplify test outcomes characterization (according to the CRASH scale) and the analysis.

JFIT high level architecture consists of the following modules (see Fig. 1):

- **Controller**. It coordinates all the modules to correctly perform the entire process. First, it collects all configuration data, such as the list of methods to be tested and the faults to inject. Then, it produces an xml document defining the testing campaign. Using such a document, the Controller properly executes the application so that it can reach the necessary state to perform the test (i.e., the invocation of the method target of the injection). Finally, it orchestrates the data collection process in order to store obtained results into the Experiment Repository.
- **Interceptor**. The interception mechanism acts as a *wrapper* between DDS middleware APIs and the workload application. It is in charge of triggering the injection process when some conditions are met: the target method is invoked; the state to perform the test is reached; there is a fault to inject in the library. It is placed outside the middleware to assure robustness testing representativeness by stressing validity checkers, which are likely placed in the more external layers.
- **Injector**. The module is in charge of performing the fault injection process. It works along with Interceptor module, for accomplishing the concrete injection. Every time the Interceptor activates it, one of the input values of intercepted method is mutated according to the mutation rules stored in the Injection Library. Actually, the faulty parameter substitution works with "native" input values, such as boolean, byte, char, short, int, long, float and double, and with java.lang.String. The user-defined types, such us object types, are substituted by *NULL* value.

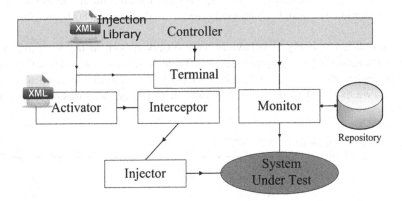

Fig. 1 JFIT Architecture

- **Monitor**. The monitoring of the injection actions and the collection of the achieved outcomes are managed by the Monitor module. This module accomplishes the monitoring task by logging the experiments outputs, and saving the obtained results in the repository, so that they can be analyzed quickly and accurately in a post-processing phase.
- **Terminal**. This module has been introduced in order to coordinate networked tests, which typically consist of several entities running on different nodes by exchanging data thought the DDS middleware. To synchronize tests and entities involved in the communication, the Terminal service uses a simple protocol based on *sync* signals.

Further details on the JFIT implementation can be found in [9].

5 Experimental Tests and Results Analysis

The experimental campaign has been carried out on actual OMG DDS implementation utilized in many mission critical systems, spanning from Defence to Aerospace, such as the SWIM-BOX[R] project. The involved middleware makes use of shared memory to interconnect publishers and subscribers to a daemon, which performs the message sending towards other nodes.

All experiments have been executed on a machine equipped with Intel Xeon 2.5 Ghz (4 core) CPU, 8 GB of RAM, running 64 bit Red-Hat Linux Operating System. Two scenarios have been taken into account, i.e., a local one, in which a single node hosts both Publisher and Subscriber, and a networked one, which involves two separate nodes on a LAN, one for the Publisher and one for the Subscriber. These two different scenarios are chosen due to a peculiarity of the considered middleware: when communicating entities reside on the same node, the middleware exploits shared memory resources of the OS to distribute information between them, otherwise the networking utilities of the OS are exploited (e.g., multicast or unicast facilities). In our experiments, the fault library accounts a total of 33 mutation rules and 27 methods, for a total of about 800 tests for each scenario.

Three different kinds of behaviors were observed both in the local and networked scenario, which are summarized in Table 3. Since the considered DDS is a mature and well-tested system and it is adopted in several mission critical applications, we expected to find very few robustness issues. As a matter of fact, no

Table 3 Results for locale and networked tests	Restart (%)	Silent (%)	Robust (%)
Local	49	11	40
Networked	47	13	40
Average	48	12	40

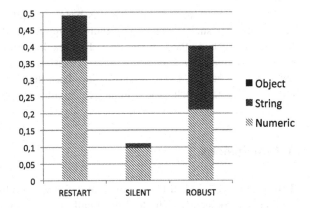

Fig. 2 Failures grouped by rules category

catastrophic, abort, and hindering events have been encountered. However only the 40 % of the tests ended with an exception compliant with DDS specification.

In average 12 % of the tests have risen a *Silent* problem, i.e., no exceptions has been thrown even if an invalid parameter was provided to the middleware. It is worth noting that, in most of the cases, the test terminated properly, i.e., all messages have been delivered, while just in few cases messages have not been delivered to the subscriber. Further analysis has been made to investigate this behavior. In particular, in Fig. 2, the obtained failures are grouped by considering the type of input injected, i.e., *numeric, string* and *object*. It is worth to note that most of the observed silent events are due to numeric mutation rules. Hence, to avoid possible unnoticed misbehaviors developers have to enforce numerical input checkers.

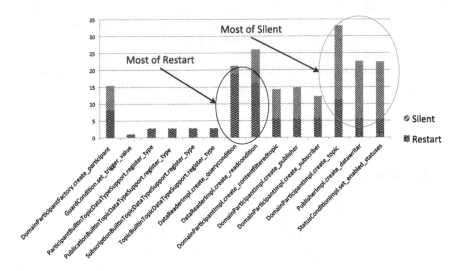

Fig. 3 Failures grouped by method

As for *Restart*, another analysis has been conducted to discover the methods responsible for such a behavior. Figure 3 shows the distribution of the type of failure for each method under test. The results show that few methods, e.g., *create_readcondition*, and *create_querycondition*, are the cause of most the restart outcomes. Moreover, Fig. 2 suggests that these methods are strongly subjected to induce a "Restart" behavior if numerical inputs are improperly used.

6 Conclusions

This paper proposed JFIT, a novel tool for the evaluation of DDS-compliant middleware robustness. The tool drastically reduces the cost of robustness testing by automatizing test executions and outcome analysis. Furthermore, it can provide to developers useful insights for the fixing of the robustness-related fault since it helps pinpointing the function and the type of input related to the robustness issue.

The tool was exploited to perform a robustness testing campaign of a DDS middleware solution that implements the DDS standard. The tool helped revealing two types of middleware misbehaviors, which according to the CRASH scale, were classified as Silent and Restart. Silent misbehavior refers to invalid input parameters that do not raise any exceptions, as instead described in the middleware documentation. However, in our tests Silent misbehavior seems not critical because the message deliveries were in most of the cases correctly performed. Restart misbehavior refers to exceptional or invalid inputs that lead to middleware unresponsiveness. This misbehavior was critical since the restart of the middleware was the only mean to recover from this failure.

These aforementioned misbehaviors were especially observed when invalid numerical inputs were injected in the input parameters of *create_readcondition*, and *create_querycondition* API. Hence, the developers could exploit these results to enforce numerical input checkers of those methods.

Future activities will be devoted to the execution of different kind of robustness tests, which take into account several QoS policies, and exceptional inputs coming from operating systems callbacks. Moreover, we plan to use the tool to assess the robustness of other DDS-compliant middleware and compare observed performance.

References

1. Eugster, P., Felber, P., Guerraoui, R., Kermarrec, A.M.: The many faces of publish/subscribe. ACM Comput. Surv. (CSUR) **35**(2), (2003)
2. Esposito, C., Cotroneo, D., Gokhale, A.: Reliable publish/subscribe middleware for time-sensitive internet-scale applications. In: Proceedings of the 3rd ACM International Conference on Distributed Event-Based Systems (DEBS 09), Nashville, pp. 1–12 (2009)

3. Esposito, C., Cotroneo, D., Gokhale, A., Schmidt, D.: Architectural evolution of monitor and control systems—issues and challenges. Int. J. Netw. Protoc. Algorithms **2**(3), 1–17 (2010)
4. IEC 61508: Functional safety of electrical/electronic/programmable electronic safety-related systems, Geneva (2005)
5. RTCA SC-167, E.W.: Software considerations in airborne systems and equipment certification. In: DO-178B, Washington (1992)
6. IEEE Std 610.12-1990: Standard glossary of software engineering terminology. IEEE, New York (1990)
7. van Moorsel, A., Madeira, H.: D2.2 State of the art in resilience assessment, measurement and benchmarking, chapter 13 robustness testing. Amber Project Deliverable. http://www.amber-project.eu/stateart.php (2009)
8. OMG Data-Distribution Service for Real-Time Systems. http://www.omg.org/spec/DDS/1.2/PDF/
9. Napolitano, A., Carrozza, G., Bovenzi, A., Esposito, C.: Automatic robustness assessment of dds-compliant middleware. In: Proceedings of the IEEE 17th Pacific Rim International Symposium on Dependable, Computing. Pasadena, pp. 174–183 (2011)
10. Forrester, J.E., Miller, B.P.: An empirical study of the robustness of windows nt applications using random testing. In: Proceedings of the 4th Conference USENIX Windows Systems Symposium. Seattle, pp. 59–68 (2000)
11. Kropp, N., Koopman, P., Siewiorek, D.: Automated robustness testing of off-the-shelf software components. In: Proceedings of the 28th International Symposium on Fault-Tolerant, Computing. Munich, pp. 30–37 (1998)
12. Rodriguez, M., Salles, F., Fabre, J.C., Arlat, J.: Mafalda: microkernel assessment by fault injection and design aid. In: Proceedings of the Third European Dependable Computing Conference on Dependable Computing. Prague, pp. 143–160 (1999)
13. Marsden, E., Fabre, J.C.: Failure mode analysis of corba service implementations. In: Proceedings of the IFIP/ACM International Conference on Distributed Systems Platforms. Heidelberg, Germany, pp. 216–231 (2001)
14. Laranjeiro, N., Vieira, M., Madeira, H.: Experimental robustness evaluation of JMS middleware. In: Proceedings of the IEEE International Conference on Services Computing. Honolulu, pp. 119–126 (2008)
15. Koopman, P., DeVale, J.: Comparing the robustness of posix operating systems. In: Proceedings of the 29th Annual International Symposium on Fault-Tolerant, Computing. IEEE CS Press, Madison, pp. 30–37 (1999)
16. Laranjeiro, N., Vieira, M., Madeira, H.: Robustness validation in service-oriented architectures. Architecting Dependable Systems VI, LNCS 5835/2009 (2009)
17. Martins, E., Rubira, C.M.F., Leme, N.G.M.: Jaca: A reflective fault injection tool based on patterns. In: Proceedings of the International Conference on Dependable Systems and, Networks. IEEE Computer Society, Bethesda, pp. 483–482 (2002)

Part II
Fault Injection

This section is focused on techniques and tools for Fault Injection, and on their adoption in the assessment of complex computer systems. There are several important aspects that have to be considered in the design of a fault injection campaign, which are discussed in this section. Some of these aspects are the definition of an appropriate fault model, the need for automated and non-intrusive tools, and the collection and analysis of data in order to obtain useful dependability measures. In particular, the first chapter describes technical issues in the injection of *software faults* in *C* and *C++* software, and how these problems have been dealt with in the context of two tools developed in CRITICAL-STEP. The second chapter discusses the injection of software faults in *Java software*, given the increasing relevance of Java in mission-critical systems, and the challenges introduced by this technology. The third chapter proposes an approach for assessing *Publish/Subscribe services* through Fault Injection, by designing a fault model and a tool tailored for this kind of systems. Finally, the fourth chapter discusses the adoption of Fault Injection in emerging critical applications, namely the *Intel Core i7* multicore processor and the *AUTOSAR* platform for automotive systems.

Roberto Natella

Tools for Injecting Software Faults at the Binary and Source-Code Level

Anna Lanzaro, Roberto Natella and Ricardo Barbosa

Abstract *Software Fault Injection* (SFI) is an approach for the assessment of fault-tolerant software, which emulates *software faults* (i.e., *bugs*) in a software component to assess the impact of these faults on the system behavior and fault-tolerance properties. In order to make SFI feasible, support tools are required to reduce the costs of implementing the experimental testbed, to automate and to keep low the duration of SFI experiments, and to oversee the phases of SFI campaigns. The focus of this chapter is on the workflow of SFI campaigns and on their implementation and execution. We detail the steps to be performed in a SFI campaign, in order to allow a tester to reproduce them in SFI experiments, and to highlight the key aspects to which attention should be given when performing SFI. SFI is presented in the context of two SFI tools developed during the CRITICAL-STEP project, namely *SAFE*, which injects software faults by mutating the *source code* of the target, and *csXception*^{TM}*/G-SWFIT*, which injects software faults by mutating *binary code*. We also provide a comparison of the two tools in terms of accuracy (i.e., ability to inject faults that match faults in the source code), and lessons learned about the implementation of SFI tools.

A. Lanzaro (✉)
Consorzio Interuniversitario Nazionale per l'Informatica (CINI), Complesso Universitario
M.S. Angelo, Via Cinthia, 80126 Naples, Italy
e-mail: anna.lanzaro@unina.it

A. Lanzaro · R. Natella
Dipartimento di Informatica e Sistemistica (DIS), Università degli Studi di Napoli Federico
II, Via Claudio 21, 80125 Naples, Italy
e-mail: roberto.natella@unina.it

R. Barbosa
ASD-T Aeronautics, Space, Defense and Transportation Critical Software SA, Parque
Industrial de Taveiro, Lt 49 3045-504 Coimbra, Portugal
e-mail: rbarbosa@criticalsoftware.com

D. Cotroneo (ed.), *Innovative Technologies for Dependable OTS-Based Critical Systems*, 85
DOI: 10.1007/978-88-470-2772-5_7, © Springer-Verlag Italia 2013

Keywords Fault injection · Fault tolerance · Binary code mutation · Machine code mutation · Source code mutation · Testing tools

1 Introduction

The injection of software faults (*Software Fault Injection*, SFI) for the assessment of fault-tolerant software is relatively new if compared to decades of research on fault injection being focused on hardware-induced faults. Software Fault Injection aims at the realistic emulation of *software faults* (i.e., *bugs*) in a software component to assess the impact of these faults on the system behavior [1–3].

The relevance of SFI is due to the increasing risk of software faults in modern complex systems, which have been recognized as one of the major causes of system failures [4]. SFI can be adopted for the experimental evaluation of fault tolerance mechanisms, to analyze worst-case scenarios, and to benchmark alternative systems or design choices [5–7]. SFI is encompassed in recent safety standards: the ISO 26262 standard for automotive safety recommends the *"injection of arbitrary faults in order to test safety mechanisms (e.g., by corrupting software or hardware components)"* [8], and the NASA Software Safety Guidebook [9] refers to SFI as *"a technique used to determine the robustness of the software"* and *"to understand the behavior of OTS software"*.

When performing SFI of a complex software system, a huge number of software faults can be potentially injected (e.g., up to hundreds of thousands of faults in 100K lines of code). A SFI campaign requires to execute the target system several times, where at each iteration an individual fault is injected. Moreover, SFI is an elaborate process, in which several technical aspects have to be taken into account (e.g., definition of the workload and of the faultload, instrumentation of the target, collection and analysis of raw data). In order to make SFI feasible, it is therefore important to keep low the cost of experiments, in terms of effort to implement the experimental testbed and of experiment execution time [6]. Support tools are therefore required to reduce the costs of implementing the experimental testbed, to automate and to keep low the duration of fault injection experiments, and to oversee the phases of SFI campaigns.

The focus of this chapter is on the workflow of SFI campaigns and on their implementation and execution. We detail the steps to be performed in a SFI campaign, in order to allow a tester to reproduce them in SFI experiments, and to highlight what are the key aspects whose attention should be given when performing SFI. SFI is presented in the context of two SFI tools that were developed during the CRITICAL-STEP project. The first tool, SAFE, injects software faults by mutating the *source code* of the target; instead, the second tool, csXception^{TM}/ G-SWFIT, injects software faults by mutating *binary code* (i.e., the *executable code* of the target software).

The injection of software faults at *binary-level* (e.g., using csXception[TM] /G-SWFIT) is required when the target source code is not available, which is often the case of Commercial Off-The-Shelf (COTS) components. However, binary-level injection has some limitations, since it requires that programming constructs used in the source code are identified by looking only at the binary code, since the injection is performed at this level; this is a difficult and error-prone task due to the complexity of programming languages and of modern compilers, which make difficult and in some cases impossible to accurately recognize where to inject faults. For this reason, in some cases binary-level mutations do not emulate any software fault (this happens when a binary-level mutation is injected in a location in which the fault could not exist in the source code), or locations where faults could be injected are not recognized and therefore are omitted.

The injection of software faults at *source-level* (e.g., using SAFE) can achieve a high degree of accuracy: in fact, a software fault is a defective piece of source code, and injecting in the source code avoids the inaccuracies that occur when faults are injected in binary code. This approach requires the availability of the source code of the target software. It can be applied to software that has been developed *in-house*, or to third-party software that has been provided with source code (e.g., the source code may have been licensed to the buyer for safety certification purposes). Moreover, source-level injection is a viable solution in the case of *open-source* software components, which are increasingly being adopted in business- and safety-critical scenarios [10, 11].

This chapter is organized as follows. Section 2 reviews past tools and techniques that were proposed for the injection of software faults. Section 3 describes the SAFE tool for source-level SFI, and a case study to demonstrate the usage of this tool in a real-world software. Section 4 provides a description and a case study for the csXception[TM]/G-SWFIT tool for binary-level SFI. Section 5 provides a comparison of the two tools in terms of accuracy (i.e., ability to inject faults that match faults in the source code), and lessons learned about the implementation of SFI tools. Section 6 concludes the chapter.

2 Related Work

In order to emulate software faults in fault injection experiments, several studies analyzed *field data* (i.e., data collected in deployed software) about failures and faults that caused them, that were adopted to characterize faults that can realistically occur in complex software. The fault characterization schema most often adopted in SFI is the *Orthogonal Defect Classification* (ODC) [12]. ODC adopts the notion of *defect type*, which reflects the *code fix* for correcting a fault. A fault can belong to exactly one ODC defect type (i.e., types are orthogonal) among Function, Checking, Assignment, Algorithm and Interface. ODC was aimed at providing feedback during development, based on the distribution of types across development phases. In [3], ODC was extended using a classification scheme that is detailed enough for fault injection purposes, by specifying for each fault type the kind of programming construct involved in the fault (e.g., which kind of assignment should be targeted for emulating the "assignment" faults, such as initializations, assignments with constants or with expressions). That work also presented a field data study, which pointed out that the majority of the software faults belong to the set of fault types shown in Table 1, and that faults tend to follow a generic distribution (i.e., independent from the specific system).

SFI tools and techniques can be divided in three categories, according to what is actually injected: *data errors*, *interface errors*, and *code changes* (summarized in Table 2). We include tools and approaches that were adopted in past work in the context of dependability assessment of fault-tolerant systems, and do not consider tools for mutation testing (where faults are used to define test cases and not for dependability assessment) since they are out of the scope of this work.

Data errors. This approach consists of injecting errors in the data of the target (i.e., a deviation from the correct system state). This is an indirect form of SFI, as what is being injected is not the fault itself but only a possible effect of the fault. The representativeness of this type of injection is difficult to assert, as the relationship between data corruption and its possible root-cause (i.e., faults) is difficult to establish. Data error injection was adopted in early SFI studies, by using techniques for emulating hardware faults (*Software-Implemented Fault Injection*, SWIFI) [13, 14]. This approach is a practical means for inducing software failures and testing specific areas of fault tolerance [2].

Table 1 Fault types injected by G-SWFIT (see also [3])

Fault type	Description
MFC	Missing function call
MVIV	Missing variable initialization using a value
MVAV	Missing variable assignment using a value
MVAE	Missing variable assignment with an expression
MIA	Missing IF construct around statements
MIFS	Missing IF construct + statements
MIEB	Missing IF construct + statements + ELSE construct
MLAC	Missing AND in expression used as branch condition
MLOC	Missing OR in expression used as branch condition
MLPA	Missing small and localized part of the algorithm
WVAV	Wrong value assigned to variable
WPFV	Wrong variable used in parameter of function call
WAEP	Wrong arithmetic expression in function call parameter

Table 2 Categories of fault injection techniques, and some related tools

Category	Tools
Data errors	FIAT [14], csXception [20], NFTAPE [21], GOOFI [22]
Interface errors	BALLISTA [16], MAFALDA [23], Jaca [24], csXception [11]
Code changes	Ng and Chen [5], FINE and DEFINE [19], G-SWFIT [3]

Interface errors. This approach is in fact another form of error injection where the error is specifically injected at the interface between modules (e.g., system components). This usually translates to parameter corruption in functions and APIs, and it is considered a form of robustness testing. The errors injected can take many forms: from simple data corruption to syntactically valid but semantically incorrect data. As with data errors, the representativeness of the errors injected at the interfaces is not clear and there is some empirical evidence that supports the idea that injecting interface errors and changing the target code produces different effects in the target [15]. This approach is often used to interface weaknesses in individual components [16].

Code changes. Changing the code of the target component to introduce a fault is naturally the closest thing to having the fault there in the first place. Moreover, the injection of code changes is recognized by studies on mutation testing as an effective means for emulating software faults [17, 18]. However, this is not easily achieved as it requires to know exactly where in the target code one might apply such change, and what instructions should be placed in the target code. Several works followed this notion, although with some limitations: Ng and Chen [5] and the FINE and DEFINE [19] tools used code changes, although their fault model is simplistic and its representativeness is not assured. G-SWFIT [3] is the state-of-the-art technique with respect to fault representativeness, which injects the most common fault types found in the field (Table 1).

G-SWFIT (Generic Software Fault Injection Technique) injects code changes at the binary-code level. It consists of a set of *fault operators* that define *code patterns* (i.e., a sequence of opcodes) in which faults can be injected, and *code changes* to be introduced (e.g., the removal of these opcodes) to emulate software faults.[1] The proposed fault operators also provide a set of *constraints* to exclude fault locations that are not realistic (e.g., to inject an MIA fault, the IF construct must not be associated to an ELSE construct, and it must not include more than 5 statements or loops; to inject an MFC fault, the return value of the function must not be used, and the call must not be the only statement in the block). The implementation of G-SWFIT is dependent on the hardware architecture, the compiler of the target application, and compiler optimizations, since these aspects affect the binary translation of programming constructs. It was originally implemented on the x86 architecture and Microsoft Windows environment [3].

The tools considered in this work inject software faults through code changes, based on the same fault types (Table 1) adopted by G-SWFIT [3]. The csXception™/G-SWFIT tool, a R&D tool by Critical Software, implements G-SWFIT for the C language with respect to the PowerPC architecture and the GCC compiler. The SAFE tool injects the same fault types of G-SWFIT in C/C++ software, although faults are injected by mutating the source code of the target instead of the binary code, and avoids accuracy issues affecting binary-level injection.

---

[1] Each fault operator is related to a specific fault type and is denoted with the "O" prefix (e.g., the OMIA fault operator is related to the MIA fault type).

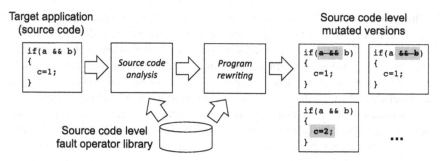

Fig. 1 Overview of the SAFE tool

3 SAFE

This fault injection tool, namely SAFE, has been developed for automating the injection of software faults in C and C++ programs. The high-level architecture of the tool is depicted in Fig. 1. It is made up of:

- A C macro pre-processor, that translates all macros (e.g., #define and #include directives) in a source code file in plain C language, in order to produce a self-contained compilation unit that will be processed by the tool.
- A C/C++ front-end, that analyzes the file and builds an Abstract Syntax Tree representation of the code. This representation guides the identification of locations where a fault type can be introduced in a syntactically correct manner, and that comply to fault types in Table 1.
- A Fault Injector that explores the Abstract Syntax Tree, and produces a set of faulty "patch" files, each containing a different software fault.

Actually, the tool consists of an executable, namely "injection", that embeds both a C/C++ front-end and the Fault Injector. The pre-processing of C macros is performed through an existing C pre-processor, namely MCPP. MCPP is a replacement for the standard pre-processor included in GCC; it is an open source (BSD-licensed) project and it is freely available at http://mcpp.sourceforge.net/. The current tool prototype supports the Fedora Linux 13 operating system, and it is intended to be used along with the GCC/G++ development tool chain, and with the "make" and "patch" UNIX utilities.

3.1 Set-Up and Usage of SAFE

We describe the use of the SAFE tool in a complex real-world system, namely the Apache web server (http://httpd.apache.org). It is a widely-adopted web server written in the C language. Version 2.2.11 will be considered, which consists of approximately 242 thousands of lines of C code. We assume that the MCPP pre-processor has already been installed. We first copy the source code of the web server and the fault injection tool in the same directory (" ~ /Desktop/demo"):

```
[~] $ mkdir ~/Desktop/demo
[~] $ cp <path>/injection ~/Desktop/demo
[~] $ cd ~/Desktop/demo
[~/Desktop/demo] $ wget http://archive.apache.org/dist/httpd/httpd-2.2.11.tar.bz2
[~/Desktop/demo] $ tar jxf httpd-2.2.11.tar.bz2
[~/Desktop/demo] $ cd httpd-2.2.11
```

Before injecting software faults in the target program, it is necessary to pre-process source files in order to translate all preprocessor macros in the program in plain C language. This can be achieved using MCPP and GCC, by compiling the target software by passing the flags "-Wp,-K,-W0-save-temps" to gcc (or to g++ in the case of C++ software). This operation will generate a set of ".i" (or ".ii" for C++) files, each corresponding to a ".c" (or ".cpp", respectively) file of the target program. They are temporary files created by GCC after preprocessing of source files. If the target program is based on the "make" build system, then it is typically possible to pass these flags using the CFLAGS and CXXFLAGS environment variables (for gcc and g++, respectively). The web server will be installed in the " ~ /Desktop/demo/installdir" directory:

```
[~/Desktop/demo/httpd-2.2.11] $ ./configure --prefix=/home/user/Desktop/demo/installdir/
...
[~/Desktop/demo/httpd-2.2.11] $ make CFLAGS="-Wp,-K,-W0 -save-temps"
...
[~/Desktop/demo/httpd-2.2.11] $ mkdir /home/user/Desktop/demo/installdir/
[~/Desktop/demo/httpd-2.2.11] $ make install
...
```

We focus on the "server" sub-directory, which includes the core components of the web server. The previous commands generate several ".i" there. The following command applies the "injection" tool to each ".i" file, and generates a set of "patch" files (in total, 5027 patches), each representing a fault to be injected in the web server code.

```
[~/Desktop/demo/httpd-2.2.11] $ ~/Desktop/demo/injection server/*.i

Target file: server/config.i
Fault injection: OMFC
Fault injection: OMVIV
Fault injection: OMVAV
...
Target file: server/connection.i
Fault injection: OMFC
Fault injection: OMVIV
Fault injection: OMVAV
...
```

In the example that follows, we inject a WPFV fault (wrong variable used in parameter of function call) in the "request.c" source file. In particular, we consider the fault contained in the "request.i_OWPFV_17.patch" file, which injects a WPFV fault at line 708: the first parameter of the "memcpy()" function call (the pointer "buf") is replaced with another variable ("save_path_info", previously declared in the function) of the same type (a character array "char *"). The tool assures that the type of the variables is the same, and that the variable has the same scope of the replaced variable. Therefore, the replacement generates syntactically correct code. The patch can be injected using the "patch" command. The faulty web server is then compiled again and installed.

```
[~/Desktop/demo/httpd-2.2.11] $ cat server/request.i_OWPFV_17.patch

--- /home/user/Desktop/demo/httpd-2.2.11/server/request.c
+++ /home/user/Desktop/demo/httpd-2.2.11/server/request.c
@@ -708,1 +708,1 @@
-            memcpy(buf, r->filename, filename_len + 1);
+            memcpy(save_path_info, r->filename, filename_len + 1);

[~/Desktop/demo/httpd-2.2.11] $ patch -p0 < server/request.i_OWPFV_17.patch

patching file /home/user/Desktop/demo/httpd-2.2.11/server/request.c

[~/Desktop/demo/httpd-2.2.11] $ make
[~/Desktop/demo/httpd-2.2.11] $ make install
```

To perform a fault injection experiment, we run the web server and generate three HTTP requests to the web server using the "wget" tool, which is a command-line HTTP client. The wget tool reports that the faulty web server is unable to reply to the requests. By inspecting the log file generated by the web server ("installdir/logs/error_log"), we notice that each HTTP request causes a crash of a server process (denoted with the "Segmentation fault" message).

```
[~/Desktop/demo/httpd-2.2.11] $ sudo ~/Desktop/demo/installdir/bin/apachectl start
[~/Desktop/demo/httpd-2.2.11] $ wget --tries=3 localhost

--2012-01-16 15:18:00--  http://localhost/
Resolving localhost... 127.0.0.1
Connecting to localhost|127.0.0.1|:80... connected.
HTTP request sent, awaiting response... No data received.
Retrying.
...
[~/Desktop/demo/httpd-2.2.11] $ cat ~/Desktop/demo/installdir/logs/error_log

[Mon Jan 16 15:17:55 2012] [notice] Apache/2.2.11 (Unix) configured -- resuming normal operations
[Mon Jan 16 15:18:00 2012] [notice] child pid 5036 exit signal Segmentation fault (11)
[Mon Jan 16 15:18:01 2012] [notice] child pid 5040 exit signal Segmentation fault (11)
[Mon Jan 16 15:18:03 2012] [notice] child pid 5039 exit signal Segmentation fault (11)
```

To terminate the experiment and restore the original code:

```
[~/Desktop/demo/httpd-2.2.11] $ sudo ~/Desktop/demo/installdir/bin/apachectl stop
[~/Desktop/demo/httpd-2.2.11] $ patch -R -p0 < server/request.i_OWPFV_17.patch

patching file /home/user/Desktop/demo/httpd-2.2.11/server/request.c
```

The steps that have been described in this section can be repeated several times, each time injecting a different fault (i.e., using a different patch file), to perform a full fault injection campaign. At each iteration, log files (e.g., "error_log", wget messages) and other relevant data (e.g., a dump of the process memory, which is generated by the OS in the case of a crash) can be collected, in order to analyze the effects of faults of the system (e.g., which kind of failure was caused by the fault, or wether the fault has been perceived by the user).

4 csXception™/G-SWFIT

csXception™ is fault injection environment developed by Critical Software© for supporting the validation activities of safety- and mission-critical systems. It relies on the advanced CPU debugging and performance monitoring features, available nowadays in all microprocessors, to inject faults and monitor their activation and impact on the target system. The csXception™ architecture (Fig. 2) is made up of two main components, namely, a front- and a back-end application. The front-end application (called Experiment Management Environment or EME) runs in a host computer and is responsible for experiment management and control. The back-end, a lightweight injection core, runs in the system being evaluated (Target System), and is responsible for the insertion of faults.

csXception™/G-SWFIT is a tool for performing SFI at binary level. It is a csXception™ plug-in component (written in Java) that extends its fault injection framework with the capability to inject software faults without the need for source code—only the binary image of the target component is required (see Sect. 2). This makes the tool useful for the assessment of COTS components such as Real-Time Operating Systems (RTOS), where the source code is rarely available to the user.

The tool translates the executable of the target software into assembly code by means of a disassembler and then it analyzes the code in order to find locations where faults can be injected (Fig. 3). A fault operator library defines code patterns and code changes to be introduced in the assembly. The plugin generates mutated versions of the original application, each one containing a software fault. Currently, the plugin supports the PowerPC™ and Intel's©x86 hardware architectures, and the GNU©GCC compiler for building target applications.

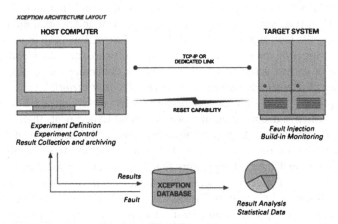

Fig. 2 High-level architecure of csXception™

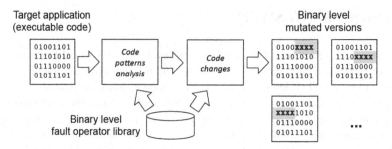

Fig. 3 G-SWFIT fault injection approach

4.1 Set-Up and Usage of csXception^TM/G-SWFIT

The plug-in provides an user-friendly GUI that allows to easily setup and execute fault injection campaigns. The EME component, which is the front-end responsible for the injection process, stores all the information related to fault definition, experiment execution and results in a relational database. Using SQL and the GUI, the user can manage the large volumes of data that may be collected by csXception^TM. The user may, for instance, execute SQL queries, crossing fault parameters, detected errors and even target processor contexts before and after each injection, in order to track the most challenging fault/error impacts. To use the csXception^TM/G-SWFIT plugin, the user should:

- Install Java runtime environment for executing csXception^TM, and a PostgreSQL database for storing the data involved in fault injection campaigns;
- Specify some architecture-specific information (e.g., CPU family, path to a binary-code disassembler for that CPU family);
- Define the working directory in which the faulty images of the target application will be located.

The first aspect to be defined is the Workload, which requires the user to provide *scripts* (i.e., small programs to be executed in an OS shell environment) for managing the fault injection process (Fig. 4). Two scripts have to be provided: a script for triggering the execution of the target software (i.e., *Workload launcher script*), and a second script that will be used for collecting the results from the target system for post-processing (i.e., *Workload output script*).

In Xception^TM, fault injection is performed by specifying a Fault Injection Campaign, which is decomposed into one or several Experiments that, in turn, are decomposed into Faults. After providing the name and description of the Campaign and its Experiment(s), the next step is to define the target application in which to inject, and the fault operators that have to be applied during the fault injection process. Figure 5 presents the *Option Selection screen* where the executable of the target ("Init.nxe") and the OMFC operator are selected.

Once the target application and fault operators are defined, the disassembler translates the selected executables into assembly code. Based on the selected

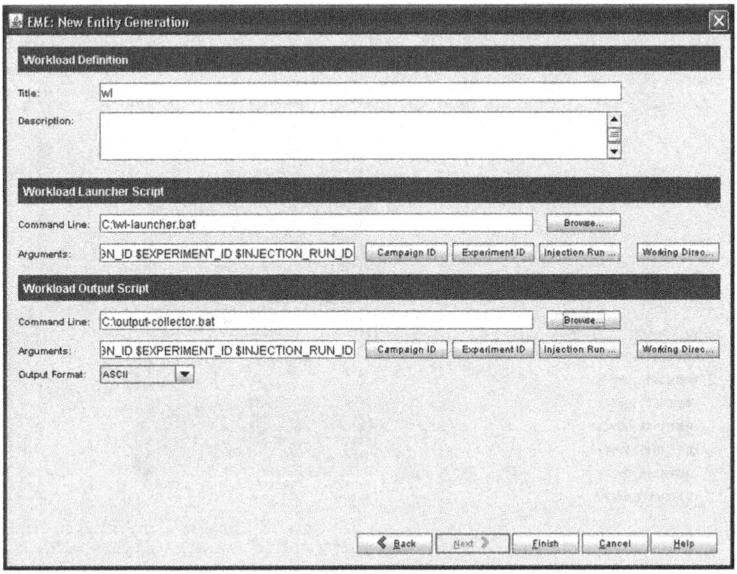

Fig. 4 Workload definition screen

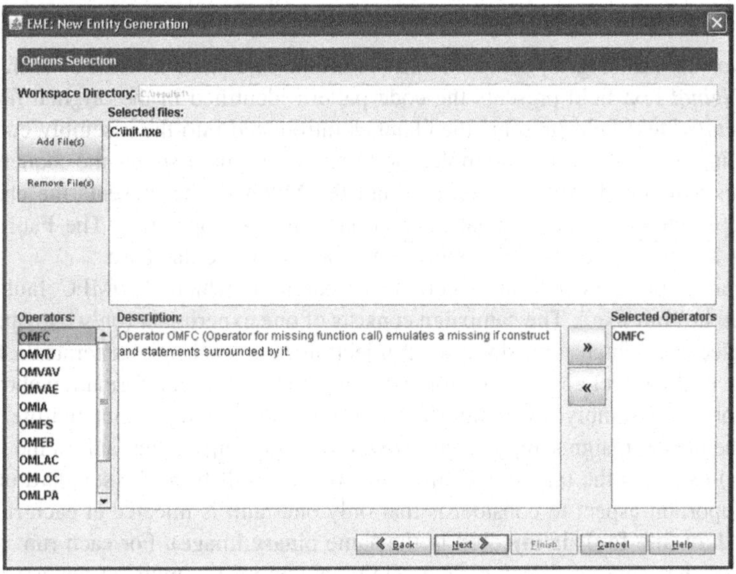

Fig. 5 Option screen

operators, the plug-in analyzes the assembly code and determines all the locations where faults have to be injected. In the example, the tool identifies in the assembly code 1806 possible locations where MFC faults can be injected. The *Fault*

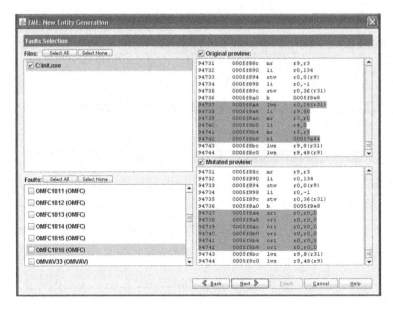

Fig. 6 Fault selection screen

Selection Screen (Fig. 6) provides a list of all the injectable faults. For each fault, the *Original* text field presents the code pattern identified in the original file and the *Mutated* text field presents the changes introduced into the assembly code for emulating the fault. In the example, the Original text field shows the sequence of opcodes associated to a function call and the Mutated one presents the changes (the replacement of the original instructions with *nop* opcodes). The Fault definitions are generated by csXception™ and stored in the database.

Figure 7 presents a fault injection campaign in which 2 OMFC faults are injected in "Init.nxe". The campaign consists of one experiment (only one operator was selected), which is made up of 2 injection runs, each one generates a faulty version of the target application; for each run, the tool stores information about the operator and assembly instructions of both the original and the mutated file.

Once the campaign setup is completed, the tool (i) injects the fault in the image file, (ii) executes the target, and (iii) collects the result from the standard output. One important aspect to consider is that only one fault is injected at each run (**no more than one fault is injected** in the same binary image). For each run, a sub-folder of the working directory is created, containing the mutated version of the target (the user can reproduce the results outside csXception™) and the text file with the execution results. During the Experiment creation, a *golden run* can be defined, where the workload is executed without any faults injected. The golden run can then be used for comparison purposes, by comparing its results with those from the execution of the faulty images.

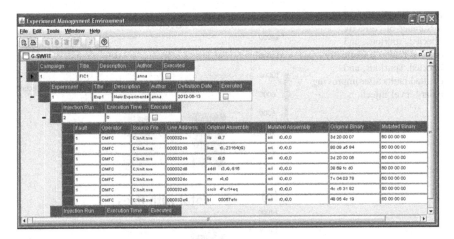

Fig. 7 Campaign, experiment, and injection run

5 Accuracy of Binary-Level Fault Injection

The SAFE and csXception™/G-SWFIT tools can inject software faults respectively at the source-code and binary level. Although binary-level injection is useful for injecting faults when source code is not available, it is difficult to assure the accuracy of the injection (i.e., faults at the binary level may not match injectable faults at source-code level). We adopted the SAFE tool (which is assumed to be accurate since faults are injected at the source-code level) to evaluate and to possibly improve the accuracy of binary-level injection, by injecting and comparing faults both in the binary and in the source code of the **same target system**. By comparing these two sets of faults, we can identify faults that are *Correctly Injected* (i.e., binary-level faults that can also be injected at source-code level), *Omitted faults* (i.e., faults injected at source-code level, but omitted at binary-level), and *Spurious faults* (i.e., faults injected at binary level that do not match any fault at source-code level). More details about the methodology adopted for the comparison can be found in [25].

Using the tools, 18,183 source-level faults and 12,380 binary-level faults were generated, respectively. Figure 8a presents the distribution of Correctly Injected, Spurious, and Omitted faults, obtained by comparing the two sets of faults. In 47.88 % of cases, faults from csXception™/G-SWFIT are Correctly Injected, while the remaining faults do not match any software fault in the source code.

By analyzing faults in detail, we identified the main causes leading to Spurious and Omitted faults. Many of them are due to C macros and inline functions: G-SWFIT generates a distinct binary-level fault for each replica of a macro or inline function (a real fault would instead be repeated in each replica). Other Omitted and Spurious faults are due to the still on-going development of csXception™/G-SWFIT at the time of writing, since the implementation of some fault

Fig. 8 Distribution of faults. **a** Number of correctly injected, spurious, and omitted faults. **b** Correctly injected, spurious, and omitted faults after improving binary-level injection

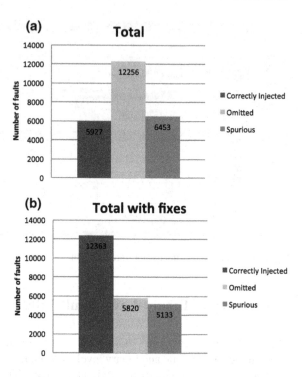

operators is simplified by choice (e.g., some operator constraints are not fully implemented). We estimated that, if operators are extended, a good degree of accuracy can be achieved by binary-level injection (Fig. 8b).

6 Conclusions

In this chapter, we described the role of tools in SFI, and presented two SFI tools, SAFE and csXception™/G-SWFIT. Using the same set of fault types and injection rules, the two tools are able to inject software faults at the source-code and binary-code level, respectively. We showed that the fault injection process can be easily automated with tools, after providing them with application-specific commands. Moreover, we discussed the problem of accuracy of binary-level injection: by comparing source-code and binary-code level injection, we found that there are some issues that cannot be avoided (e.g., incorrect binary faults due to inline functions), and that if binary-level injection is improved with the feedback from source-level injection, a good degree of accuracy can be achieved.

References

1. Christmansson, J., Chillarege, R.: Generation of an error set that emulates software faults based on field data. In: Proceedings of the Symposium on Fault-Tolerant Computing (1996)
2. Voas, J., Charron, F., McGraw, G., Miller, K., Friedman, M.: Predicting how badly "Good" software can behave. IEEE Softw. **14**(4), 15–19 (1997)
3. Durães, J., Madeira, H.: Emulation of software faults: a field data study and a practical approach. IEEE Trans. Softw. Eng. **32**(11), 849–867 (2006)
4. Gray, J.: A census of tandem system availability between 1985 and 1990. IEEE Trans. Reliab. **39**(4), 409–418 (1990)
5. Ng, W., Chen, P.: The systematic improvement of fault tolerance in the Rio file cache. In: Proceedings of the 29th International Symposium on Fault-Tolerant Computing (1999)
6. Vieira, M., Madeira, H.: Benchmarking the dependability of different OLTP systems. In: Proceedings of the International Conference on Dependable Systems and Networks (2003)
7. Pecchia, A., Pietrantuono, R., Russo, S.: Criticality-driven component integration in complex software systems. Computer Safety, Reliability, and Security (2011)
8. International Organization for Standardization: Product Development: Software Level. ISO 26262-6 (2012)
9. National Aeronautics and Space Administration: NASA Software Safety Guidebook. NASA-GB-8719.13 (2004)
10. Norris, J.: Mission-critical development with open source software: lessons learned. IEEE Softw. **21**(1), 42–49 (2004)
11. Maia, R., Henriques, L., Barbosa, R., Costa, D., Madeira, H.: Xception fault injection and robustness testing framework: a case-study of testing RTEMS. In: VI Test and Fault Tolerance Workshop (2004)
12. Chillarege, R., Bhandari, I., Chaar, J., Halliday, M., Moebus, D., Ray, B., Wong, M.: Orthogonal defect classification—a concept for in-process measurements. IEEE Trans. Softw. Eng. **18**(11), 943–956 (1992)
13. Chillarege, R., Bowen, N.: Understanding large system failures-a fault injection experiment. In: Proceedings of the International Symposium on Fault-Tolerant Computing (1989)
14. Barton, J., Czeck, E., Segall, Z., Siewiorek, D.: Fault injection experiments using FIAT. IEEE Trans. Comput. **39**(4), 575–582 (1990)
15. Moraes, R., Barbosa, R., Durães, J., Mendes, N., Martins, E., Madeira, H.: Injection of faults at component interfaces and inside the component code: are they equivalent? In: European Dependable Computing Conference (2006)
16. Koopman, P., DeVale, J.: The exception handling effectiveness of POSIX operating systems. IEEE Trans. Softw. Eng. **26**(9), 837–848 (2000)
17. Daran, M., Thévenod-Fosse, P.: Software error analysis: a real case study involving real faults and mutations. ACM Softw. Eng. Notes 21(3) (1996)
18. Andrews, J., Briand, L., Labiche, Y.: Is mutation an appropriate tool for testing experiments? In: Proceedings of the International Conference on Software Engineering (2005)
19. Kao, W.I., Iyer, R., Tang, D.: FINE: a fault injection and monitoring environment for tracing the UNIX system behavior under faults. IEEE Trans. Softw. Eng. **19**(11), 1105–1118 (1993)
20. Carreira, J., Madeira, H., Silva, J.: Xception: a technique for the experimental evaluation of dependability in modern computers. IEEE Trans. Softw. Eng. **24**(2), 125–136 (1998)
21. Stott, D., Floering, B., Kalbarczyk, Z., Iyer, R.: A framework for assessing dependability in distributed systems with lightweight fault injectors. In: Proceedings of the International Computer Performance and Dependability Symposium (2000)
22. Aidemark, J., Vinter, J., Folkesson, P., Karlsson, J.: GOOFI: generic object-oriented fault injection tool. In: Proceedings of the International Conference on Dependable Systems and Networks (2001)
23. Arlat, J., Fabre, J., Rodríguez, M., Salles, F.: Dependability of COTS microkernel-based systems. IEEE Trans. Comput. **51**(2), 138–163 (2002)

24. Martins, E., Rubira, C., Leme, N.: Jaca: a reflective fault injection tool based on patterns. In: Proceedings of International Conference on Dependable Systems and Networks (2002)
25. Cotroneo, D., Lanzaro, A., Natella, R., Barbosa, R.: Experimental analysis of binary-level software fault injection in complex software. In: Proceedings of the Ninth European Dependable Computing Conference (2012)

Survey on Software Faults Injection in Java Applications

Aniello Napolitano, Gabriella Carrozza, Nuno Antunes and Joao Duraes

Abstract Software faults are currently on of the major cause for computer-based system failures. Nowadays, no software development methodology has provided fault-free software, and fault injection is recognized as a technique to understand the effects of faults in a given software product. However, the injection of software faults is not trivial and is still an open research problem. This chapter provides an overview on the injection of software faults and focus on the injection of faults for Java-based software, highlighting the new challenges specific of this language.

Keywords Software fault injection · Software reliability · DDS middleware · System of systems · Java applications

A. Napolitano (✉) · G. Carrozza
SESM s.c.a.r.l, Via Circunvalazione Esterna di Napoli, 80014 Giugliano, Italy
e-mail: anapolitano@sesm.it

G. Carrozza
e-mail: gcarrozza@sesm.it

N. Antunes · J. Duraes
Department of Informatics Engineering, DEI, University of Coimbra,
Pólo II—Universidade di Coimbra, Coimbra 3030-290, Portugal
e-mail: nmsa@dei.uc.pt

J. Duraes
e-mail: jduraes@dei.uc.pt

D. Cotroneo (ed.), *Innovative Technologies for Dependable OTS-Based Critical Systems*,
DOI: 10.1007/978-88-470-2772-5_8, © Springer-Verlag Italia 2013

1 Introduction

Modern society has become highly dependent on computer systems; the welfare and safety of our society is now based on the continued correct behavior of many computer-based systems. The notion of correct behavior includes computers not failing, or, if they do fail, those failures are appropriately handled and recovered.

Software faults are currently recognized as the major cause behind computer-based system failures [16, 27, 32, 38]. Table 1 presents a summary of death-causing accidents related to software faults [14] (however, hundreds more cases do exist).

Despite the great amounts of testing efforts invested during development and the accumulated experience from past failure occurrences, computer-based systems field-failures remain common. The reasons behind this scenario are mainly the increasing system complexity and industry practices including shrinking time-to-market deadlines and cost-reduction in testing efforts. Generally speaking, the more complex a software system is, the higher the probability of the existence of hidden faults within that system. The infeasibility of eliminating all software faults during the development phase leads to the scenario with deployed systems having software defects but no one knowing exactly when they will reveal themselves, and what are the consequences of the activation of those software faults.

Experimental evaluation by fault injection has become an attractive approach of validating specific fault handling mechanisms and assessing the impact of faults in actual systems and helping in the estimation of fault-tolerant system mechanisms. During fault injection the system is exercised (using a workload) and faults are inserted into it. The goal is to observe how the system behaves in the presence of the injected faults, considering that these faults represent plausible faults that may affect the system. In fault injection experiments, the fault load describes which faults to inject and how to inject them (e.g., where and when), and the workload describes how the system should be exercised.

One important aspect of fault injection is the failure acceleration factor that reduces the time-effort necessary to conduct the experiments and obtain results. Instead of waiting for the natural occurrences of fault activation events, researchers

Table 1 Well-known accidents caused by software faults that resulted in loss of life

Short description of incident	Year	Deaths
Northeastern US and Canada power failure	2003	3
Radiation overdose administered in cancer treatments in Panama	2001	5
Crash of a Marine Corps Osprey tilt-rotor aircraft	2000	4
Radar fails to prevent Korean jet crash	1997	225
Lethal dose of morphine administered in medical treatment	1997	1
American Airlines jet crashes into a mountain in Colombia	1995	159
Patriot Missile fails to intercept incoming SCUD missile	1991	28
Lethal radiation overdose administered by Therac-25 medical device	1985	3

can induce these by injecting faults and thus reduce the time needed to observe how the system behaves when faults are activated.

Fault injection can be used to achieve both fault removal and fault forecasting [2, 3]. Concerning fault removal, fault injection is aimed at reducing by verification the presence of faults in the design and implementation of the fault tolerance mechanisms. This way, deficiencies existing in these mechanisms can be discovered and eliminated. Concerning fault forecasting, fault injection can be used to evaluate the effectiveness of the fault tolerant mechanisms regarding fault coverage and latency, and the behavior of the system in terms of consequences of possible unknown faults (e.g., [11, 33, 39]). Fault injection can also be used for risk evaluation, observing the behavior of the system when faults are activated and checking if this behavior is safe or if it complies with regulations. Fault injection can also be used as an enabling technology for dependability evaluation, where users and system integrators may be interested to compare system dependability properties [13, 20, 23, 35, 40], when systems are subjected to faults.

Fault injection started as a technique focused on hardware. Early fault injectors were implemented in hardware and were designed to inject faults at very low level (e.g., circuit and gate level). Hardware-implemented fault injectors are commonly known as HWIFI tools (hardware implemented fault injection tools). Some examples of hardware fault injection approaches are pin-level instrumentation to modify the values at the processor pins, insertion of probes to alter the electric current values in selected hardware points, and external hardware to expose the target to heavy-ion radiation. Some examples of HWFIT tools can be found in [2, 10, 17, 25, 28].

Given the increasing circuit scale integration and the decreasing size of the discrete system components, HWIFI tools become technically difficult to implement, in particular those that involve the physical attachment of probes to the target system. Software implemented fault injection tools (SWIFI tools) provided a cheaper and more versatile technology for the injection of faults. At the same time, software started to became the predominant source of faults, and SWIFI started to focus on more complex fault models and on faults that try to mimic problems existing at the software level (e.g., data corruption, wrong instructions, bad input values, etc.). Some examples of SWIFI tools for the injection of faults in software systems are: FIAT [37], FERRARI [21], FINE [24], and Xception [5] among others).

These tools, using trap routines and other processor-specific mechanisms can, for instance, intercept the use of a given memory address and overwrite its contents to emulate a fault in that memory position (which can be used to simulate a hardware fault at that memory position, e.g., a stuck-at fault, or it can be used to simulate a missing variable initialization type of software fault).

Table 2 (from [19]) presents an example of early fault classes and injection methods. The table comprises both software and hardware faults. It is worth noting that there are two distinct forms of injection related to software faults (line 1 and 2 of the table): the injection of software faults and the injection of software errors. The injection of a software fault is aimed at the reproduction of the actual fault and

Table 2 Examples of low-level fault injection methodologies

Fault class	Example of injection method
Software fault	Code segment modification
Software error	Data segment modification
Memory fault	Memory bit-flip and stuck-at
CPU fault	Register bit-flip
BUS fault	Bit-flip on the transmitted data
Network fault	Corruption, delayment and deletion of messages

involves the modification of the target code; the injection of a software error is aimed at the reproduction of the consequence (error) of some software fault through the modification of the program data state and therefore is an indirect form of injection of software fault and cannot be viewed as the injection of a software fault in the strict sense. Given the fact that there is no guarantee of a one-to-one relationship between intended-fault and injected error, the accuracy of this emulation process is not as assured as the actual fault injection.

Although SWIFI tools are currently the dominant type of fault injection tools (an overview can be found in [19, 18]), the injection of software faults remains a difficult problem. One key issue contributing to this difficulty is the lack of proper understanding of what exactly are software faults. Software faults are defects inserted in the software that remain hidden and go with the finished product into the operational scenario. However, this definition is too broad. These defects can be small mistakes made by the programmers, wrong algorithms, incorrect design, and even incomplete user specification. These broad range what fault definition makes it very hard to simulate (inject) the existence of such defects into a given target. The knowledge about what exactly are software defects can only be discovered through field studies and these are uncommon as they involve very large quantities of hard to find data (such as bug reports) and the investment of large periods of time. Thus, not many studies on field data about on software defects can be found in the literature. Some examples of such works are [8, 12, 16, 26].

Even considering a specific subset of software faults, such as programmers' mistakes, there is the need to understand exactly what software faults are. In this case, it is required to be able to describe to a tool (the fault injector) what to do when injecting a fault. To main approaches do exist surrounding the notion of emulating programmer mistakes: the injection of data errors (these emulate an errors—not a fault—meaning the possible consequence of a fault), and the injection of code changes (the injection of a programmer mistake) (e.g., see [9, 22]). The first is mostly used in robustness testing, while the second is more close to the notion of injecting actual faults. Injecting code changes requires the knowledge of *what* exactly to inject and *where*. This is a difficult knowledge to obtain, as not all changes are related to valid (that is, syntactically valid) code changes, or meaningful code changes. The where problem is also very relevant as the same code change in one place could be related to a realistic software defect, while in another may be not as it might result in a defect that would stop the program from working altogether and thus, it would certainly be discovered and corrected. The definition of the what and where, together with fault classification schemes are required to be able to specify to a fault injector which actions to perform to simulate the existence of specific software defects. Among others, the ODC [8] and the G-SWIFT [12] works contributed to the improvement on the classification and definition of software faults for fault injection.

From the above, it is clear that not all faults are equally interesting to inject, and it is both unfeasible and wrong to inject all possible faults into a given target. It is unfeasible because the time requirements are too large (even in small software, all possible code changes on all possible valid locations amount to very a large number), and it is uninteresting because injecting all possible faults means injecting faults that are very unlikely to appear in the operational scenario, and this would skew the results making fault injection less attractive for dependability benchmarking, risk evaluation, just to mention a few scenarios. Understanding which faults are the representative ones is a two-fold problem:

- From all the possible defects that a programmer can make, some do appear more often in the operational scenario than others (which means that some fault types, for some reason, elude more easily testing procedure than others). Those fault types that do appear more often in the operational scenario are more relevant to inject (usually, it is unfeasible to inject all possible faults due to time constraints). To understand which are the most common faults it is required to once again use field data studies and fault classification schemes. Two such studies can be found in [8, 12]. These two studies identified the faults more common in the operation scenario, which means that these faults did elude testing procedures. The work [12] proposed a simple classification to characterize faults based on the notion of syntactic constructs of the high level language where faults are either missing, extraneous or wrong constructs (variable initializations, expressions in conditions, and so on) (see Table 3). It also proposes a technique (G-SWFIT) to emulate those at binary level code (not requiring the source code of the target). The injection strategy is relatively straight forward: using a fault emulation library (containing patterns of instruction sequences and code changes to apply for each given fault type), the fault injection tool seeks appropriate locations within the target and applies the necessary code changes for the intended fault type.
- Another way to identify the most interesting faults to inject is to analyze the fault activation probability of each fault type. The reasoning behind this logic is that the faults which are more difficult to activate are those that will tend to elude whatever testing case is being used and go with the product into the operational scenario. A study on the representativeness of software faults using this notion can be found in [31].

Faults types are related to the Orthogonal Defect Classification from [8] (ASG = Assignment, CHK = Checking, INT = Interface, ALG = Algorithm, FUN = Function).

Table 3 Most common software fault types found in the operation scenario according to [12]

Fault nature	Fault specific types	# Faults	ODC types ASG	CHK	INT	ALG	FUN
Missing	*if* construct plus statements (**MIFS**)	71				✓	
	AND sub-expr in expression used as branch condition (**MLAC**)	47		✓			
	function call (**MFC**)	46				✓	
	if construct around statements (**MIA**)	34		✓			
	OR sub-expr in expression used as branch condition (**MLOC**)	32		✓			
	small and localized part of the algorithm (**MLPA**)	23				✓	
	variable assignment using an expression (**MVAE**)	21	✓				
	functionality (**MFCT**)	21					✓
	variable assignment using a value (**MVAV**)	20	✓				
	if construct plus statements plus *else* before statements (**MIEB**)	18				✓	
	variable initialization (**MVIV**)	15	✓				
Wrong	logical expression used as branch condition (**WLEC**)	22		✓			
	algorithm - large modifications (**WALL**)	20					✓
	value assigned to variable (**WVAV**)	16	✓				
	arithmetic expression in parameter of function call (**WAEP**)	14			✓		
	data types or conversion used (**WSUT**)	12	✓				
	variable used in parameter of function call (**WPPV**)	11			✓		
Extraneous	variable assignment using another variable (**EVAV**)	9	✓				
Total faults for these types in each ODC type		452	93	135	25	192	41
Coverage relative to each ODC type (%)		**68**	**65**	**81**	**51**	**72**	**100**

Most works on software faults used non-oriented programming languages such as C for their research. However, many large software systems are currently being built using object oriented languages, Java being one of the most used ones. This raises the question of how to inject software faults, as many of the results obtained in previous works may not apply to objected oriented languages, and in particular to Java. The following are relevant research questions:

- The fault classification schemes, including the identification of the most commonly found software faults, resulting from previous studies may not apply to Java. Some studies already exist for Java language, but their results should be confirmed and generalized.
- The syntax of Java is stricter than that of C (for instance, strict data types usage, and buffer limit enforcement), and many fault types possible in C are simply no longer possible in Java. Fault classification schemes must be revised to accommodate this reality.
- Java works inside the Java Virtual Machine sandbox and many effects of software defects are minimized or even eliminated by the Virtual Machine. This directly impact on the notion of the representative fault types, and it means that new studies must be devised and performed to access which faults are more relevant to inject for Java language.
- Object oriented languages, such as Java, raises the possibility of new fault types which are not foreseen in existing fault classification schemes based on C or

similar languages. The new types of faults must be identified and its relevance investigated.

The injection of code changes in Java follows a different logic than in platform-native executable programs. For the latter, one could modify the binary file prior to execution, or perform code changes accessing the process memory space; in the case of Java, there are other options, such as reflection mechanisms. However, the Java Virtual Machine imposes very strict rules concerning the modification of code and fault injection tools must be redesigned (note that changing the target at source code level is basically the same for C and Java, but I is not an interesting option as it requires source code which may not be available for some of the fault injection application scenarios). Two examples of difficult scenarios for fault injection in java are the web servers and application servers. These have custom class loaders which prevents one possible mechanism for fault injection which is class manipulation upon class loading.

2 The Industrial Applications

Applications written in Java language are increasingly spreading in several and heterogeneous contexts. The appeal of Java derives from improved developer productivity, reduced software maintenance costs, higher software reliability, enhanced functionality, and improved generality, all of which lead to expanded software longevity. In the traditional business information processing marketplace (financial record keeping, customer relations management, inventory controls, billing, payroll, etc.), the Java programming language has replaced C++ as the predominant programming language, largely because Java programmers are approximately twice as productive when developing new code, and five to ten times as productive during maintenance of existing code [7, 34]. In [41] a comparison among the main development languages, such as C, C++, Ada and Java, is provided, highlighting that Java language is becoming better than the other languages.

Stemming from the above facts, the industrials are also starting to develop components for mission critical applications using of the Java language.

Lockheed Martin,[1] one of the world leaders in the field of military combat systems, has chosen the Java language for developing many critical components of the Aegis Combat System, which is an integrated a complex naval weapons system for supporting Navy units during war. This is just a first example of this growing trend, which is bringing the use of the Java language into several sectors, such as airborne, ground, missile, space, as well as simulation/training and command and control [41, 42].

---

[1] www.lockheedmartin.com

In Air Traffic Management (ATM), the same trend has been followed, and in the last years more and more components of Air Traffic Control (ATC) systems have been developed in Java.

The SWIM [43] (System Wide Information Management) platform is an European example of this trend, about which is worth spending more words, for. This platform provides technological services designed to facilitate and enable the wide sharing of information, such as airport operational status, weather information, flight and surveillance data, among several ATM/ACC centers. It makes use of Commercial Off-The-Shelf (COTS) hardware and software components to support the SOA approach aiming to facilitate dynamic system composition and to increase common situational awareness.

The overall system is a grid of SWIM nodes, physically deployed at the stakeholders' premises and referred to as "legacy" nodes, which are the actual users of the SWIM common infrastructure. These nodes are allowed to access the SWIM bus through a SWIM-BOX [6] component (see Fig. 1). Only SWIM-BOX instances can directly exchange data and invoke services over the net, acting as mediators between legacy nodes and the SWIM-BUS. It is very likely that existing legacy systems are not aware of the SWIM service semantics. Indeed, they could either have been built according to different technologies or using different data models. This is the reason why a further software layer, named Adapter, has been introduced. On one hand, this provides technology independence, which is one of the SWIM-BOX fundamental requirements. On the other hand, it guarantees that all the nodes involved into the network comply with the IGOC standard data model. The Adapter is one of the critical components in SWIM infrastructure, and it is actually developed in Java language.

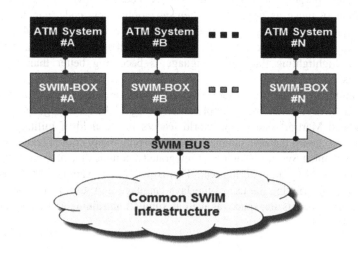

Fig. 1 SWIM network architecture

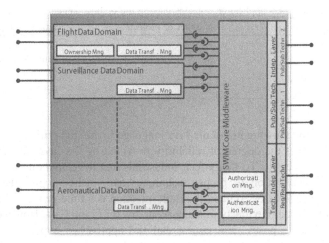

Fig. 2 SWIM-BOX architecture

Figure 2 shows the SWIM-BOX two-layered architecture which is made up of (i) the Core layer providing a set of basic and common facilities (e.g., security, data distribution, and registry); and (ii), the Domain Specific (DS) layer, in charge of providing domain-related services (e.g., Flight Data Description (FDD), or surveillance subscription, incoming flight notifications).

The Publish Subscribe Service (Pub/Sub) component is in charge of distributing the data provided from domain level components by means of the publisher/ subscriber pattern. In order to assure technology transparency, Pub/Sub actually provides an abstraction layer able to easily substitute the underlying technology without impacting the uppermost domain level components. This has been achieved through the definition of an interface (in order to limit the impact on the performance) that issues the basic operations needed to subscribe and publish data over the SWIM bus.

Subscriptions can be requested according to push and pull paradigms. The former lets the subscriber not to be blocked while waiting for incoming data (asynchronous, push-style). The latter, instead, provides a cache (i.e., pull-point) from which it is possible to retrieve data periodically. Filtering criteria are also provided in this case, both at subscription and at execution time, to select only needed data.

The Publisher/Subscriber layer can make use of different distributions for sharing the data, such as OpenSplice DDS® [44], RTI DDS® [45], and the open source Java Messaging Service (JMS) [46]. The tests carried out to assess the performance of the three frameworks provided the results that Java-based framework is comparable with the commercial ones, natively developed in C or C++ language.

The aforementioned systems are just some example of the Java use in mission and critical applications. Table 4 provide a summary of application domains in which the Java language is explored for developing mission critical applications.

Table 4 Mission critical application domains making use of Java language

Application domain	Number of projects	Example application
Command and control	45	Command center
Military-airbone	40	Embedded sensors
Military-ground	52	Combat center
Military-space	18	Attitude control system

Despite of the growing use of the Java language in mission critical applications, the need to assess the degree of reliability provided by the Java for these applications is still present. To that effect, industrials and developers need to be supported by the definition of proper techniques and methodologies that provide automated ways to assess reliability. Fault injection is a time-proven technique to reach the goal, used previously in many scenarios for C and C++. However, its use for Java language poses new issues, and the approaches explored so far for applications written in C and C++ are not entirely appropriate. In fact, due to the structure of the Java language, the approach described for C and C++ in [12] cannot be 100 % directly applied, and new fault types and fault injection strategies have to be derived allowing an effectiveness assessment of the Java applications reliability.

3 Why and How Injecting Software Faults in Java Applications

Java is nowadays the most widely used programming language [41]. It is increasingly being used to build mission and critical applications, comparing with the classic language such as C and C++, mainly because of the mass of COTS components developed in Java available on the market. This increased adoption raises the crucial need of assessing the dependability of Java applications. Fault injection plays a fundamental role as the most effective mean for dependability evaluation and assessment of software systems. Although several academic studies and tools addressed the dependability issues for C and C++ applications, few of them can be found in literature to perform fault injection in applications written with the Java language.

The Object-Oriented language model creates different fault injection requirements that the ones of C language, a problem that is not new. However, the characteristics of Java also make it different from C++, which made necessary and possible the development of new fault injection techniques and tools [15]. The rigid type-safety, standardized ranges and sizes of primitive types, and bounds-checking avoids some of the faults possible in other languages. Additionally, running inside a virtual machine and the mandatory use of garbage collection also avoids some types of faults related to resource management. Concerning methodologies for fault injection, it is possible to inject faults into the bytecode level, something that doesn't exists for traditional C/C++, and the reflection mechanisms built into Java allowing meta-programming and dynamic code generation at run-time, which can be used for fault injection.

Jaca [29] is a tool based on reflection to inject interface faults in Java applications with the purpose of performing robustness testing without the need for the source code of the target application. However, this tool injects only interface faults, which is used mainly for robustness testing purposes only and causes different impact in the system when compared with the injection of actual software faults. Empirical evidences presented in Moraes et al. [30] support this difference between injecting errors at the interfaces and injecting actual faults. GOOFI [1] is a tool developed in Java, highly adaptable and portable. However, it disregards the use of fault patterns, namely the ones detailed in the field studies [12].

Java Software Fault Injection Tool (J-SWIFT) [36] was proposed as a tool that allows the injection of software faults in Java systems in a scalable way. J-SWIFT can inject more types of faults including specific Java software faults (i.e., software faults that are characteristics from the Java language and object-oriented paradigm). It is completely based on the G-SWFIT technique [12], meaning that J-SWFIT follows the same methodology of type of faults (adding new fault types for Java/OOP) and fault operators and basic methodology. Current implementation also does not require the source code to perform the injection. The manipulations of the classes are made directly at byte code level, using the framework Object Web ASM.[2]

In [4] Basso et al. presented a field data study on real Java software faults. The field study was based on the analysis of correction patches available for open source software. The differences between the faulty application and the correction patches are analysed using a diff tool that highlighting the changes introduced in the sources (following similar methodology of [12] used for G-SWFIT). The correction analysis allows identifying the software faults. More than 550 faults were analysed and classified, determining the representativeness of these faults. The authors also define new operators, specific to this programming language structure, guiding the definition of a Java faultload.

Following the generic G-SWFIT strategy, the J-SWIFT methodology consists in analysing byte code files, finding specific areas where faults could exist, inject each fault independently according to the emulation operator library (i.e. Missing IF Construct plus Statements or Missing Function Call), run the system with the fault present, monitor its outcome, and finally compare the behaviour in the presence and absence of each fault. The faultload used is the one from [4]. Until now only two operators have been implemented: Missing IF Construct plus Statements (MIFS) and Missing Function Call (MFC) from those typical for Java language, which are summarized in Table 5.

---

[2] http://asm.ow2.org/

Table 5 Proper faults operators for Java language from [4]

Fault nature	Fault specific type
Missing construct	Missing interface implementation (MII)
	Missing throw statement (MTS)
	Missing try/catch/finally statement around statements (MTCFAS)
	Missing try/catch/finally statement plus statements (MTCFS)
	Missing Synchronized statement around statements (MSAS)
	Missing throws specification in method (MTSM)
	Missing extended class (MEC)
	Missing Synchronized statement (MSS)
Wrong construct	Wrong extended class (WEC)
	Wrong parameter passed to an object constructor (WPOC)
Extraneous construct	Extraneous try/catch/finally statement (ETCFS)
	Extraneous synchronized statement (ESS)

4 Conclusions

The detection of faults in software applications is a hard challenge to be faced. Several tools and techniques have been proposed and developed during the last years to address this challenge, and fault injection is one technique that has proven itself to be effective in aiding the mitigation of software defects, particularly. In the last decade Java has become as a popular programming language for developing computer-based systems, including mission critical scenarios. Because Java has significant differences from the languages used to establish previous fault injection techniques, it is now needed to rethink fault injection techniques and tools to address the differences present in Java language, as well as make use of the language characteristics that may prove to be useful when building fault injection tools, such as reflection.

References

1. Aidemark, J., Vinter, J., Folkesson, P., Karlsson, J.: GOOFI-a generic fault injection tool. In: Proceeding of DSN'01, Gothenburg, Sweden (2001)
2. Arlat, J., Aguera, M., Amat, L., Crouzet, Y., Fabre, J.C., Laprie, J.C., Martins, E., Powell, D.: Fault injection for dependability validation: a methodology and some applications. IEEE Trans. Softw. Eng. **16** (1990)
3. Avresky, D., Arlat, J., Laprie, J.C., Crouzet, Y.: Fault injection for formal testing of fault tolerance. IEEE Trans. Reliab. **45**(3), 443–455 (1996)
4. Basso, T., Moraes, R., Sanches, B.P., Jino. M.: An investigation of java faults operators derived from a field data study on java software faults. In: Workshop de Testes e Tolerância a Falhas—WTF 2009, João Pessoa, Brasil (2009)
5. Carreira, J., Madeira, H., Silva, J.G.: Xception: Software fault injection and monitorintg in processor functional units. IEEE Trans. Softw. Eng. **24**, 125–136 (1998)

6. Carrozza, G., Di Crescenzo, D., Napolitano, A., Strano, A.: Data distribution technologies in wide area systems: lessons learned from the SWIM-SUIT project experience. Netw. Protoc. Algorithms **2**(3), 100–115 (2010)
7. Chen, Y., Dios, R., Mili, A., Wu, L, Wang, K.: An empirical study of programming language trends. IEEE Softw. **22**(3),73–78 (2005)
8. Chillarege, R.: Orthogonal defect classification. In: M. Lyu, (ed.) Handbook of Software Reliability Engineering. IEEE Computer Society Press, McGraw (1995)
9. Christmansson, J., Hiller, M., Rimén, M.: An experimental comparison of fault and error injection. In: Proceedings of the 9th International Symposium on Software Reliability Engineering, ISSRE'98 (1998)
10. Cusick, J., Koga, R., Kolasinski, W.A., King, C.: SEU vulnerability of the Zilog Z-80 and NSC-800 microprocessors. IEEE Trans. Nucl. Sci. **NS-32**, 4206–4211 (1986)
11. Durães, J., Madeira, H.: Characterization of operating systems behavior in the presence of faulty device drivers through software fault emulation. In: Proceedings of the Pacific Rim International Symposium on Dependable Computing, PRDC-02 (2002)
12. Duraes, J., Madeira, H.: Emulation of software faults: a field data study and a practical approach. IEEE Trans. Softw. Eng. **32**(11), 1105–1118 (2006)
13. Durães, J., Vieira, M., Madeira, H.: Web server dependability benchmarking. In: Proceedings of the 23th International Conference on Computer Safety, Reliability and Security—SAFECOMP'04 (2004)
14. Gage, D., McCormick, J.: Why Software Quality Matters, Baseline Magazine, Kent (2004)
15. Gosling, J., Joy, B., Steele, G., Bracha, G.: Java (TM) Language Specification, The (Java (Addison-Wesley)), Addison-Wesley Professional, New York (2005)
16. Gray, J.: A Census of tandem systems availability between 1985 and 1990. IEEE Trans. Reliab. **39**, 409–418 (1990)
17. Gunneflo, U., Karlsson, J., Torin, J.: Evaluation of error detection schemes using fault injection by heavy radiation. In: Proceedings of the Fault Tolerant Computing Symposium—FTCS-19 (1989)
18. Hsueh, M.C., Tsai, T.K., Iyer, R.K.: Fault injection techniques and tools. IEEE Comput. **30**, 14–15 (1997)
19. Iyer, R.K.: Experimental evaluation. In: Proceedings of the 25th IEEE International Symposium on Fault Tolerant Computing, FCTS-25, Special Issue FTCS-25 Silver Jubilee (1995)
20. Kalakech, A., Jarboui, T., Arlat, J., Crouzet, Y., Kanoun, K.: Benchmarking operating system dependability: Windows 2000 as a case study. In: Proceedings of the IEEE Pacific Rim International Conference on Dependable Computing—PRDC'04 (2004)
21. Kanawati, G.A., Kanawati, N.A., Abraham, J.A.: FERRARI: A tool for the validation of system dependability properties. In: Proceedings of the 22th IEEE International Fault Tolerant Computing Symposium, FTCS-22 (1992)
22. Kanawati, G.A., Kanawati, N.A., Abraham, J.A.: FERRARI: a flexible software-based fault and error injection system. IEEE Trans. Comput. **44**, 286–291 (1995)
23. Kanoun, K., Arlat, J., Costa, D., Cin, M.D., Gil, P., Laprie, J. C., Madeira, H., Suri, N.: DBench: dependability benchmarking. In: Proceedings of the Supplement of the IEEE/IFIP International Conference on Dependable Systems and Networks—DSN'01 (2001)
24. Kao, W.I., Iyer, R.K., Tang, D.: FINE: A fault injection and monitoring environment for tracing the UNIX system behavior under faults. IEEE Trans. Softw. Eng. **19**, 1105–1118 (1993)
25. Karlsson, J., Gunneflo, U., Lidén, P., Torin, J.: Two fault injection techniques for test of fault handling mechanisms. In: Proceedings of the IEEE International Test Conference (1991)
26. Knuth, D.E.: The Errors of TeX, Softw. Pract. Experience **19**, 607–685 (1889)
27. Lee, I., Iyer, R.K.: Software dependability in the tandem GUARDIAN system. IEEE Trans. Softw. Eng. **21**(5), 455–467 (1995)
28. Madeira, H., Rela, M., Moreira, F., Silva, J.G.: RIFLE: a general purpose pin-level fault injector. In: Klaus, E., Dieter, H., David, P. (eds.) Proceedings of the European Dependable

Computing Conference—EDCC-1, Lecture Notes in Computer Science vol. 852, Spinger (1994)

29. Martins, E., Rubira, C., Leme. N.: Jaca: A reflective fault injection tool based on patterns. In: Proceedings of the 2002 International Conference on Dependable Systems & Networks, Washington, (2002)

30. Moraes, R., Barbosa, R., Durães, J., Mendes, N., Martins, E., Madeira, H.: Injection of faults at component interfaces and inside the component code: are they equivalent? In: Proceeding of Sixth European Dependable Computing Conference—EDCC'06 (2006)

31. Natella, R., Cotroneo, D., Duraes, J., Madeira, H.: On fault representativeness of software fault injection. IEEE Trans. Softw. Eng. **99**(9), 1–17 (2012)

32. Newman, P.: The Risks Digest, Forum on Risks to the Public in Computers and Related Systems. ACM Comittee on Computers and Public Policy **1** (1986) to **21** (2001)

33. Ng, W.T., Chen, P.M.: Systematic improvement of fault tolerance in the RIO file cache, In: Proceedings of the 29th IEEE International Fault Tolerant Computing Symposium, FTCS-29, Madison, (1999)

34. Nilsen, K.: Quantitative analysis of developer productivity in C vs. real-time java. Defense advanced research projects agency Workshop on Real-Time Java (2004)

35. Ruiz, J.C., Yuste, P., Gil, P., Lemus, L.: On benchmarking the dependability of automotive Engine control applications. In: Proceedings of the IEEE International Conference on Dependable Systems and Networks—DSN'04 (2004)

36. Sanches, B.P., Basso, T., Moraes, R.: J-SWFIT: A java software fault injection tool. In: 5th Latin-American Symposium on Dependable Computing (2011)

37. Segall, Z., Vrsalovic, D., Siewiorek, D., Kownacki, J., Barton, J., Dancey, R., Robinson, A., Lin, T.: FIAT—Fault injection based automated testing environment. In: Proceedings of the 18th IEEE International Symposium on Fault Tolerant Computing—FTCS'88 102–107 (1988)

38. Sullivan, M., Chillarege, R.: Software Defects and their Impact on Systems Availability—A Study of field failures on Operating Systems. In: Proceedings of the 21st IEEE Fault Tolerant Computing Symposium, FTCS-21 (1991)

39. Tsai, T.K., Iyer, R.K.: Measuring fault tolerance with the FTAPE fault injection tool. In: Proceedings of the 8th International Conference on Modeling Techniques and Tools for Computer Performance Evaluation (1995)

40. Vieira, M., Madeira, H.: A dependability benchmark for OLTP application environments. In: Proceedings of the 29th International Conference on Very Large Database Systems, VLDB'03 (2003)

41. Wood, D.: Java emerges as solution for military software modernization. VITA Technologies (VME and Critical Systems) (2007)

42. http://www.javelocity.com/collateral/calix.pdf

43. http://www.sesarju.eu/programme/workpackages/wp-14-swim-technical-architecture–201

44. http://www.prismtech.com/opensplice

45. http://www.rti.com/products/dds/

46. http://openjms.sourceforge.net/

Evaluating Fault-Tolerance of Publish/ Subscribe Services

Christian Esposito

Abstract Publish/subscribe services are being increasingly used in innovative critical systems to federate their internal components. Industrial practitioners require a rigorous methodology for assessing the behaviour of the adopted service in case of fault occurrences, both for satisfying demands of safety standards but also for selecting the best product to use. In this paper, we propose to use fault injection for this purpose and to present the description of the fault model to be used, the analysis of failure modes and the dependability measures for describing middleware behaviour in case of fault manifestations and the implementation of a fault injection tool. We also present the results of a fault injection campaign on three publish/subscribe service implementations, representative of the different technologies currently used in several industrial cases.

Keywords Publish/subscribe middleware · Fault injection · Reliability

1 Introduction

Publish/subscribe services [1] are middleware adopting an event-based architecture and offering data-centric communications. They are implemented by using an abstraction, called Notification Service, which mediates between interacting applications, and provides strong decoupling properties, which motivates their

C. Esposito (✉)
Consorzio Interuniversitario Nazionale per l'Informatica (CINI), Complesso Universitario
M.S. Angelo, via Cinthia, 80126 Naples, Italy
e-mail: christian.esposito@unina.it

D. Cotroneo (ed.), *Innovative Technologies for Dependable OTS-Based Critical Systems*, 115
DOI: 10.1007/978-88-470-2772-5_9, © Springer-Verlag Italia 2013

wide adoption for realizing large-scale data dissemination infrastructures, such as Market Data Platforms, Mobile Asset Management or Digital Services.

Critical systems are recently undergoing a radical rethinking due to the strong growth of their size and moving towards federated architectures [2]. To this aim, industrial practitioners are looking for a suitable middleware for efficient data dissemination so to federate the different components within such innovative critical systems, and publish/subscribe services are imposing themselves as the most appealing candidates. In fact, there are several concrete examples of publish/subscribe services being imposed as key reference technologies for architecting such innovative critical systems; here just few examples:

- the novel European framework for the Air Traffic Management under development by EuroControl, i.e., Single European Sky ATM Research (SESAR);
- a wide-area federated infrastructure, namely North American Synchro-Phasor Initiative network, for monitoring and control of power grids;
- the next generation of information system for collecting data from roadside sensors or neighbor cars as well as interconnecting sensors and actuators within a car[1];
- the upcoming federation of Health Information Systems for allowing a seamless clinical data sharing across Italy.[2]

Due to their critical nature, such systems impose stringent requirements on the adopted middleware, and strong importance is devoted to fault-tolerance, requiring the publish/subscribe to be equipped with proper mechanisms to avoid their violation. Industrial practitioners are interested in assessing the fault-tolerance mechanisms available at current publish/subscribe services, as typically demanded by strict standards that regulate the overall development cycle of critical systems. Specifically, they need to evaluate the behaviour of a given publish/subscribe service under the manifestation of several kinds of faults, observing if it brings up a failure of the system and if such failure implies a violation of the system requirements. Due to the importance of the middleware in such novel federated systems, this activity plays a key role in ensuring that the developed product actually meets the customer needs in terms of non-functional properties. In addition, the outcomes on such evaluation can be also used to compare the different available marketed products for finding the one that best fits the customer requirements.

Fault-tolerance represents a key aspect of safety, since a safety critical system should handle all possible faults and fault tolerance is required at various points across the system so to imply the absence of catastrophic consequences [7]. Therefore, it is worth to give a look to the several regulations that designed to

---

[1] April 6, 2009 Real-Time Innovations (RTI), The Real-Time Middleware Experts, today announced that Volkswagen AG, Electronics and Vehicle Research department, is using RTI's real-time messaging middleware across different projects to integrate advanced driver assistance systems into the car.

[2] www.ehealth.icar.cnr.it/

Table 1 Validation activities as specified in recent standards

Standard	Scope and procedures
IEC 61508 [3]	Each software module shall be tested by means of proper methods. Fault Injection is mandatory to validate the correct implementation of fault tolerance mechanisms in modules with all safety integrity levels, i.e., indication that its failure has the potential for major on-site injuries or a fatality, when the required diagnosis coverage is at least 90 %
ESA PSS-05-0 [4]	Compliance to safety requirements can be tested by deliberately causing problems under controlled conditions and observing the system behaviour when faults occur during tests. Safety analysis classifies events and states according to how much of a hazard they cause to people or property and identifies functions whose failure may cause a catastrophic or critical hazard
DO 178B [5]	It is needed to detect and report errors that may have been introduced during the software development processes. This is not simply testing, since it, in general, cannot show the absence of errors. To implement the software testing objectives, two categories of test cases should be included: normal range test cases and robustness (abnormal inputs and conditions) test cases
ISO 26262 [6]	Validation has to prove that the safety exhibited by the item is appropriate for the defined requirements. The following methods shall be applied: reproducible tests with specified procedures (such as fault injection, stress tests, highly accelerated life testing and simulations), analyses (e.g., FMEA), long-term tests, user tests under real life conditions, and reviews

ensure the safety of products, activities or processes in certain application domains, and to analyze which technique they recommend for evaluating fault-tolerance in safety critical systems. From Table 1, it is evident that *Fault-Injection* [8] is highly recommended by different safety regulations to be included as part of the dependability analysis of the critical systems under development. Therefore, in this paper we investigate how to use it for introducing fault events within the notification infrastructure and observing how the middleware reacts, and propose a framework that helps industrial practitioners in assessing publish/subscribe services. For this reason, we define in Sect. 3.1 a fault model derived from an analysis of failure causes and effects, based on the current literature of the field and our past experience on reliable publish/subscribe services [9]. Then, we identify in Sect. 3.2 the failure modes that could arise due to the occurrence of the faults contained in the mentioned model. Last, we describe in Sect. 3.3 a tool that we have implemented for performing fault injection campaigns for publish/subscribe systems, and in Sect. 3.4 the testbed where tests have been conducted.

An experimental campaign is presented in Sect. 4 by selecting well-known publish/subscribe service implementations, and testing by means of fault injection their reliability mechanism under a representative workload for large-scale critical systems. Results are discussed by describing the failure modes observed in each product when a given fault is injected, and by comparing the obtained behaviour with the one exhibited when no faults happen. Last, we conclude in Sect. 5 with some final remarks on the lessons learnt in this work and future activities.

2 Background

Fault-Injection [8] consists in the artificial introduction of faults into a given system to assess the system behaviour in faulty conditions. It represents a powerful technique for the evaluation of non-functional properties, such as fault-tolerance, of a software artifact [10], and it has been successful used in several different application domains and kinds of hardware and software systems. Traditionally, there are two different kinds of fault injection approaches: fault can be injected at hardware level, according to the so-called *Hardware-implemented Fault Injection* (HWIFI), i.e., injection is performed into the physical components of a system (e.g., by interfering with the voltage within a circuit); or injection is performed at software level, according to the so-called *Software-implemented Fault Injection* (SWIFI), i.e., faults consist of introducing of bugs into a program (e.g., effects of physical faults are emulated at software level or common programming errors are intentionally introduced within the code).

From our analysis of the current literature [11], we have noticed that only SWIFI approaches are used within the context of communication systems. In addition, we can distinguish between four different kinds of fault injection methods, based on where, within the classic abstraction of distributed systems (shown in Fig. 1a), a fault is injected:

1. a fault can consist in invoking middleware functionalities with exceptional parameters, namely *Invalid Inputs*, or even receiving unexpected and/or malicious messages coming from remote applications (we can define them as *Byzantine Messages*);
2. a fault can be wrong code, emulated by transforming parts of the middleware source code (namely *Code Mutation*), i.e., changing variable names or arithmetic operators in expressions, according to [12];

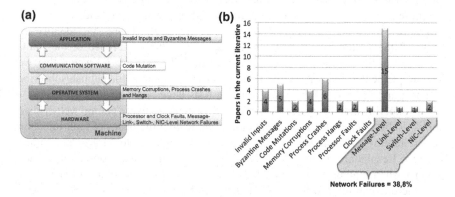

Fig. 1 a Abstraction of a node within a distributed system and faults injectable at each abstraction layer. **b** Analysis of the Fault Model within recent fault injection efforts on communication software (for details, refer to [11])

3. a fault can be seen as a return of invoked system call with exceptional values or even a failure of an entity: (i) *Memory Corruptions*, (ii) *Process Crashes*, which is the sudden termination of a process, and (iii) *Process Hangs*, which is a process that is not terminated but it is not reactive to incoming inputs;
4. a fault can be seen as an erroneous behaviour of some hardware devices: *Processor Faults*, such as corruptions within the registers, and *Clock Faults*, such as crash or strong drifts. In addition, we can also include in this class the *Networking Failures*, i.e., incorrect behavior exhibited by the adopted network, since they are seen as faults by the communication software. In particular, they can be at level of Message (i.e., losses, excessive delays, reordering or duplication), NIC (*network interface down*), Link (i.e., crashes), or Switch (i.e., crashes).

We have analyzed most of all the recent published works on fault injection within the context of communication software (in total 26 different approaches starting from 1995, as presented in Table 1 of [11]), aiming at finding what kind of faults have been applied in each of them. From the outcomes of such analysis, shown in Fig. 1b, we can say that the most considered faults are message-level networking failures (in fact, 30.6 % of the analyzed works assume them within their fault model), and in general, network failures (38.8 %). They are followed by process crashes (12.24 %) the application-level faults (i.e., 10.2 % focus on byzantine messages, while 8.2 % of the analyzed works study invalid inputs), and memory corruptions (8.2 %). Few tools deal with the other faults.

From our analysis, it is evident that the different fault injection experiences do not agree on which faults to inject when studying communication software, and in particular, this is true also for publish/subscribe services. In this work, we have considered all the faults contained in Fig. 2 with the only exception of some of them, since the scope of their injection is not related to the evaluation of fault-tolerance mechanisms:

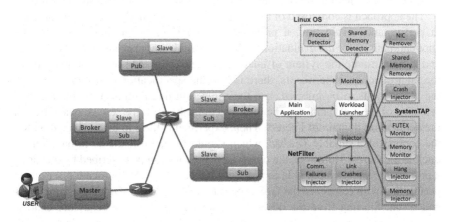

Fig. 2 Deployment of the ICeFiSh tool, and its internal organization

1. Exceptional parameters are commonly useful for testing the robustness of a software artifact, i.e., evaluating how it reacts when not properly used. On the contrary, we are interested to evaluate the dissemination quality when the publish/subscribe service is used as expected.
2. Code mutation usage in fault injection has a close intent to "bebugging" [13] (or fault seeding), i.e., introducing known faults via source code mutation for the purpose of monitoring the rate of detection and removal of a particular test methodology. Altering internal data and structure of the publish/subscribe service implies that the assessed dissemination quality can not be referred to the given implementation, but simply to a different one.
3. Injecting unexpected and/or malicious messages presents several affinities to the *Vulnerability Testing*, which aims at identifying a potential security flaw in the system (in fact, in the literature there have been previous works, such as [14], which used this kind of faults for performing vulnerability testing). Although security is an important feature, we are more interested in assessing other dependability aspects, such as reliability and timeliness.

3 Approach

Our proposed approach for evaluating the fault-tolerance mechanisms of publish/subscribe services consists of two phases. In the first one, called *Golden run*, the evaluation application is executed for observing the behaviour of the system under test in normal conditions. In the second one, called *Faulty run*, the application is executed by running the fault injection tool so to observe the behaviour when a certain fault condition occurs. A comparison of the behaviour measured in the two phases provides indications on the tolerance of the given injected fault, i.e., if the measured behaviour diverge, then we can infer that the fault is not tolerated. Moreover, in case a fault is not tolerated, the mentioned comparison is able to indicate the notification service degradation caused by the applied fault condition.

The approach is composed of five main elements. Similarly to common practice in performance evaluation, a proper *Workload* (i.e., the business logic of the application used for the evaluation), which should be representative of the domain and closely mimic the system of interest, is needed. In addition, to properly drive the fault injection experiments, there is also the specification of a *Faultload* (i.e., the set of faults to be injected, and their injection distribution over time), representative of the real faults experienced by a publish/subscribe service when used in the application domain of interest. Then, experiments have to be conducted within the context of a suitable *Testbed*, which should be controllable so to have reproducible measures. Moreover, the observed behaviour can be described by means of a proper *Characterization* able to precisely indicate how the notification service is performing with respect to the QoS properties of Reliability, Ordering, Timeliness and so on. Starting from the observed effects captured by the behaviour characterization between the Golden run and the Faulty run, it is possible to easily evaluate if a given fault has been completely tolerated, thanks to the mechanisms available in the publish/subscribe service, or not.

Nowadays, the specification of workload and measures does not represent an open issue. In fact, in the first case, there are standardized workloads in the current literature, such as the one in [15], or it is simple to obtain a workload by analyzing the specific system under development where the publish/subscribe service should be used. While, in the second case, it is easy to find the proper metrics for a given QoS aspect in publish/subscribe services thanks to the available related works, such as [16]. On the contrary, the specification of the other elements are still felt as issues, and will represent the topics of the following subsections.

3.1 Fault Model

To define a suitable fault model that will drive out fault injection experiments, we have conducted a study of the failure causes and effects, based on our past experience on reliable publish/subscribe services [9], and related works on this topic. Specifically, we have decomposed a publish/subscribe service in components, and investigated the effects of the faults identified in Sect. 2 (more details on such study can be found in [11]). From the outcomes of such study, we have defined the fault model for publish/subscribe services presented in Table 2 and structured considering four dimensions: (i) Location, i.e., where the faults have to be injected, (ii) Type, i.e., what kind of faults can be injected in a given location, (iii) Persistence, i.e., for how long the faults will be continuously present, and (iv) Trigger, i.e., when the faults will start to be injected.

Table 2 Fault model for publish/subscribe services

	Location	Type	Persistence
		Omission	Intermittent
			Bursty
		Corruption	Intermittent
Network	Message level	Reordering	Bursty
		Duplication	Intermittent
		Delay	Intermittent
			Bursty
	Link level	Crash	Transient
		Crash	Permanent
	Process level		Transit
		Hang	Permanent
Nodes			Transit
		Leak	Permanent
	Memory level	Shared memory Destruction	Permanent
	NIC level	Down	Permanent

Such a fault model contains the locations of all the possible causes directly came out from the failure causes and effects analysis that we have conducted, and described in [11], with the exception of hardware failures, which will not be directly injected, but will be only emulated by injecting their effects (as common in all SWIFI techniques). The possible locations where faults can be injected are the network and nodes, the main components originated by the mentioned analysis, in particular at message- or link-level with respect to network-related faults, or process-, memory- and NIC-level with respect to node-related faults.

With respect to the persistence of each fault, we have taken as starting point the characterization contained in [7], where persistence is defined by means of two distinct values: *Permanent*, i.e., after the fault is applied it is never deactivated (i.e., continuous in time), and *Transient*, i.e., a fault can be deactivated (i.e., its presence is bounded in time). From this characterization, we have identified two sub-classes within the context of transient faults, related to the case of network-related fault. Without loss of generality, let us assume message losses; studies, such as [17], have proved that such faults can occur in two different manners: *Intermittent*, i.e., there may be more than one sporadic manifestation of losses, and *Bursty*, i.e., several consecutive messages can be dropped at the same time, and there may be more than one burst during the monitoring time. Although intermittent and bursty network-related faults are sub-classes of transient faults, we have decided to leave them distinct in our fault model. In fact, to inject Transient faults, the client has to specify only activation and deactivation time; on the other hand, Intermittent and Bursty faults require some additional information. In addition to the activation time, the first one requires also the probability to apply the fault for a given message, while the second one needs the average burst length. For this reason we have characterized persistence considering all the previous four classes of faults.

Table 2 contains the overall fault characterization we have obtained from our investigation and used in our fault injection campaigns. In particular, let us consider some assumptions upon which we have based the content of this table. First, we have not indicated the trigger in the table since, as evident, we only assume temporal triggers for our fault model. In fact, due to the decoupling properties no particular event can trigger a certain fault, as may happen in other, synchronous, middleware solutions, such as CORBA, where a failure in a given component can propagate to other components. Second, crashes and hangs of processes can be both permanent or transient if the process can be restarted or not. Last, link crashes are only transient and not permanent. In fact, the Internet routing protocols are designed to automatically reconfigure and recompute routing tables when they detect a link crash [18], and lost connections are fast re-established.

3.2 Behaviour Characterization

By definition, a failure consists in the deviation from correct service [7], which is expressed in a series of functional and non-functional requirements. When

Table 3 QoS of publish/subscribe services

Reliability	Notifications are assured to be delivered despite of failures
Durability	Notifications are available even for late-joiners subscribers
Persistency	Notifications are available even if their source are no more active
Ordering	Delivery of notifications may respect the temporal order of their publication
Timeliness	Notifications have to be delivered before the expiration of a temporal constraint

evaluating the fault-tolerance of a given system, our attention is only directed towards the latter ones, which in case of publish/subscribe systems can be formulated by means of the QoS properties available in [16] and introduced in Table 3. It is possible to have quantitative measures of the experienced QoS, able to characterize the behaviour of the publish/subscribe service under study. In particular, such QoS properties can be measured by means of different well-known metrics:

- Latency, namely λ_i, indicates the mean time elapsed between the publication of a notification and its delivery to the ith subscriber. It can be averaged over the total number of subscribers, namely λ_μ, and also used to compute its standard deviation, namely λ_σ.
- Delivery Success Rate, namely ρ_i, indicates the fraction of notifications received by the ith subscriber over the total number of published notifications.
- Out-of-order Rate, namely ω_i indicates the fraction of notifications received out of order by the ith subscriber over the total number of published notifications.
- Liveliness, namely v_i, indicates, if negative, that a certain entity, such as a subscriber, is no more active and suddenly terminated.
- Connectivity, namely κ_i, indicates, if negative, that the ith subscriber is no more connected and is not receiving any notifications from a certain time instance.

In particular, Latency is related to Timeliness, Out-of-order Rate to Ordering, while the other ones to the remaining QoS properties.

Starting from these measures, we have classified, in Table 4, the possible cases we can have when comparing the values assumed by the measures obtained in the Golden run and the ones assumed in the Bursty run:

- *No Effects*, i.e., there is no deviation from the behaviour measured during the golden run;
- *Performance Degradation*, i.e., there is a deviation in terms of performance when a given fault is injected (i.e., the difference between the mean or standard deviation of Latency observed when the fault is applied and the one measured during the golden run, indicated in figure with $\Delta()$ is not null);
- *Reliability Degradation*, i.e., one or more subscribers experienced omissions of some notifications;
- *Ordering Degradation*, i.e., one or more subscribers experienced the out-of-order reception of some notifications;
- *Node Termination*, i.e., there has been the sudden termination of the application;

Table 4 Failure modes for publish/subscribe services

Fault effect	Description
Performance degradation	$\Delta(\lambda_\mu) \neq 0$ or $\Delta(\lambda_\sigma) \neq 0$
Reliability degradation	$\exists i : \rho_i < 1$
Ordering degradation	$\exists i : \omega_i > 0$
Entity termination	$\exists! i : v_i < 0$
Entity isolation	$\exists i : \kappa_i < 0$
Catastrophic failure	$\nexists i : \kappa_i > 0$
No effect	Otherwise

$\Delta()$: Comparison between golden run and faulty run

- *Node Isolation*, i.e., despite the application is still active, it stopped to receive notifications;
- *Catastrophic*, i.e., due to the injected fault, none of the active subscribers is able to receive any notification.

Table 4 provides a qualitative characterization of experienced QoS, indicating the manner to describe the effects caused by a fault occurrence. In this work we are not interested to assign any severity measure to each of these effects. In fact, if a given fault effect represent a treat or not for a given critical system highly depends on its requirements. For a concrete example, the loss of a certain notification would be generally catastrophic for an Air Traffic Management system (i.e., if the current position of a flight is not timely known it is not able to predict and avoid any possible collision with other flights), but would not represent a treat for a Power Grid Management system (i.e., if the current power level of transmission lines is lost, the new one is probable to come before the occurrence of an event that needs attention by the system). Generally speaking, to establish if a given fault can be tolerated or not, we can have the following cases:

1. No effects are obtained by injecting the given fault, so it is completely tolerated (*Strong Tolerance*);
2. Degradation effects happen after injecting the given fault, so, since the consideration of these effects as failures depends on the specific requirements of the application running on top of the publish/subscribe service, we can assume that the given fault is weakly tolerated (*Weak Tolerance*);
3. One, or more, of the last effects in Table 4 occurs for injecting the given fault, we can say that the injected fault has not been tolerated (*Intolerance*).

3.3 Fault Injection Tool

From our analysis of the related work in [11], we have noticed that none of the existing fault injection tools is able to cover all the fault types in our model, but each only focuses on a particular group of faults. As a concrete example, let us consider the following related works:

- [19] performs a dependability analysis of CORBA platforms and focuses only on message faults and not on the other ones, such as node faults;
- [20] describes a framework for evaluating the fault tolerance in distributed systems, but injecting only message faults and memory leaks, without caring of process faults;
- [21] analyses a middleware solution for exchanging Air Traffic management (ATM) data by injecting process and memory faults, but without considering message ones.

Therefore, we have decided to implement ex-novo a tool called *ICeFiSh* (fault-InjeCtion For publish/subscribe Services). Such tool is composed of two different applications coded in Perl: one, called *Master*, runs on the user machine, while the other ones, called *Slaves*, run on the testbed machines. The duty of the master is (i) to get in an XML file user preferences for the injection campaign, in terms of deployment of benchmarking applications, description and location of faults to be injected and duration of the campaign, (ii) to activate the slaves on all the nodes of the testbed and (iii) to drive the fault injection campaign based on user preferences. On the other hand, the slaves have to launch the benchmarking applications (such as publishers, subscribers, and, when present in the chosen publish/subscribe service, even brokers), and to perform the injection. Such architecture of ICeFiSh is depicted in Fig. 2, where there is also a repository, e.g., a directory within the file system or even a database that collects all the results of an injection campaign. ICeFiSh works in the two distinct phases, according to our approach, but with a slight difference: the golden run is not only used to have a baseline behaviour of the middleware without faults, but also to monitor the resources used by the executed applications (in terms of processes, memory allocations, mutex, or connection links), so to allow the user to properly select which faults have to be injected depending on the resources currently used by the middleware.

ICeFiSh has been implemented by using functionalities provided by the Linux OS and by two other tools: SystemTAP (sourceware.org/systemtap) and NetFilter (www.netfilter.org). SystemTAP allows the user to define a probe point at a given system call, so to perform proper actions before and/or after its invocation. On the other hand, NetFilter defines mechanisms within the networking stack for (i) passing messages out of the stack for queueing to userspace, (ii) placing these messages back into the kernel with a verdict specifying what to do with the messages (such as ACCEPT or DROP), and (iii) modifying content in userspace prior to re-injecting messages back into the kernel. As illustrated in the right side of Fig. 2, the slave application is composed of several modules, some for the monitoring phase while others for the injection phase:

1. SystemTAP is used with respect to process hangs and memory leaks. In the first case, since it is not possible to directly inject such fault, we have decided to artificially introduce its cause, i.e., causing a deadlock by altering the release of *futex*. Specifically, the input parameters of the futex system call are changed by placing the first parameter always equal to 0 (which indicates a wait), and

setting the second equal to 0 (i.e., indefinite wait). In the second case, we alter the return of *write* and *read* system calls by returning always −1, which indicates an error occurred and the operation has not been performed; in addition, in case of *write*, the buffer passed in input is placed to *null* (so to avoid that the kernel would perform the *write*).

2. Injecting process crashes, destroying shared memory segments and marking a NIC as "down" are done using Linux OS utilities. In the first case, known the PID of the target process by using the *ps* command, we will force it to terminate with the *kill* command; if the crash is transient the workload launcher will invoke again the crashed application. In the second case, we have implemented a kernel module so to use *unmap* for detaching shared memory segments. Last, in the third case, we use the *ifconfig* command, and put a given NIC in the "down" state so that the system will not attempt to transmit messages through that interface.

3. We have used NetFilter for injecting network-related faults. Specifically, we properly manipulate messages so to apply intermittent and bursty message-level faults. While, link crashes are emulated by discarding all the messages towards a given destination.

3.4 Testbed

A software system can be experimentally evaluated through on-field measurements by using prototypes in real wide-area testbeds. A crucial feature of such testbeds is represented by controllability, in order to have reproducible measures after the execution of an evaluation campaign and to be sure that measured behaviours are due to injected faults and not due to some uncontrollable phenomena of the testbed. With small-scale testbed, such as a cluster of nodes, this requirement is trivial to be satisfied; however, large-scale testbeds still face some problems. One of the most known large-scale testbed is *PlanetLab* [22]; however, it does not exhibit controllable behaviour. For a concrete example, we have performed some comparisons between a cluster of computers interconnected by a dedicated LAN, and some nodes in Planetlab by running a publisher and a subscriber on two distinct nodes, which exchange ping-pong messages though a DDS implementation. We have measured the notification latency, and Fig. 3 shows the measures for a specific link between London (UK) and Naples (IT) (but we have registered similar trends also in other six considered links in Europe): measures on LAN exhibit lower variability (as demonstrated by an Interquartile Distance of 20), while on Planetlab we have higher performance fluctuations (as demonstrated by an Interquartile Distance of 37672.5). This allows us to say that Planetlab is not a suitable testbed for assessing publish/ subscribe services. This result is not surprising because Planetlab has not been designed to perform controlled experiments and to achieve reproducible results, as also stated by its developers in [23].

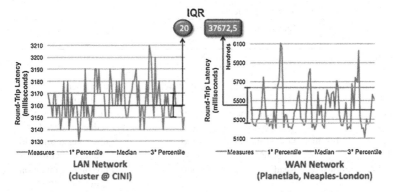

Fig. 3 Comparison of latencies on a LAN and on Planetlab

The issues that affect real wide-area testbeds can be addressed by using a small-scale testbed, such as a cluster of nodes, where wide-area network dynamics are emulated (*Network Emulation*). This is different to another related approach called *Network Simulation*, in which an entire distributed system is simulated by means of models and run by a single machine. In network emulation, only the network which connects end-systems is emulated, not the end-systems themselves, which runs in different machines connected to the network emulator. Although there are several network emulators available in the current literature, most of them cannot be used in our work since they are affected by scalability limits due to the limited numbers of real machines that they can interconnect. The use of virtualization can ease such an issue by increasing the number of machines usable for the experiments; therefore, we have used *Neptune* [24] in our work. Neptune is an open-source network emulator that provides the ability of interactively designing multiple virtual network topologies, which are then deployed onto a cluster of real machines and used as if they were dedicated physical testbeds, and is based on XEN for node virtualization, and on XEN virtual interfaces and NETEM for link emulation.

4 Experimental Results

The presented assessment methodology and tool have been used for the evaluation of two pub/sub services: OpenSplice DDS, and Apache Active MQ.[3] The last one is an open source implementation of the popular *Java Message Service* (JMS) specification for pub/sub services, adopting a broker-based architecture.[4] As workload, we have used a publisher and a subscriber exchanged a message with

---

[3] activemq.apache.org/

[4] www.oracle.com/technetwork/java/jms/index.html

Table 5 Fault model for pub/sub services

Middleware	Target	Injection type	Effect type	Effect description
Opensplice DDS	Publisher	Futex	No Effect	–
Opensplice DDS	Subscriber	Futex	Catastrophic	Subscriber in hang
Opensplice DDS	Publisher	Shared memory removal	Abort	Publisher termination due to a crash
Opensplice DDS	Subscriber	Shared memory removal	Abort	Subscriber termination due to a crash
Opensplice DDS	Publisher	Read	Abort	Publisher termination due to a crash
Opensplice DDS	Subscriber	Write	Abort	Subscriber termination due to a crash
Opensplice DDS	Publisher	Omission	Performance degradation	Increase of the communication latency
Opensplice DDS	Subscriber	Omission	Performance degradation	Increase of the communication latency
Active MQ	Broker	Futex	Catastrophic	Broker and subscriber in hang
Active MQ	Broker	Read	Abort	Broker termination due to a crash
Active MQ	Broker	Write	Abort	Broker termination due to a crash
Active MQ	Broker	Crash	Catastrophic	Interruption communications between publishers and subscribers
Active MQ	Broker	Omission	Performance degradation	Increase of the communication latency

structure as defined within the context of the SESAR project (i.e., with a size of about 100 MB) with a publication of 100 messages per second. While as faultload, we have used a subset of Table 2 (i.e., we focused on the most considered faults in Fig. 1, leaving for future work the other ones). Both middleware solutions have been set to offer reliable dissemination.

Table 5 presents the results of our injection campaign. We have classified the effects of the injection according to the following characterization: (i) *No Effect*, i.e., there is no deviation from the behaviour measured during the golden run when the injection is performed; (ii) *Degradation*, i.e., there is a deviation in terms of performance (i.e., delivery time is increased) and/or delivery properties (i.e., some sporadic messages are lost); (iii) *Failure*, i.e., there is an unexceptional behaviour such as sudden termination of the application (*Abort*), or impossibility to send/ receive messages (*Catastrofic*). In particular, we have focused on the broker for Active MQ due to its key role for the delivery of messages between publishers and subscribers, while for OpenSplice DDS we have injected on the daemon activated both at publisher and subscriber side.

We have observed that manipulating *futex* allowed us to cause hangs, with the only exception at the publisher for OpenSplice DDS, which caused the interruption of message flows within the pub/sub service. The removal of the shared memory in OpenSplice DDS is critical since it implies the crash of publishers and subscribers; we had the same effect when manipulating *read* and *write* systems call. If the crash of a subscriber in OpenSplice DDS did not have any serious consequences on the overall service, the same is not true then is the publisher or the broker to crash. In particular, the crash of the broker in Active MQ does not imply a mere interruption of messages flows as seen for the crash of the publisher in OpenSplice DDS, but it has a direct effect on the active publisher and subscriber application: after the crash of the broker, both publisher and subscriber are suddenly terminated returning an error message of "Communication protocol with broker unexpected terminated". Last, omissions (intermittent with PTF of 0.4) are recovered by both middleware with no notification losses, but only performance degradations. As a concrete example, in Active MQ, the latency is increased in average passing from 0.009 s during the golden run to 12.75 s when omissions are injected.

5 Final Remarks

Pub/sub services are increasingly adopted within the context of critical systems, making demanding their evaluation not only with respect to performance aspects, as done in the current literature, but also from a dependability perspective. This paper has presented a methodology for the rigorous assessment of pub/sub services in the presence of faults. We have illustrated what kind of faults can affect such middleware solutions, and how to use fault injection to inoculate such faults during the assessment of pub/sub service. In the future, we aim to perform a complete experimental assessment of several kinds of pub/sub services so to investigate what guarantees they provide and if there is a relation between the adopted architecture and the provided quality of service with faults.

References

1. Eugster, P., Felber, P., Guerraoui, R., Kermarrec, A.M.: The many faces of publish/subscribe. ACM Comput. Surv. **35**(2), 114–131 (2003)
2. Esposito, C., Cotroneo, D., Gokhale, A., Schmidt, D.: Architectural evolution of monitor and control systems—issues and challenges. Int. J. Netw. Protoc. Algorithms **2**(3), 1–17 (2010)
3. International Electrotechnical Commission (IEC): Functional safety of electrical/electronic/ programmable electronic safety—related systems (2005)
4. European Space Agency (ESA): Guide to software verification and validation (1995)

5. Radio Technical Commission for Aeronautics (RTCA): Software considerations in airborne systems and equipment certification (1992)
6. International Organization for Standardization (ISO): Road vehicles—functional safety, draft international standard (2009)
7. Avizienis, A., Laprie, J.C., Randell, B., Landwehr, C.: Basic concepts and taxonomy of dependable and secure computing. IEEE Trans. Dependable Secure Comput. **1**, 11–33 (2004)
8. Hsueh, M.C., Tsai, T., Iyer, R.: Fault injection techniques and tools. IEEE Comput. **30**(4), 75–82 (1997)
9. Esposito, C., Cotroneo, D., Gokhale, A.: Reliable publish/subscribe middleware for time-sensitive internet-scale applications. In: Proceedings of the 3rd ACM International Conference on Distributed Event-Based Systems (2009)
10. Arlat J., et al.: Fault injection for dependability validation: a methodology and some applications. IEEE Trans. Softw. Eng. **16**(2), 166–182 (1990)
11. Esposito, C.: How assessing quality-of-service of publish/subscribe services by means of fault injection techniques. Mobilab Technical Report (www.mobilab.unina.it) (May 2011)
12. Howden, W.: Weak mutation testing and completeness of test sets. IEEE Trans. Softw. Eng. **4**(8), 371–379 (1982)
13. Koopman, P.: What wrong with fault injection as a benchmarking tool?. In: Proceedings of the Workshop on Dependability Benchmarking (2002)
14. Wenliang, D., Mathur, A.: Testing for software vulnerability using environment perturbation. In: Proceedings International Conference on Dependable Systems and Networks (2000)
15. Sachs, K., Koumev, S., Bacon, J., Buchmann, A.: Performance evaluation of message-oriented middleware using the SPECjms2007 benchmark. Performance Evaluation **66**(8), 410–434 (2009)
16. Corsaro, A., Querzoni, L., Scipioni, S., Tucci-Piergiovanni, S., Virgillito, A.: Quality of service in publish/subscribe middleware. In: Baldoni, R., Cortese, G., Davide, F., Melpignano, A. (eds) Emerging Communication: Studies in New Technologies and Practices in Communication—Global Data Management, IOS Press, vol. 8, (2006)
17. Paxson, V.: End-to-end routing behavior in the internet. ACM SIGCOMM Comput. Commun. Rev. **36**(5), 43–56 (2006)
18. Coffman, E., Ge, Z., Misra, V., Towsley, D.: Network resilience: exploring cascading failures within BGP. In: Proceedings of the 40th annual Allerton Conference on Communications, Computing and Control, (2002)
19. Marsden, E., Fabre, J.C., Arlat, J.: Dependability of CORBA systems: service characterization by fault injection. In: Proceedings of the 21st IEEE Symposium on Reliable Distributed Systems (2002)
20. Meling, H.: A framework for experimental validation and performance evaluation in fault tolerant distributed system. In: Proceedings of the IEEE International Parallel and Distributed Processing Symposium (2007)
21. Cotroneo, D., Pecchia, A., Pietrantuono, R., Russo, S.: A failure analysis of data distribution middleware in a mission-critical system for air traffic control. In: Proceedings of the 4th International Workshop on Middleware for Service Oriented, Computing (2009)
22. Bavier, A., Bowman, M., Culler, D., Chun, B., Karlin, S., Muir, S., Peterson, L., Roscoe, T., Spalink, T., Wawrzoniak, M.: Operating system support for planetary-scale network services. In: Proceedings of the First Symposium on Networked Systems Design and Implementation (2004)
23. Spring, N., Peterson, L., Bavier, A., Pai, V.: Using planetLab for network research: myths, realities, and best practices. ACM SIGOPS Oper. Syst. Rev. **40**(1), (2006)
24. Di Gennaro, P., Bifulco, R., Canonico, R.: Link multiplexing in a Xen-based network emulation system. In: Proceedings of NGNM 2009, 6th International Workshop on Next Generation Networking Middleware, co-located with MANWEEK 2009, Multicon Lecture Notes 11 (2009)

Leveraging Fault Injection Techniques in Critical Industrial Applications

Antonio Pecchia, Anna Lanzaro, As'ad Salkham, Marcello Cinque and Nuno Silva

Abstract The importance of fault injection techniques is widely recognized by the critical systems industry. Fault injection allows evaluating error handling/mitigation mechanisms and assessing system safety properties under exceptional conditions. Even of more relevance, the use of fault injection is currently recommended by many international standards, such as ISO-26262 and DO-178B, to support the system validation and certification process. This chapter introduces design and technical challenges of fault injection techniques in the context of real industrial applications. Discussion starts from a generic framework that presents the functional components implementing a fault injection campaign. The adoption of the framework to support system evaluation by means of fault injection is shown for Intel Core i7 and AUTOSAR.

A. Pecchia (✉) · A. Lanzaro · M. Cinque
Dipartimento di Informatica e Sistemistica (DIS), Università degli Studi di Napoli
Federico II, Via Claudio 21, 80125 Naples, Italy
e-mail: antonio.pecchia@unina.it

M. Cinque
e-mail: macinque@unina.it

A. Lanzaro
Consorzio Interuniversitario Nazionale per l'Informatica (CINI), Complesso Universitario
M.S. Angelo, Via Cinthia, 80126 Naples, Italy
e-mail: anna.lanzaro@unina.it

A. Salkham · N. Silva
ASD-T Aeronautics, Space, Defense and Transportation Critical Software SA , Parque
Industrial de Taveiro, Lt 49, 3045-504 Coimbra, Portugal
e-mail: asad.salkham@criticalsoftware.com

N. Silva
e-mail: nsilva@criticalsoftware.com

D. Cotroneo (ed.), *Innovative Technologies for Dependable OTS-Based Critical Systems*,   131
DOI: 10.1007/978-88-470-2772-5_10, © Springer-Verlag Italia 2013

132

A. Pecchia et al.

Keywords Fault injection · Error handling · Dependability · Intel Core i7 ·
AUTOSAR

1 Introduction

Critical application domains, such as defense, automotive, space, e-health, and power supply infrastructures, increasingly rely on computer systems. Assessing dependability properties of this type of systems plays a key role to engineers. For example, analysis allows identifying architectural bottlenecks, implementing strategies to reduce maintenance costs, and designing effective recovery and mitigation means to avoid catastrophic effects of system failures. Approaches aiming to explore dependability issues become even more crucial to validate new architectures and protocols before operations.

Fault injection is a well established technique in the area of dependability evaluation. It consists in the deliberate introduction of faults in a system with the aim of understanding its behavior under exceptional conditions and evaluating the effectiveness of its fault-tolerance mechanisms [1]. The importance of fault injection techniques is widely recognized by the critical systems industry. They allow for validating error handling mechanisms by triggering code paths that are hard to test under regular operations and achieving insights into the safety properties of the system. More important, fault injection is currently recommended, if not mandatory, and regulated by many **international standards**, such as ISO-26262, IEC-61508, NASA-STD-8719.13B, DO-178B, to support the system validation and certification process and to develop robust software. For example, fault injection is an important constituent of the ISO 26262 [2] standard to supplement software unit and integration testing. This process allows ensuring the correctness of a given implementation in terms of specification, technical and functional safety requirements.

This chapter discusses design and technical challenges of fault injection techniques in the context of real industrial applications. The chapter introduces relevant tools and a generic framework to present the functional components implementing a fault injection campaign. Instances of the framework to support system evaluation by means of fault injection are shown for the Intel Core i7 processor and the AUTOSAR platform for automotive systems. Discussion highlights that, even if the application domains considered in the study share the same functional components, engineers must perform specific choices about the fault model and injection strategies depending on the target systems.

The rest of the chapter is organized as follows. Section 2 introduces tools and industrial challenges of fault injection. Section 3 describes the generic fault injection framework supporting experimental campaign. Industrial case studies are described in Sect. 4, while Sect. 5 concludes the chapter.

2 Background and Industrial Challenges

Safety-critical industries increasingly rely on fault injection to improve and automate the dependability assessment and qualification process. Nevertheless, **industrial needs** for fault injection goes beyond assessing dependability properties. Fault injection makes it possible to accomplish other requirements, imposed by the market, such as compliance to standards, contributing with evidences to safety cases, or supplementing the set of tests to achieve fault coverage or code coverage including error-handling mechanisms. While industrial needs are very well defined, **time-to-market** and production **cost restrictions** drive crucial decisions about the use of a specific injection technique and the number of experiments. Furthermore, technical limitations regarding hardware or software interfaces supporting the injection process, affects the fault models used in industrial applications. The existence of appropriate and complete interfaces drives the creation of the *faultload*, i.e., the set of faults to be injected, and the extent fault injection is possible into hardware and software entities composing the architecture under test.

Fault modes for **hardware** include emulation of hardware deficiencies, forcing errors or register corruption, bus errors, memory modifications and corruptions, and so on. Early work in the area of fault injection aimed at emulating such problems by injecting **physical faults** (e.g., by means of radiation, shorting connections on circuit boards and interacting with the hardware device at pin-level) in the system [3]. This approach is not straightforward because of the growing systems and hardware complexity. Even more important, it does not cope properly with evolving industrial needs. Critical systems industries usually rely on low-cost and more controllable ways to inject faults. For these reasons, **software implemented** fault injection (SWIFI) has gained popularity. SWIFI approaches allow emulating the effects of hardware faults through software, and overcomes limitations of physical fault injection by ensuring a controlled and repeatable framework to perform experiments. Examples of SWIFI tools are Xception [4] and NFTAPE [5]. Another technique that is currently widespread in industry is **scan chain implemented** fault injection (SCIFI), which is supported by csXception. SCIFI is based on the Boundary-scan (BSCAN) hardware specification adopted in the early nineties by IEEE.

Fault modes for **software** includes introducing common coding errors, forcing error-handling mechanisms, triggering non-nominal behaviors, variable corruption, etc. Recent efforts address the issue of injecting software faults [6, 7]. For example, the generic software fault injection technique (G-SWIFT) [6] emulates software faults by means of changing the binary code of the program. Alternatively, injection can be accomplished by modifying the source code of the program. Nevertheless, changing the code at varying levels is not always acceptable by industry. Industrial systems increasingly rely on the integration of existing services and components (built-in-house and, occasionally, Off-The-Shelf) and the source code might not be available. Assessment approaches based on the use of fault injection cannot always assume the ability to modify the source code.

Above-mentioned techniques are quite mature and provide a valuable help for industry that requires fault injection to improve system dependability. However, they are usually connected to the technologies, either hardware or software, under development. For these reasons, the number of commercial fault injection tools is not very large (csXception is among the few proposals supporting several techniques for different technlogies/architectures) although the number of academic tools is acceptable. Several companies actually prefer to develop their own tools addressing very specific purposes.

3 Fault Injection Framework

A framework supporting fault injection experiments consists of different functional components. Figure 1 shows a high-level framework representation [8] that applies to both the case studies discussed in the chapter. The unit under test is the component, or even the whole system, whose properties, such as error-handling mechanisms and safety-related aspect, are assessed in presence of activated faults. Components shown in Fig. 1 are described in the following, along with key implementation challenges that arise in case of industrial applications of fault injection:

- **Workload** exercises the unit under test during the injection process. For each experiment, it should be ensured that the workload is able to activate the injected fault. Moreover, to assess the extent the unit under test guarantees the continuity of the workload under errors, strategies must be adopted to make it

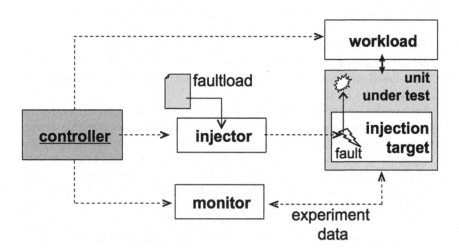

Fig. 1 High-level fault injection framework

sure that the workload is actually executed at the time the fault is activated. For example, the mentioned objectives can be achieved by profiling the unit before fault injection experiments or by leveraging operating system supports to cope with scheduling issues of processes.

- **Injector** is the entity responsible for introducing faults into the target. For example, it can be implemented by a debugger or a software module. If the injector is implemented via software, the injector must not interfere either with the workload and the unit under test. If not, the injection process might bias analysis results. Faults are selected from a **faultload**, again, the set of faults that will be injected in the unit under test. The injector has to cope with spatial and timing features, such as the location where the fault is injected (e.g., line of code, data/instruction register) and the time the fault is injected.

- **Monitor** is responsible for collecting data produced during the experiment. Example data include system logs, values of variables and parameters of interest, and output produced by the unit under test. Strategies have to be implemented to avoid data loss caused by faults leading to severe manifestations, such as crashes of system reboot. Again, monitor and data collection procedures should not interfere with the system under analysis.

- **Controller** is the entity responsible of iterating fault injection experiments. For each fault in the faultload, it coordinates the workload, the injector and the monitor. For example, the controller might interact with the workload running on the top of the unit under test, activates/deactivates injector module(s), and stores monitoring data for the subsequent analysis.

4 Industrial Applications

Instances of the framework to support system evaluation by means of fault injection are shown in the context of two critical application. The **Intel Core i7** processor is gaining increasing popularity in the safety-critical and embedded domain because of power efficiency features. **AUTOSAR** provides a standardized and open source architecture to develop automotive systems.

4.1 Emulation of Machine Check Errors in the Intel Core i7

Multicore processors are being more and more recognized as a valid option for industrial applications because of high-performance and power efficiency properties. This applies also to safety-critical and embedded systems, which are becoming more sophisticated by means of new functionalities that require higher computing power and reduced SWaP (size, weight, and power consumption). In domains, such as automotive and avionic, manufacturers are gradually adopting multicore processors; studies about the use of multicore in avionics systems were conducted to investigate possible interactions between applications of different safety-criticality [9].

The complexity introduced by multicore in the design, development and verification of software applications requires the implementation of specific methodologies supporting dependability assessment. The framework shown in Fig. 1 has been instanced to support the analysis of dependability properties of multicore systems, such as Intel Core i7 2670QM [10]. This processor consists of four cores implementing the simultaneous multi-threading (SMT) technology. A point-to-point communication link connects the cores integrated on the same chip. Proposed framework leverages the error-reporting mechanism of the processor to emulate problems affecting different hardware units, e.g., TLB, memory controller, interconnection, and cache.

The error reporting architecture of the target processor is also referred to as **machine check architecture** (MCA), and consists of a set of registers whose values provide detailed information about errors occurring in the system. Figure 2a shows the registers composing the MCA, called Machine Specific Register (MSRs), for a single core of the processor. The MCA is composed by 9 banks of registers replicated for each core and associated to specific hardware units. Each bank is composed by 5 registers: two control registers (MCi_CTL and MCi_CTL2), a status register (MCi_STATUS), an address register (MCi_ADDR), and a miscellaneous error information register (MCi_MISC). Proposed approach accomplishes the emulation of realistic errors by writing into the registers of the MCA. Error codes are inferred from available processor documentation and represent problems that can actually affect the execution [11]. Preliminary experiments described in this chapter focus on a subset of errors that the processor is not able to correct, i.e., **uncorrected errors**, but for which it can signal that a recovery action is required (SRAR), optional (SRAO) or not required (UCNA).

As shown in Fig. 2b, the workload running on the top of the i7 processor is the Linux OS kernel (version 3.1.10). Experiments aim to assess the operating system

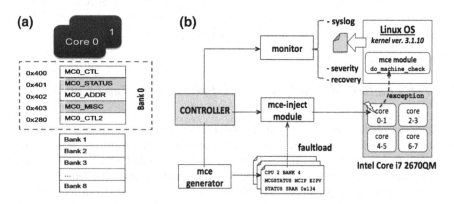

Fig. 2 Proposed fault injection approach **a** MCA registers. **b** Experimental framework

Fig. 3 MCE description and error severity levels. **a** Machine check error. **b** Linux severity levels

(a)

| CPU 2 BANK 8 |
| MCGSTATUS MCIP RIPV EIPV |
| STATUS UNCORRECTED 0x0000 |
| ADDR 0x11111111 |
| MISC 0x11111111 |
| NOBROADCAST |

(b)

Level	Severity	Description
0	NO	No Action
1	KEEP	No panic
2	SOME	No panic
3	AO	Action Optional
4	UC	Uncorrectable
5	AR	Action Required
6	PANIC	Panic

machine check exception handler, namely do_machine_check(). The handler is triggered by the kernel when a machine check error (MCE) affects the system, i.e., a specific interrupt occurs, and it is responsible for initiating recovery actions. The injector is represented by the **mce-inject** toolset [12] that allows to change the values in the registers of the MCA through a kernel module. An example file containing the values describing the error that is injected by the tool during an experiment is shown in Fig. 3a.

The entire set of MCEs to be injected (i.e., the faultload) is automatically created by **mce generator**, i.e., a bash script that generates the files representing the errors used by the injection module. Each experiment of the campaign consists in injecting a single MCE and collecting experiment data via a **monitor** (reported in Fig. 2b). We collect results about the error *severity* determined by the kernel (reported in Fig. 3b) and the *recovery action* triggered by the kernel. Such an information is inferred from the system log produced by the OS. The whole fault injection campaign is coordinated by the **controller**, responsible of iterating among fault injection experiments.

Preliminary experimental campaigns have been conducted to validate the proposed framework. Some results are presented in Fig. 4a, b. Results demonstrate that the Linux exception handler does not discriminate errors affecting different hardware units (e.g., the severity distribution of memory controller and TLB errors is almost the same). Moreover, the only recovery actions implemented by the handler are *process kill* or *kernel panic* (as indicated by Fig. 4b). Experiments show that the handler is not able to properly manage a significant number of errors (e.g., resulting in a *spurious* severity level) and that only two experiments triggered a specific recovery action, i.e., AR severity.

This preliminary fault injection campaign has been useful, for instance, to point out the MCE coverage of the Linux kernel, and to possibly suggest modifications of the handler to face uncovered MCEs. The approach can be potentially extended

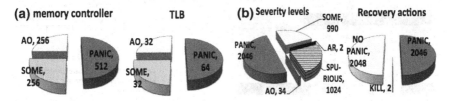

Fig. 4 Preliminary experimental results. **a** Severities by HW unit. **b** Overall severities and recovery actions

to other kernel versions and OSs to perform comparisons (e.g., dependability benchmarks), and to assess the performance impact of the MCE handling mechanism on running applications. This is relevant to evaluate the temporal impact introduced by such mechanisms in time-critical applications, such as real-time control loops.

4.2 CDD-Based Fault Injection for AUTOSAR Systems

AUTomotive Open System Architecture (AUTOSAR) [13] has emerged as a collective effort among the different elements in the automotive industry in order to provide standardized and open software architecture for different types of vehicles. The development process of automotive systems is driven by the ISO 26262 (tailored from IEC 61508) standard, which provides the guidelines to achieve functional safety requirements. ISO 26262 recommends the adoption of fault injection techniques to test automotive systems; however, there is a lack of details concerning the strategies that should be adopted to implement such techniques.

Proposed fault injection approach leverages the complex device driver (CDD) cross-layer, which is shown in Fig. 5a, to implement a minimally-intrusive framework to assess AUTOSAR systems. The main idea behind this approach is to trigger faults from the very base layer, i.e., microcontrollers (μCs), and to monitor the behaviour of the AUTOSAR system with the aim of evaluating its safety as a whole. Figure 5a shows how the components of the framework described in Sect. 3 get implemented in the context of the AUTOSAR architecture. The controller and a monitoring service are implemented as AUTOSAR software components (SWCs) and drive the injection performed at the CDD level. Each fault injection module is specialized in emulating given types of errors, e.g., communication-related, WatchDog Timer (WDT) or NVRAM-related: emulation is

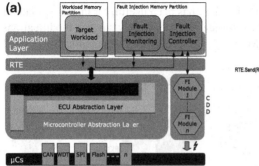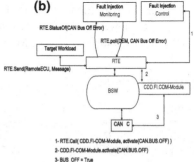

Fig. 5 Fault injection In AUTOSAR. **a** CDD-based fault injection. **b** Communication-related error fault injection scenario

achieved by corrupting the status, behaviour or content of the μCs through the CDD. It must be observed that μCs are not our test target and that the corruption aims to trigger the error handling and safety mechanisms at the Basic Software (BSW) and/or at the SWCs that rely on the integrity of such μCs. For this reason, it is sufficient to have the needed μC for a specific fault-triggering scenario being accessible and adjustable. The framework consists of two further entities, i.e., the target workload and the FI monitoring component. The target workload is implemented by one or more SWCs that use the BSW in a way that can exercise error-prone activities such as memory access or communication. The monitoring SWC is responsible for gathering information concerning the system status. Typically, it will require polling, through the RTE, components that are responsible for receiving error reports or possibly those performing mitigation. For example, monitoring may involve the Diagnostic Event Manager (DEM), which is responsible for most of the housekeeping, CAN interface, workload SWC, NV memory manager. The FI controller coordinates the described entities and is responsible for iterating through the FI experiments composing a campaign. It is worth noting that we exploit AUTOSAR memory partitioning to isolate the FI software from the system targeted by the injection. Essentially, controlling and monitoring software components run on a separate partition from that of the workload. This ensures that the FI software will be isolated from any potential memory errors that could occur at the workload partition. The controller is able to activate/deactivate a given injection module at the CDD and run the workload through the RTE. Furthermore, the controller stores results produced by the monitoring component during each experiment, which will be used to perform subsequent analysis.

An example of communication-related errors is the CAN Bus Off error which is raised when there is a CAN communication channel loss. As per the error information path, the CAN driver is responsible for polling its dedicated μC to check the status of the CAN bus readiness, i.e., the communication channel aliveness. The CAN driver is able to discover the CAN Bus Off error as the μC updates its register where the driver then tries to cancel all pending messages and informs the CAN interface about the error using a dedicated API. The CAN interface hence changes its mode to "stopped" and reports the error to the CAN state manager using a similar dedicated API. The CAN state manager starts the recovery and counts the error events. If the error is confirmed, the DEM, the BSW state manger and the communication manager are notified. The recovery includes resetting the CAN μC and enabling/disabling the transmit path. If the error is successfully mitigated, its event is removed from the DEM and the CAN state manager informs the involved elements. Indeed, the relevant SWCs are always updated through the communication manager using the RTE about the detection and the recovery of the error at hand. In order to test for the CAN Bus Off error, an FI scenario (See Fig. 5b) involves a situation where the target workload is trying to send a message to a remote ECU that eventually requires accessing the CAN bus. Following the target workload request, the CAN Bus Off error is triggered as the CAN μC is forced to be offline by the CDD fault injection module. The latter was instructed through the RTE to make the CAN bus inaccessible as part of the fault injection logic. Throughout the process, the fault injection monitoring SWC polls the DEM through the RTE in order to register a successful or a fail error handling for that case. Moreover, the fault injection monitoring SWC considers that the error is successfully handled if its relevant event is no more present at the DEM.

5 Conclusions

This chapter described the application of fault injection in two relevant industrial application domains. A generic framework has been presented to show similarities between the reference scenarios, such as the presence of a workload, an injector, a monitor and a controller. Nevertheless, the differences between the targeted systems impose different choices about the fault models and the strategies that are adopted to perturb the normal system function. Specifically, in the case of multicore processors, the machine check architecture has been exploited to emulate the occurrence of errors and to assess the error handling mechanism implemented by the operating system. On the other hand, in the case of AUTOSAR systems, the complex device driver is exploited to introduce specific faults in the controllers and to assess the functionalities of applications under errors. In both cases, errors are injected via software. Future efforts will be devoted to the improvement and the extensive use of the framework, and to conduct thorough fault injection campaigns with the aim of assessing dependability and safety properties in a variety of industrial applications.

References

1. Arlat, J., Aguera, M., Amat, L., Crouzet, Y., Fabre, J., Laprie, J., Martins, E., Powell, D.: Fault injection for dependability validation: a methodology and some applications. IEEE Trans. Softw. Eng. 16(2), 166–182 (1990)
2. International Organization for Standardization: Product development: software level. ISO 26262-6 (2012)
3. Gunneflo, U., Karlsson, J., Torin, J.: Evaluation of error detection schemes using fault injection by heavy radiation. In: Proceedings of the International Symposium on Fault-Tolerant Computing. Chicago (1989)
4. Carreira, J., Madeira, H., Silva, J.G.: Xception: a technique for the experimental evaluation of dependability in modern computers. IEEE Trans. Softw. Eng. 24(2), 125–136 (1998)
5. Stott, D.T., Floering, B., Burke, D., Kalbarczpk, Z., Iyer, R.K.: NFTAPE: a framework for assessing dependability in distributed systems with lightweight fault injectors. In: IEEE Proceedings of the International Computer Performance and Dependability, Symposium, pp. 91–100(2000)
6. Duraes, J., Madeira, H.: Emulation of software faults: a field data study and a practical approach. IEEE Trans. Soft. Eng. 32(11), 849–867 (2006)
7. Natella, R., Cotroneo, D., Duraes, J., Madeira, H.: On fault representativeness of software fault injection. IEEE Trans. Softw. Eng. (2011) PrePrint. doi: 10.1109/TSE.2011.124

8. Hsueh, M., Tsai, T., Iyer, R.: Fault injection techniques and tools. IEEE Comput. **30**(4), pp. 75–82 (1997)

9. Nowotsch, J., Paulitsch, M.: Leveraging multi-core computing architectures in avionics. In: European Dependable Computing Conference. Springer, Berlin (2012)

10. Intel 64 and IA-32 Architectures Software Developer's Manual Vol. 3: system programming guide. http://www.intel.com/

11. Lanzaro, A., Cotroneo, D., Duraes, J., Silva, N., Barbosa, R.: Multicore systems: challenges for creating a representative fault model for fault injection. In: Proceedings of the International Conference on Data Systems In Aerospace (2012)

12. Kleen, A.: Machine check handling on Linux, SUSE Labs (2004)

13. AUTOSAR consortium, specification of multi-core OS architecture v1.0, AUTOSAR release 4.0 (2009)

Part III
Security

Either you think at large scale and distributed software systems or at nano devices used to share, process and transmit digital signals, security is an issue. Web based applications and Service Oriented Architectures (SOAs), consisting of several interacting software packages, are more and more used even for critical missions. Their worldwide deployment threats security. Smaller in size but even more complex in structure, embedded systems are spreading into everyday life both for stand alone systems and interconnected in a all size network. Resource constraints of these devices represent the trickiest issue to handle for improving security and dependability. Several COTS tools are available for security improvement and assessment of computer systems and networks, and many techniques have been developing for protecting critical systems and infrastructure from any attack. Papers in this section face the problem of security assessment and improvement from different perspectives and at different layers, from web services security and vulnerabilities to embedded systems challenges for security. A wide set of security evaluation tools has been analysed, showing the lacks and weaknesses of such products. All the papers present novel ideas and propose solutions from improving and assessing information systems security. However, they show that research is still due in this field if we want to get the challenge of having secure and trustable systems even in mission and critical scenarios.

Gabriella Carrozza

Using Vulnerability Injection to Improve Web Security

José Fonseca and Francesca Matarese

Abstract This chapter presents a methodology to evaluate and benchmark web application vulnerability scanners using software fault injection techniques. The most common software faults are injected in the web application source code, which is then checked by the scanners. Using this procedure, we evaluated three leading commercial scanners, which are often regarded as an easy way to test the security of web applications, including critical vulnerabilities such as XSS and SQL Injection. Our idea consists of providing the scanners with the input they are supposed to handle, which is a web application with software faults and possible vulnerabilities originated by such faults. The results of the scanners are compared evaluating the efficiency in identifying the potential vulnerabilities created by the injected fault, their coverage of vulnerability detection and false positives. However, the results show that the coverage of these tools is low and the percentage of false positives is very high.

Keywords Risk management · Vulnerability · Threat · Web security

J. Fonseca (✉)
DEI/CISUC, University of Coimbra, 3030-290 Coimbra, Portugal
e-mail: josefonseca@ipg.pt

J. Fonseca
Polytechnic Institute of Guarda, Guarda, Portugal

F. Matarese
SESM S.c.a.r.l, Via Circumvallazione Esterna di Napoli 80014 Giugliano, Italy
e-mail: fmatarese@sesm.it

D. Cotroneo (ed.), *Innovative Technologies for Dependable OTS-Based Critical Systems,*   145
DOI: 10.1007/978-88-470-2772-5_11, © Springer-Verlag Italia 2013

1 Introduction

The goal of a security program is to choose and implement cost effective countermeasures that mitigate the vulnerabilities that will most likely lead to loss. This chapter discusses how Vulnerability Management is one of the few countermeasures easily justified by its ability to optimize risk.

One of the most difficult issues security managers have is justifying how they spend their limited budgets. For the most part, information security budgets are determined by percentages of the overall IT budget. This implies that security is basically a "tax" on IT, as opposed to providing value back to the organization. The fact is that security can provide value to the organization, if there is a discussion of risk with regard to IT, as much as there is a discussion of risk with regard to all other business processes. Calculating a return on investment for a security countermeasure is extremely difficult as you rarely have the ability to calculate the savings from the losses you prevented.

However, if you start to consider that Security is actually Risk Management, you can start determining the best countermeasures to proactively and cost effectively mitigate your losses. By determining the vulnerabilities that are most likely to create loss, you can then compare the potential losses against the cost of the countermeasure. This allows you to make an appropriate business decision as to justifying and allocating a security budget. More importantly, if you can make such a business decision, you can justify increasing security budgets for additional countermeasures. The key is to be able to specifically identify an area of potential loss, and identify a security countermeasure that cost effectively mitigates that loss [7].

Vulnerability injection is an innovative technique that can effectively increase vulnerability management by identifying the countermeasures that are really needed. Traditional countermeasures like network firewalls, intrusion detection systems (IDS), and use of encryption can protect the network but cannot mitigate attacks targeting web applications, even assuming that key infrastructure components such as web servers and database management systems (DBMS) are fully secure. Hence, hackers are moving their focus from network to web applications where poor programming code represents a major risk. This can be confirmed by numerous vulnerability reports available in specialized sites like www.securityfocus.com, www.ntbugtraq.com, www.kb.cert.org/vuls, etc.

The Open Web Application Security Project released its ten most critical web application security vulnerabilities [6] based on data provided by Mitre Corporation [5]. This report ranked XSS as the most critical vulnerability, followed by Injection Flaws, particularly SQL injection.

Computer Security Institute/FBI concluded in a survey [4] that defacement of web sites is a problem for many organizations, as 92 % of the respondents reported more than 10 web site incidents. An Acunetix audit result says "on average 70 % of websites are at serious and immediate risk of being hacked... and... 91 % of these websites contained some form of website vulnerability, ranging from the more serious ones such as SQL Injection and Cross Site Scripting (XSS)..." [1].

These attacks basically take advantage of improper coded applications due to unchecked input fields at user interface. This allows the attacker to change the SQL commands that are sent to the database (SQL Injection) or through the input of HTML and a scripting language (XSS). The high risk of these exploitations is due to: the easiness of finding and exploiting such vulnerabilities; the importance of the assets they can disclosure; and the level of damage they may inflict. These allow attackers to access unauthorized data (read, insert, change or delete), gain access to privileged database accounts, impersonate another user, mimicry web applications, deface web pages, get access to the web server, etc.

To prevent this scenario developers are encouraged to follow the best coding practices, perform security reviews of the code and regular auditing, to use code vulnerability analyzers, etc. However, developers normally focus on functionalities and user requirements, and tend to neglect security aspects due to time constraints.

Web vulnerability scanners are often regarded as an easy way to test the security of web applications, including critical vulnerabilities such as SQL injection and XSS. Web application developers and system administrators often rely on them to test web applications against vulnerabilities. Therefore, for them, trusting the results of web vulnerability scanners is essential. To what extent can one trust the verdict delivered by web vulnerability scanners, especially when the tool report suggests that there are no vulnerabilities in the web application? The answer to this question is the focal point of assessing the performance of these scanners using the proposed methodology.

2 Security Risk and Vulnerabilities

Security risk assessment is fundamental to the security of any organization. It is essential in ensuring that controls and expenditure are fully commensurate with the risks to which the organization is exposed.

The risk deliberated can be defined by the following formula:

$$Risk = Likelihood\ of\ the\ threat * vulnerability$$
$$* consequences\ of\ the\ exploitation.$$

A threat is, in a general approach, anything that might trigger a risk. However, it is important to point out that a threat is effective only if it is connected to a vulnerability. The risk is thus dependant on the vulnerability and on the threat. Threats are mitigated through vulnerability analysis over the assets. According to the vulnerability analysis, the threats can be eliminated or reduced to a point where the value of the risk is acceptable.

This chapter is therefore intended to explore vulnerability analysis as one of the basic elements of risk, and to introduce vulnerability injection to help ensure compliance with security policies, external standards and with legislation.

2.1 Web Application Vulnerability Scanners Benchmarking Approach

The approach to evaluate and benchmark the web application vulnerability scanners consists of injecting software faults into a web application code and checking if the scanners can detect the potential vulnerabilities created by the injected faults. The existence of vulnerabilities is confirmed manually in order to get accurate measures of the detection coverage and false positives. The characteristics of the faults injected are derived from the adaptation the web application environment of generic software faults not related with security issues, resulting from a field study [3].

2.2 Web Application Testing Methodology

Web application vulnerability scanners execute their procedures based on the knowledge of a large collection of signatures of known vulnerabilities, different versions of web servers, operating system and also of some network configurations. These signatures are updated regularly as new vulnerabilities are discovered. They also have a pre-defined set of tests of some generic types of vulnerabilities like XSS and SQL Injection. In the search for vulnerabilities like XSS and SQL Injection, the scanners execute lots of pattern variations adapted to the specific test in order to discover the vulnerability and to verify if it is not a false positive. The tests for these vulnerabilities, including both the sequences of input values and the way to detect success or failure, are quite different from scanner to scanner, so the results obtained by different tools vary a lot. This is actually one of the reasons why it is so important to have means to compare vulnerability scanners.

Two of the most widely spread and dangerous vulnerabilities in web applications are XSS and SQL Injection, because of the damage they may cause to the victim business. Trusting the results of web vulnerability scanning tools is of utmost importance. Without a clear idea on the coverage and false positive rate of these tools, it is difficult to judge the relevance of the results they provide. Furthermore, it is difficult, if not impossible, to compare key figures of merit of web vulnerability scanners.

The proposed methodology assumes typical topologies of web application installation and web servers. In a common setup, we need two computers connected by an Ethernet network. One computer acts as a server executing the functions of a web server, an application server and a database server. For the evaluation of server side security mechanisms like web application firewalls, IDSs, it is in this computer where they run. The other computer acts as a client with a web browser. For the evaluation of client side security mechanisms like web application vulnerability scanners, it is in this computer where the scanners are executed.

The methodology of injecting software faults into a web application, one fault at a time, consists of three main stages described in the following paragraphs.

2.3 First Stage

In the First Stage, the code of the target web application is examined in order to identify all the points where each type of fault can be injected, resulting in a list of possible faults. This proposal is based on the G-SWFIT software fault injection technique [3] focusing on the emulation of the most frequent types of faults.

Although the G-SWFIT fault operators were also evaluated for other languages, none of them are typical programming languages used for the development of web applications (usually scripting languages, like PHP or PERL). Thus, small adaptations in the fault operators proposed had to be introduced to use them for our web application purposes. The biggest change was in the "Missing function call (MFC)" operator. In web application programming there are normally lots of functions subject of security problems that process a parameter and returns data that will be used by the program. For example, in PHP code it is quite common to have code like this:

```
<? echo 'test.php?id='. urlencode($id); ?>
```

where the `urlencode` function encodes the string variable `$id` to be passed as a GET parameter in the URL. If the developer forgets to use the `urlencode` (`$id`) therefore using only the `$id` variable, the code can still be interpreted without any problem by the web server. So it is feasible that the software developer may forget to use this function and pass the `$id` directly as the GET parameter. However according to [3] it is not possible to insert this kind of fault because it fails to follow the restriction of the MFC rules. The MFC should be applied only when the return value of the function is not being used by any of the subsequent instructions. To overcome this situation we relaxed the restriction and created a new operator named "Missing function call extended (MFCext.)".

When the list of faults that can be injected in a web application is very large (because the application code is extensive, resulting in lots of possible locations for each fault type), only a percentage of the fault locations is used, keeping the relative percentages shown in Table 1.

2.4 Second Stage

The Second Stage comprises the injection of each fault, which corresponds to the insertion of the code change (defined by the fault operator) in the web application. After injecting each fault, the web application is scanned by the security tools under assessment and their results are gathered.

The testing of a client side security mechanism, like web application vulnerability scanners starts, with a "gold run" where the web application is tested once by each vulnerability scanner without any faults injected. The web application may already have some vulnerabilities and this run will be able to find most of them.

Table 1 Most frequent software fault types, derived from a field work (modified from [3])

Fault types	Description	% of total observed in the field	ODC class
MIFS	Missing "If (*cond*) {statement(s)}"	9.96	Algorithm
MFC	Missing function call	8.64	Algorithm
MLAC	Missing "AND EXPR" in expression used as branch condition	7.89	Checking
MIA	Missing "if (*cond*)" surrounding statement(s)	4.32	Checking
MLPC	Missing small and localized part of the algorithm	3.19	Algorithm
MVAE	Missing variable assignment using an expression	3.00	Assignment
WLEC	Wrong logical expression used as branch condition	3.00	Checking
WVAV	Wrong value assigned to a value	2.44	Assignment
MVIV	Missing variable initialization using a value	2.25	Assignment
MVAV	Missing variable assignment using a value	2.25	Assignment
WAEP	Wrong arithmetic expression used in parameter of function call	2.25	Interface
WPFV	Wrong variable used in parameter of function call	1.50	Interface
Total faults coverage		50.69	

Because of the existence of (at least) two computers, some operations need to be performed in the server computer and some in the client computer, in synchronism and this is guaranteed by a Control Tool specially developed for this operation. After the "gold run", the Control Tool reads the file with fault definitions (set of faults to inject, identified in the first fault injection stage) that will be used in the tests. Then, for each fault, the following procedure is executed (Fig. 1):

1. Every test starts with the clean initial setup: the web server is restarted; the database is restored; and the web site files are copied from a clean backup.
2. The next fault is injected into the web application.
3. The web application vulnerability scanner is started and at the end, the results are saved into a file. The file name includes a reference to the web application file and the type of fault injected. The Control Tool monitors the scanner application in order to detect when its execution stops before continuing the next test.

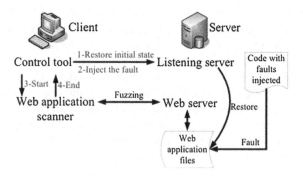

Fig. 1 View of the client and server algorithmic procedures

4. This procedure is repeated from 1 to 3 until all the faults are injected.
5. This procedure (from steps 1 to 4) is also repeated until all the web application vulnerability scanners have been evaluated.

2.5 Third Stage

Finally in the Third Stage, the resulting data is analyzed in order to obtain a comparative evaluation of the security tools. This procedure can be used, for example, to compare the detection capabilities of web application vulnerability scanners, WAFs, IDSs, etc.

After all tests have been performed, every file resulting from the execution of the scanners is manually analyzed using the algorithm presented in Fig. 2. This

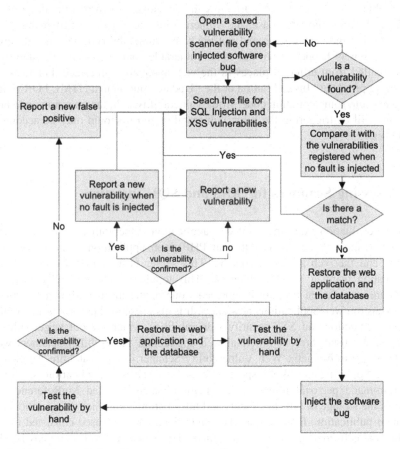

Fig. 2 Algorithm applied to the scanner generated files

data convey the decisions of the scanners regarding every vulnerability that was injected. Their results must be analyzed in order to be classified.

In these experiments, we are only interested in XSS and SQL Injection vulnerabilities, so when the scanner reports other types of vulnerabilities they are ignored. All the reported vulnerabilities are manually checked for false positives. It is also verified if the vulnerability is derived from the fault injected or if it is a vulnerability that was already present in the application and has not been detected in the "gold run".

To verify the accuracy of the scanners, it is possible to test if they found every vulnerability present in the web application, or to test if they found every trigger of every vulnerability. The former test allows comparing the scanners by the number of alarms raised. However, a scanner can be able to find more places that trigger a given vulnerability and fail to detect other vulnerabilities, while another scanner may find more vulnerabilities, even if it does not detect every input places where these vulnerabilities can be triggered. For practical reasons it was considered this later results, because they are more accurate for the corrections purpose. This is the main objective of the scanners: to allow the developers to correct the flaws of the web application. For this case, the vulnerabilities are also verified manually to confirm that they are unique and not the same vulnerability tested in a different way. This may happen when the same vulnerable source code is executed even when called from different places in the web application interface. For instance, when we press the "Insert" button or the "Update" button in a HTML FORM they may execute some common code. If the vulnerability is in the common code both actions will be triggering the same vulnerability and it should only be accounted only once.

3 Assessing Scanners for XSS and SQL Injection

For the evaluation experiments of web application vulnerability scanners we used LAMP (Linux, Apache, MySQL and PHP) web applications. The server runs Linux and the web server is Apache. This server hosts a PHP developed web application using a MySQL database. This topology of operating system and software was chosen because it represents one of the most used technologies to build custom web applications nowadays. It is also responsible for a large number of SQL Injection and XSS security vulnerabilities, which are our target vulnerabilities. We used three commercial web application vulnerability scanners were under test: the Acunetix Web Vulnerability Scanner 4, the Watchfire AppScan 7 and the Spi Dynamics WebInspect 6.32. As test bed web application we used a custom-made personal reference information manager called MyReferences. It allows the storage of pdf documents and information about their title, authors and year of publication, for example. The underlined database used consisted in 114 publications from an overall of 311 authors. The web application code has 12 PHP files with 1,436 lines of code.

Table 2 Detailed results

Fault types	# Faults	Acunetix		AppScan		WebInspect		Total distinct vulnerabilities found by scanners			
		XSS	SQL	XSS	SQL	XSS	SQL	XSS	SQL	#	%
No fault Injected	0	7	0	1	1	11	1	12	2	14	–
MIFS	23	1	1	0	0	1	1	1	1	2	9
MFC	26	0	0	0	0	0	0	0	0	0	0
MFCext.	71	8	5	2	16	6	36	20	39	59	83
MLAC	48	2	0	0	0	0	0	2	0	2	4
MIA	55	4	7	2	1	1	8	5	10	15	27
MLPC	97	0	0	0	0	0	0	0	0	0	0
MVAE	80	0	0	0	0	0	0	0	0	0	0
WLEC	76	3	7	3	3	0	8	7	12	19	25
WVAV	13	0	0	0	0	0	0	0	0	0	0
MVI	8	0	0	0	0	0	0	0	0	0	0
MVAV	13	0	0	0	0	0	0	0	0	0	0
WAEP	1	0	0	0	0	0	0	0	0	0	0
WPFV	148	0	13	0	0	0	12	2	19	21	14
Total injected	659	25	33	8	21	19	66	49	83	118	18

3.1 Overall Results

For the experiments with the MyReferences web application we injected the 12 most frequent types of faults described in Table 1 and derived from the results of a field study on common software bugs [3]. Every source code file was analyzed, looking for possible locations for each fault type. We injected 659 faults and we executed the scanners looking for them. The detailed results of the experiments are depicted in Table 2.

The faults injected produced application bugs and application malfunctioning, but they also produced a considerable amount of security vulnerabilities, 18 %. Note that some injected bugs contributed to more than one type of vulnerabilities (XSS and SQL Injection) and some produced more than one vulnerability of the same type.

One aspect that should be highlighted is the high number of vulnerabilities found even before the start of the tests (they are latent errors). These are the 14 vulnerabilities that were present before any fault was injected by the experiments.

3.2 XSS and SQL Injection Comparison

Table 2 shows that, from the 12 fault types only six produced vulnerabilities. These fault types are the "Missing "If (cond) {statement(s)}" (MIFS)", the "Missing function call extended (MFCext.)", the "Missing "AND EXPR" in

Table 3 Type of vulnerabilities of the MyReferences application

	XSS	SQL Injection
#	37	81
%	31	69

expression used as branch condition (MLAC)", the "Missing "if (cond)" sur-rounding statement(s) (MIA)", the "Wrong logical expression used as branch condition (WLEC)" and the "Wrong variable used in parameter of function call (WPFV)". Every one of these six fault types generated both XSS and SQL Injection vulnerabilities.

The distribution of XSS and SQL Injection is shown in Table 3. Fault injection produced more than the double of SQL Injection type than XSS.

3.3 Coverage

The analysis of the individual results of the scanners shows that all the scanners have detected some vulnerabilities that none of the others have. After having the data supporting this conclusion, we suspected that the scanners might leave some vulnerabilities undetected, which is also stated by other studies [2]. To search for the vulnerabilities left undetected by the scanners and, therefore, analyze the scanners coverage, a human tester was used to perform a manual inspection of both the PHP code and the browser results.

The overall coverage is depicted in Fig. 3. The intersection area of the circles represents vulnerabilities detected by more than one scanner. The actual number of vulnerabilities detected is also shown.

Analyzing Fig. 3 we can see that the circle representing the manual scan does not intersect the other circles, which means that the vulnerabilities detected by manual inspection were not detected by any of the tools evaluated. The radius of each circle is proportional to the number of vulnerabilities detected, providing a comparative visual image of the coverage of each tool. The observation of Fig. 3 clearly shows that WebInspect is the best scanner concerning overall coverage of vulnerability detection, followed by Acunetix and AppScan.

The manual scan detected 17 vulnerabilities that have not been detected by none of the vulnerability scanners, which corresponds to 9 % of all vulnerabilities found. For the BookStore application, a complete hand scan could not be done due to time constraints, however some quick tests uncovered the existence of some second order vulnerabilities that were not detected by the scanners, which confirms the trend observed in the MyReferences experiments.

Looking at the details of the coverage of the individual vulnerability types (Fig. 4 for XSS and Fig. 5 for SQL Injection) it is possible to conclude that the best scanner for SQL Injection is not necessarily the best for XSS.

Fig. 3 Total coverage of the
MyReferences application

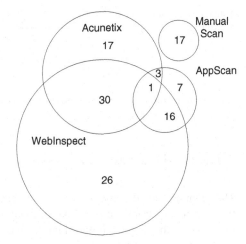

Fig. 4 SQL Injection
coverage of the
MyReferences application

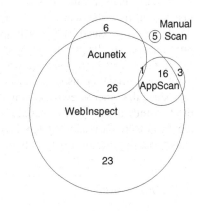

Fig. 5 XSS coverage of the
MyReferences application

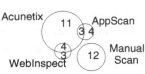

Given the high price of these commercial scanners, they leave many vulnerabilities undetected. While some of these vulnerabilities should have been detected by the scanners, there are others that will be difficult to be detected by a tool using only the black-box approach. Other types of vulnerabilities undetected are logic errors and second order vulnerabilities, which are vulnerabilities that need some reasoning to detect them. Although a human tester can uncover them, they are not easily automated (and implemented by the scanners) and generalized for every web application.

Another difficulty for the scanners occurs when the exploit needs some specific tokens to be present. These tokens may be the right number of parenthesis in a SQL Injection attempt, or some precise HTML code in an XSS attack. Although

Table 4 False positives of the MyReferences application

	Acunetix	AppScan	WebInspect
#	13	43	45
%	20	62	38

the scanners have some fuzzy variations of tests, these will hardly cover all the possible combinations.

3.4 False Positives

The scanners found some vulnerabilities but they also detected many false positives, as depicted in Table 4. Like in many other related fields, the false positive rate tends to be directly proportional to the ability to detect vulnerabilities.

We also analyzed the possible reasons for the false positives to provide some insights on how the scanners could be improved. Some false positives occurred due to an error issued by the web application in normal execution because of the fault injected. In the penetration test, the same error was shown and that triggered the scanner. This error message was found in 10 cases using the Acunetix, in 43 cases using the WebInspect, and in 40 cases using the AppScan. We could not reproduce the other three remaining cases of false positives found by Acunetix and the two remaining by WebInspect. The three remaining false positives found by AppScan were curiously triggered by the data stored in the back-end database: the cause was the title of a paper about SQL Injection.

4 Conclusions

In this chapter we proposed an approach to evaluate and compare web application vulnerability scanners, in order to eliminate the threats or reduce them to a point where the value of the risk is acceptable. It is based on the injection of realistic software faults in web applications in order to compare the efficiency of the different tools in the detection of the possible vulnerabilities caused by the injected bugs. The results of the evaluation of three leading web application vulnerability scanners show that different scanners produce quite different results and that all of them leave a considerable percentage of vulnerabilities undetected. The percentage of false positives is very high, ranging from 20 to 77 % in the experiments performed. The results obtained also show that the proposed approach allows easy comparison of coverage and false positives of the web vulnerability scanners. In addition to the evaluation and comparison of vulnerability scanners, the proposed approach also can be used to improve the quality of vulnerability scanners, as it easily shows their limitations. Even the common widely used Rapid Application Development environments produce code with vulnerabilities. For some critical web applications several scanners should be used and a manual scan should not be discarded from the process. In fact, it should be mandatory for critical applications.

Each one of the web application vulnerability scanners analyzed cannot be used as a "One tool to rule them all" solution. Even the results of the three scanners combined do not cover the vulnerabilities thoroughly. Through a different set of experiments, using PHP, Java, ASP.NET and ASP applications and also testing for JavaScript related problems, Ananta Security compared the same brand scanners and their conclusions are similar to ours [2]: the scanners have a huge false positive rate and the black-box scanning using automated tools is not enough to assure complete security. The disturbing conclusion is that, even if the scanners do not find any vulnerability we cannot assure that the web application is free of vulnerabilities.

References

1. Acunetix: Acunetix Web Security Survey Report, Acunetix (2007). http://www.acunetix.com/news/security-audit-results.htm
2. Ananta Security: Web Vulnerability Scanners Comparison (2009). http://anantasec.blogspot.com/2009/01/web-vulnerability-scanners-comparison.html
3. Durães, J., Madeira, H.: Emulation of software faults: a field data study and a practical approach, IEEE. Trans. Softw. Eng. **32**(11), 849–867 (2006)
4. Gordon, L.A., Loeb, M.P., Lucyshyn, W., Richardson, R.: CSI Computer Crime & Security Survey, Computer Security Institute (2006)
5. MITRE Corporation: Common Vulnerabilities and Exposures (2012). http://cve.mitre.org/
6. OWASP Foundation: OWASP Top 10—2010, OWASP Foundation (2010)
7. Winkler, I.: Justifying IT Security Managing Risk & Keeping Your Network Secure. Qualys Inc., Redwood City (2010)

Security Testing in SOAs: Techniques and Tools

Nuno Antunes and Marco Vieira

Abstract Web Applications and Services are often deployed with critical software bugs that may be maliciously exploited. The adoption of Service Oriented Architectures (SOAs) in a wide range of organizations, including business-critical systems, opens the door to new security challenges. The problem is that developers are frequently not specialized on security and the common time-to-market constraints limit an in depth test for vulnerabilities. Additionally, research and practice shows that the effectiveness of existing vulnerability detection tools is very poor. This highlights the need for tools capable of efficiently detecting vulnerabilities in SOAs. This chapter discusses these problems and proposes new techniques and tools to improve services security by detecting vulnerabilities in a SOA in an automated manner.

Keywords Service oriented architectures · Services · Security testing · Software vulnerabilities · Vulnerability detection · Command injection vulnerabilities · Penetration testing · Static code analysis

N. Antunes (✉) · M. Vieira
Department of Informatics Engineering, University of Coimbra, DEI, Pólo II—Universidade de Coimbra, 3030-290 Coimbra, Portugal
e-mail: nmsa@dei.uc.pt

M. Vieira
e-mail: mvieira@dei.uc.pt

D. Cotroneo (ed.), *Innovative Technologies for Dependable OTS-Based Critical Systems,*   159
DOI: 10.1007/978-88-470-2772-5_12, © Springer-Verlag Italia 2013

1 Introduction

Service Oriented Architectures (SOAs) are used in a wide range of organizations and scenarios, including business-critical systems. These architectures consist of several interacting software resources designed to support the infrastructure of the organization. These resources are packaged as services, which are well-defined, self-contained, standard-based and protocol-independent modules that provide standard business functionalities and are independent from the state or context of other services [1]. SOAs can be implemented using different types of services and technologies, but Web Services are frequently the implementation of choice [24].

Research and practice show that, in general, web-based applications present dangerous flaws [1, 29], and services are no exception, as shown in two previous studies [20, 27] for web services and messaging middleware, respectively. Such services provide a simple interface between a provider and consumers [10] and are based on exchange of messages over the network using, for example, HTTP or HTTPS protocols. The service and the format of the messages to be exchanged is defined in a description file (e.g., WSDL [11] for SOAP WS or WADL [22] for REST WS).

Existing studies also show the predominance of injection vulnerabilities (namely SQL Injection), which are among the most common and dangerous vulnerabilities in the Web [29]. Injection attacks try to take advantage of improperly coded applications to execute commands specified by the attacker, enabling, for instance, access to critical data and resources [29]. SQL Injection and XPath injection vulnerabilities are particularly relevant [27], as services frequently use a data persistence solution over a relational or a XML database. As a matter of fact, hackers are moving their focus from the network to applications' code, searching for these vulnerabilities by exploiting applications' inputs with specially tampered values. These application level attacks are performed through ports used for regular web traffic and thus cannot be mitigated by traditional security mechanisms such as firewalls and intrusion detection systems [24].

To prevent vulnerabilities, developers should apply best coding practices, perform security inspections, execute penetration tests, etc. [6]. However, many times, developers focus on the satisfying user's functional requirements and time-to-market constraints, disregarding security aspects. However, web applications are so exposed that hackers will most probably uncover any existing security vulnerability. Under this scenario, automated vulnerability detection tools have a very important role on helping the developers to produce less vulnerable code.

Different techniques for the detection of vulnerabilities have been proposed in the past [25], including penetration testing and static analysis. Penetration testing, by far the most used by web developers, is a technique in which the application is stressed from the point of view of the attacker ("black-box" approach) by issuing a large amount of malicious interactions. As the application is tested from the user point of view, there is no need to access or modify the source code. The main problem is that, in practice, vulnerability identification can only rely on the analysis of the web application output. This way, the effectiveness of penetration testing is always limited by the lack of visibility on the internal behavior of the application. The limited effectiveness of penetration testing tools is confirmed by several studies [5, 12, 27, 28]. Static analysis is a "white-box" approach based on the analysis of the source code to identify specific code patterns that are prone to security vulnerabilities. However, it lacks a dynamic view of the real behavior of the service in the presence of a realistic workload (e.g., it does not find vulnerabilities introduced in the runtime environment). In fact, the number of false positives reported reduces the effectiveness of this technique, as shown in [5, 9]. Additionally, both providers and consumers can use penetration testing, but only providers can apply static analysis, as it requires access to the code of the service.

The impact of such problems increases in the context of a SOA, with new challenges being raised. First, it is still necessary to test each service offline for vulnerabilities, thus we need efficient vulnerability detection tools. Second, these architectures are usually build using services that are controlled by multiple providers creating the need for different types of vulnerability detection tools. Finally, SOAs are dynamic in nature, facing changes in the services used and in the way they interact, which brings the need for automated approaches able to continuously test the whole architecture in an automated way. This chapter presents existing techniques and tools and discusses these challenges in details, also proposing ways to overcome them.

The structure of this chapter is as follow. The next section introduces the most frequently used security testing techniques. Section 3 presents commercial tools that implement those techniques and discusses their limitations. Section 4 discusses security requirements in a services environment. Section 5 presents a security testing approach for SOAs and Sect. 6 concludes the paper.

2 Security Testing Techniques

To detect security issues, we must focus not only on testing the functionalities of the application but also on addressing security aspects. For this purpose two main approaches are usually considered: white-box analysis and black-box testing.

2.1 White-Box Vulnerability Detection

White-box analysis consists of examining the code of the application without executing it. This can be done in one of two ways: manually during code inspections and reviews or automatically by using automated analysis tools.

A code inspection is the process by which a programmer delivers the code to his peers and they systematically examine it, searching for programming mistakes that can introduce bugs [14]. A security inspection is an inspection that is specially targeted to find security vulnerabilities. Inspections are the most effective way to guarantee that an application has a minimum number of vulnerabilities and are a crucial procedure when developing software for critical systems. Nevertheless, they are usually very long, expensive and require inspectors to have a deep knowledge on web security. A less expensive alternative is code reviews [14]. Code reviews are a simplified version of code inspections and can be considered when analyzing less critical code. Reviews are also a manual approach, but they do not include a formal inspection meeting. The reviewers perform the code review individually and the moderator is in charge of filtering and merging the outcomes from the several experts. Although also a very effective approach, it is still quite expensive.

The solution to reduce the cost of white-box analysis is to rely on automated tools, such as static code analyzers. Static code analysis tools vet software code, either in source or binary form, in an attempt to identify common implementation-level bugs [25]. The analysis performed by existing tools varies depending on their sophistication, ranging from tools that consider only individual statements and declarations to others that consider dependencies between lines of code. Among other usages (e.g., model checking and data flow analysis), these tools provide an automatic way for highlighting possible coding errors. The main problem is that exhaustive source code analysis may be difficult and cannot find many security flaws due to the complexity of the code and the lack of a dynamic (runtime) view.

Although of great importance, the use of static code analysis tools sometimes affects programmer's productivity, predominantly because of the false positive warnings reported (that lead to useless additional work) [9]. To avoid this situation, developers need policies to ensure that the tools are being correctly used (and also time for learning and using those tools). For instance, it is necessary to specify rules to classify and select the warnings to be fixed, and the time to fix them. Also, the analysis tools shall be correctly configured to report only the warnings that are, in fact, relevant to the current development context. Developers that do not adopt effective practices for using static analysis usually end up not taking advantage of all their functionalities and underestimating their real benefits.

2.2 Black-Box Vulnerability Detection

Black-box testing refers to the analysis of the program execution from an external point-of-view. In short, it consists of exercising the software and comparing the execution outcome with the expected result. Testing is probably the most used technique for verification and validation of software.

There are several levels for applying black-box testing, ranging from unit testing to integration testing and system testing. The testing approach can also be more formalized (based on models and well defined test specifications) or less formalized (e.g., when considering informal "smoke testing"). Robustness testing is a specific form of black-box testing. The goal is to characterize the behavior of a system in presence of erroneous input conditions. Penetration testing, a specialization of robustness testing, consists of the analysis of the program execution in the presence of malicious inputs, searching for potential vulnerabilities. In this approach the tester does not know the internals of the web application and it uses fuzzing techniques over the web HTTP requests [25]. The tester needs no knowledge about the implementation details and tests the inputs of the application from the user's point of view. The number of tests can reach hundreds or even thousands for each vulnerability type.

Penetration testing tools provide an automatic way for searching for vulnerabilities avoiding the repetitive and tedious task of doing hundreds or even thousands of tests by hand for each vulnerability type. The most common automated security testing tools used in web applications are generally referred to as **web security scanners** (or web vulnerability scanners), which allow easily testing applications against vulnerabilities. These scanners have a predefined set of test cases that are adapted to the target application, saving the user from define all the tests to be done. In practice, the user only needs to configure the scanner and let it test the application. Once the test is completed the scanner reports existing vulnerabilities (if any detected). Most of these scanners are commercial tools, but there are also some free application scanners often with limited use, since they lack most of the functionalities of their commercial counterparts.

3 Vulnerability Detection Tools

Penetration testing and static code analysis can be performed manually or automatically. Manual tests or inspections require resources specialized in security and larger amounts of time. Additionally, many times, developers focus on the implementation of functionalities and on satisfying the costumer's requirements and disregard security aspects. Under this scenario, automated vulnerability detection tools have a very important role on helping the developers to produce less vulnerable code. An important aspect when discussing the limitations of vulnerability detection tools is that it is quite hard to test for security. Indeed, it is very difficult to measure the security of an application: it can be easy to find some of the vulnerabilities, but very hard to guarantee that there is no vulnerability left in the application [15].

3.1 Penetration Testing Tools

The most common automated security testing tools used in web applications are generally referred to as **web security scanners** (or web vulnerability scanners). Three brands lead the market: HP WebInspect [16], IBM Rational AppScan [17] and Acunetix Web Vulnerability Scanner [2].

HP WebInspect is a tool that "performs web application security testing and assessment for today's complex web applications, built on emerging Web 2.0

technologies. HP WebInspect delivers fast scanning capabilities, broad security assessment coverage and accurate web application security scanning results" [16]. This tool includes pioneering assessment technology, including simultaneous crawl and audit (SCA) and concurrent application scanning. It is a broad application that can be applied for penetration testing in web-based applications.

IBM Rational AppScan "is a leading suite of automated Web application security and compliance assessment tools that scan for common application vulnerabilities" [17]. This tool is suitable for users ranging from non-security experts to advanced users that can develop extensions for customized scanning environments. IBM Rational AppScan can be used for penetration testing in web applications, including web services.

Acunetix Web Vulnerability Scanner "is an automated web application security testing tool that audits a web applications by checking for exploitable hacking vulnerabilities" [2]. Acunetix WVS can be used to execute penetration testing in web applications or web services and is quite simple to use and configure. The tool includes numerous innovative features, for instance the "AcuSensor Technology" [3].

3.2 Static Code Analysis Tools

A solution to reduce the cost of white-box analysis is to rely on static code analyzers. In fact, the use of automated code analysis tools is seen as an easier and faster way to find bugs and vulnerabilities in web applications. The following paragraphs briefly introduce some of the most used and well-known static code analyzers, including both commercial and free tools.

FindBugs is an open source tool that "uses static analysis to look for bugs in Java code" [26]. Findbugs is composed of various detectors each one specialized in a specific pattern of bugs. The detectors use heuristics to search in the bytecode of Java applications for these patterns and classify it according to categories and priorities. Some of the highest levels of priorities are usually, among other problems, security issues.

Fortify 360 is a suite of tools for vulnerability detection commercialized by Fortify Software [13]. The module Fortify Source Code Analyzer performs static code analysis. According to Fortify, it is able to identify the root-cause of the potentially exploitable security vulnerabilities in source code. It supports scanning of a wide variety of programming languages, platforms, and integrated development environments.

IntelliJ IDEA is a commercial and powerful IDE for Java development that includes "inspection gadgets" plug-ins with automated code inspection functionalities [18]. IntelliJ IDEA is able to detect security issues in java source code. These functionalities are available also in a community edition that is distributed free and open source since 2009.

Yasca (Yet Another Source Code Analyzer) is a "framework for conducting source code analyses" [23] in a wide range of programming languages, including Java. Yasca is a free tool that includes two components: the first is a framework for conducting source code analyses and the second is an implementation of that framework that allows integration with other static code analyzers (e.g., FindBugs, PMD, and Jlint).

Pixy is a free and open source program that performs automatic static code analysis of PHP 4 source code, aimed at the detection of XSS and SQL injection vulnerabilities [19]. As referred in Pixy's webpage, "Pixy takes a PHP program as input, and creates a report that lists possible vulnerable points in the program, together with additional information for understanding the vulnerability".

3.3 Limitations of Vulnerability Detection Tools

Both penetration testing and static code analysis tools have intrinsic limitations. Penetration testing is based on the effective execution of the code and, in practice, vulnerability identification is based only on the analysis of the web application output. This way, the effectiveness of penetration testing is limited by the lack of visibility on the internal behavior of the application. On the other hand, static code analysis is based on the analysis of the source code. The main problem here is that exhaustive source code analysis may be difficult and cannot find many security flaws due to the complexity of the code and the lack of a dynamic (runtime) view. Of course, penetration testing does not require access to the source code while static code analysis does.

The effectiveness of vulnerability detection tools is frequently very low, thus using the wrong tool may lead to the deployment of applications with undetected vulnerabilities. Figure 1 presents the main findings of a practical study that compares the effectiveness (in terms of coverage and false positives) of very well known and largely used penetration testing and static analysis tools in the detection of SQL Injection vulnerabilities in Web Services [5]. Results show that the coverage of static code analysis tools (including *FindBugs, Yasca*, and *IntelliJ IDEA*; anonymized as SAx in the figure) is typically much higher than penetration testing tools (including *HP WebInspect, IBM Rational AppScan*, and *Acunetix Web Vulnerability*; anonymized as VSx in the figure). False positives are a problem for both approaches, but have more impact in the case of static analysis. A key observation is that different tools implementing the same approach frequently report different vulnerabilities in the same code. The problem is that, although we frequently trust vulnerability detection tools, results highlight their limitations showing that we need to improve the state of the art in vulnerability detection, for instance by combining different approaches.

4 Security Requirements in SOAs

Service Oriented Architectures are typically based on services that can be under the control of multiple different providers. Furthermore, they are highly dynamic, in terms of the services used over time, and of their interactions. Figure 2 presents

Fig. 1 Penetration testing
versus static code analysis [5]

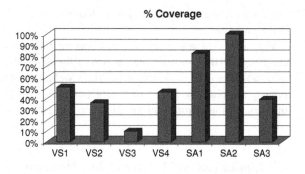

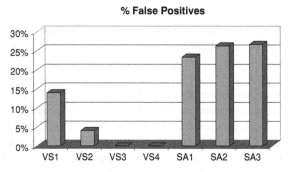

a simple example of a SOA, which will guide the analysis of the main security
requirements and challenges in the next paragraphs.

The ellipse represents the parts of the system controlled by provider **P0**. The
services and resources represented outside the ellipse are known and within-reach
but are not controlled by P0. The cloud represents parts of the system about which
P0 has no information, but that can be used by some of the services that are not
under his control. **C0** is a consumer that uses services **S0** and **S2**.

To start, this is a simplified view of a SOA, meaning that these systems are
frequently much more complex than the represented one. Additionally, these are
dynamic architectures (i.e., they change over time) making testing a frequent and
difficult process. This way, we need a tool able to automatically discover and test
the services involved in a SOA, starting from the knowledge of the entity that is
testing the system (provider P0 in the example in Fig. 2). A key aspect is that
different services are usually owned or controlled by more than one provider.
Thus, the users of the testing tool may have different types of access to the services
to be tested and are allowed to use different techniques in different services.
This creates the need for a tool that includes multiple vulnerability detection
approaches. Furthermore, such tool must be able to continuously test each of the
services using the technique or set of techniques that have the highest probability
of detecting vulnerabilities, depending on the specific situation. In practice, three
scenarios may be considered:

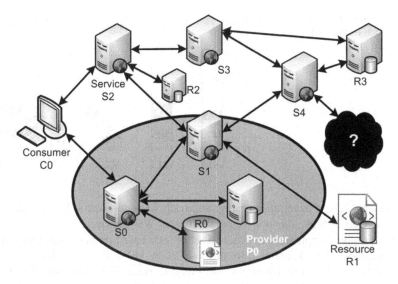

Fig. 2 Example of a service oriented architecture

- *Scenario 1:* a service is within reach but not under control, like in the case of S2 in Fig. 2. This means that it is not possible to access the source code and only black-box testing techniques can be used. This scenario also simulates the point-of-view of the consumer.
- *Scenario 2:* a service is under control but some of the resources that it uses are not, like in the case of S1 (it uses resource R1 that is not under control). In this case, it may not be possible to access the source code. However, all the interfaces between the service and the external environment are well known, which allows one to obtain relevant input domain information.
- *Scenario 3:* a service is under control and also the resources that it uses are, like in the case of S0. It is possible to use all kinds of vulnerability detection techniques, including the ones that require access to the source code (e.g. static analysis).

To address these scenarios, different types of security testing tools are necessary. Depending on the parts of the architecture that each tool addresses it will require different types of information. The following sections present a set of tools developed to address these situations.

4.1 Scenario 1: Services Within-Reach

Although the results of penetration testing will always be limited by the output of the services we believe that the effort necessary to improve these techniques is very important, as penetration testing is the only technique available for service's

Fig. 3 Results for the
penetration testing tool
presented in [7]

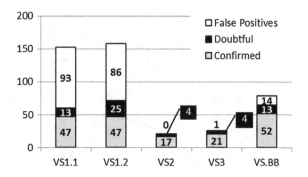

consumers. A new penetration testing approach was proposed in [7], focusing on the detection of SQL injection vulnerabilities in Web services.

The proposed approach consists of a set of tests based on malicious parameters (i.e., attacks) that is applied to disclose code vulnerabilities. Web services responses are analyzed based on well-defined rules that help confirming the existence of vulnerabilities and avoiding false positives. Comparing to existing penetration testing tools, our approach has four key improvements:

- It uses representative workloads to exercise the services and understand the expected behavior (i.e., the typical responses in the presence of valid inputs).
- The set of attacks performed is a compilation of all the attacks performed by a large set of scanners plus many attack methods that can be found in the literature;
- It applies well defined rules to analyze the web services responses in order to improve coverage.
- It includes different techniques for confirming the existence of vulnerabilities (e.g., robustness testing), which allow reducing the number of false positives.

Figure 3 summarizes the results of the experimental evaluation. As we can observe, the prototype tool that implements the proposed approach (VS.BB) was able to perform much better than the commercial tools, namely *HP WebInspect*, *IBM Rational AppScan*, and *Acunetix Web Vulnerability* (anonymized as VSx for results presentation) achieving higher coverage while reporting a much lower number of false positives. Details on the technique can be found at [7] as well as the results of the experimental evaluation (also summarized in Fig. 3).

4.2 Scenario 2: Services Partially Under Control

Although penetration testing is based on the execution of the code, vulnerability detection is based essentially on the analysis of the web services responses, which limits the visibility on the internal behavior of the service. The Sign-WS technique addresses this limitation [8].

Fig. 4 Coverage and false positive rates for Sign-WS and commercial penetration testers. Results from [8]

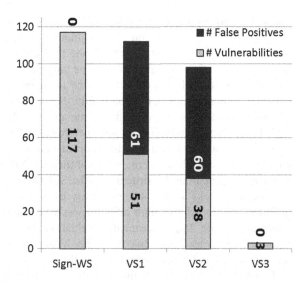

The idea is to use attack signatures and interface monitoring for the detection of injection vulnerabilities in web services. The goal is to improve the penetration testing process by providing enhanced visibility, yet without needing to access or modify the WS code. The key assumption is that most injection attacks manifest, in some way, in the interfaces between the attacked web service and other systems (e.g., database, operating system, gateways) and services. For example, a successful SQL Injection attack leads the web service to send malicious SQL queries to the database. Thus, these attacks can be observed in the SQL interface between the service and the database server.

Comparing to traditional penetration testing, this approach allows achieving higher effectiveness, as it provides the information needed to increase the number of vulnerabilities detected and reduce the number of false positives. Still, the application is tested as a black-box as the only requirement is to monitor the interface between the application and the used resources as allowed in this specific scenario.

Figure 4 summarizes the results of the experimental evaluation for this approach. As expected, the approach was able to achieve much higher detection coverage than the market-leading penetration testing tools *HP WebInspect*, *IBM Rational AppScan*, and *Acunetix Web Vulnerability* (again, anonymized as VSx for results presentation) while reporting zero false positives. Further details can be found at [8].

4.3 Scenario 3: Services Under Control

Although the signatures system presented above achieves high coverage while avoiding false positives, there is room for improvement. In the scenario where it is possible to access the source code (or p-code) information about the internal behavior of the application can be used to achieve maximum effectiveness. This way, a new approach based on runtime anomaly detection was proposed to detect SQL and XPath injection vulnerabilities [4]. Contrarily to static analysis that ignores the runtime perspective of the application, this approach takes full advantage of the behavior of the service including the available internal information. Command Injection Vulnerability Scanner for Web Services (CIVS-WS) combines penetration testing with runtime anomaly detection with for uncovering SQL Injection vulnerabilities in web services with high effectiveness.

The approach is based on the instrumentation of the tested web services, requiring access to their internals (it is intrusive). Vulnerabilities are identified at runtime by comparing the structure of the SQL/XPath commands executed in the presence of attacks to the ones previously learned in the absence of attacks. This makes it able to achieve high effectiveness when completely profiling the application is possible. The experimental evaluation shows that the approach is able to automatically detect SQL Injection and XPath Injection vulnerabilities in web services with much higher effectiveness than the remaining tools.

Figure 5 presents the summary of the experimental evaluation. As expected, CIVS-WS was able to achieve much higher detection coverage than the penetration testing tools (VS.BB and *HP WebInspect, IBM Rational AppScan*, and *Acunetix Web Vulnerability;* anonymized as VSx for results presentation) without reporting false positives. It is also possible to observe that CIVS-WS was able to present higher detection coverage than static analysis tools *FindBugs, Yasca*, and *IntelliJ IDEA* (anonymized as SAx), again while avoiding false positives. Details can be found at [4].

5 Towards an Integrated Security Testing Approach for SOAs

A testing tool for Service Oriented Architectures needs to be able to cope with the complexity and dynamicity of such architectures. This tool must be able to automatically discover and test the services at runtime (i.e., after the deployment of the application). Furthermore, the tool must test each of the services using the techniques that are most effective considering the deployment scenario (as exemplified in Fig. 2).

Traditional black-box techniques focus on testing the interface between the external users and the service. However, this service may also interact with other services or resources, making it possible the existence of vulnerabilities in these interfaces. The services and resources are discovered using interface monitoring techniques to monitor all the traffic starting in the services that are totally or partially *Under Control*. Using these techniques to monitor all the accessible interactions among services and resources allows testing the service for the relations between the services and, consequently detecting also these vulnerabilities.

Fig. 5 Comparing CIVS-WS
with vulnerability scanners
and static code analyzers.
Results from [4]

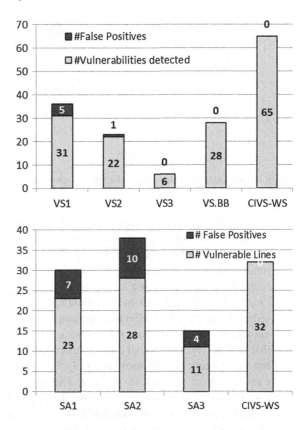

The idealized solution is based in a key concept: an iterative testing process that uses interface monitoring to discover services and resources and performs runtime detection of vulnerabilities. This process is represented in Fig. 6 and consists of three main steps:

(1) The tool provides a GUI in which the user can provide a basic description of the SOA to be tested. The user has to specify the services that act as entry points for the system but, if possible, information about all the Services Under Control should be provided. The specification of a service includes the definition of the input domain, potentially using EDEL [21], a language that allows developers to express domain dependencies between parameters, defining domains in a more complete way. It has also to be possible to specify additional services as well as some of the relations among them. Based on this specification, the application creates a representation of the system in an xml format that can be updated when new services or relations are discovered during the testing process.

(2) Starting from the services previously described, the tool issues a set of profiling interactions to discover new resources and services available, and to gather information for the training phase of CIVS-WS (only for the Services

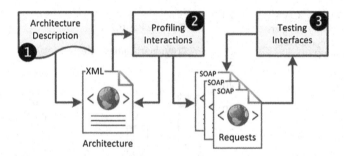

Fig. 6 Representation of the proposed approach's workflow

Under Control). These interactions are built using the EDEL definition, when available. This is a progressive process that finishes when no more services are discovered and the learning phase is finished for all the services to which runtime anomaly detection is to be applied. A key feature of this process is to select the workload taking into account code coverage.

(3) Finally, the tool proceeds to the vulnerability detection phase. Each service is tested using the most effective technique available (i.e., depending on the knowledge available about the service). Although improbable, it is possible that new services are found during this process (which should then be tested), but these services will most probably be *Services Within-reach*, making it unnecessary to go back to phase 2. During the testing phase, some of the invalid and/or malicious inputs cause the application to raise internal exceptions that prevent a more complete code testing coverage, leaving some paths of code untested (and their vulnerabilities undetected). To circumvent this problem and improve the testing process, exception-handling techniques may be used to avoid the interruption of code execution. Again, this is only possible for the Services Under Control.

6 Conclusions

Services used in Service Oriented Architectures are often deployed with security vulnerabilities with potential to be maliciously exploited. Research and practice shows that the effectiveness of existing vulnerability detection tools is very poor highlighting the need for more efficient tools to detect vulnerabilities in SOAs.

The particularities of the Service Oriented environment, typically highly dynamic and interconnecting very different services that can be provided by multiple different providers, raise new security requirements and challenges that must also be addressed in an efficient way.

This chapter discussed these challenges and requirements of security testing in SOAs and presented potential ways for endowing developing teams with effective methodologies and tools to perform automated detection of security vulnerabilities in SOAs. This is extremely useful for service providers to improve their solutions and for consumers to select the services that best fit their needs.

Future work includes implementing the proposed Security Testing Approach for SOAs and developing efficient techniques to evaluate these vulnerability detection techniques. As important as providing the developing teams with the tools to detect vulnerabilities, is to provide them with tools that allow them to select the most efficient ones.

References

1. Acunetix: 70 % of websites at immediate risk of being hacked! http://www.acunetix.com/news/security-audit-results.htm
2. Acunetix: Acunetix web vulnerability scanner. http://www.acunetix.com/vulnerability-scanner/
3. Acunetix: AcuSensor technology. http://www.acunetix.com/vulnerability-scanner/acusensor.htm
4. Antunes, N., Laranjeiro, N., Vieira M., Madeira, H.: Effective detection of SQL/XPath injection vulnerabilities in web services. In: 2009 IEEE International Conference on Services Computing (SCC 2009) (2009)
5. Antunes, N., Vieira, M.: Comparing the effectiveness of penetration testing and static code analysis on the detection of sql injection vulnerabilities in web services. In: 15th IEEE Pacific Rim International Symposium on Dependable Computing. IEEE Computer Society, Shanghai, pp. 301–306 (2009)
6. Antunes, N., Vieira, M.: Defending against web application vulnerabilities. IEEE Comput. **45**(2), 66–72 (2012)
7. Antunes, N., Vieira, M.: Detecting SQL injection vulnerabilities in web services. In: Fourth Latin-American Symposium on Dependable Computing, LADC'09. IEEE Computer Society, Washington (2009)
8. Antunes, N., Vieira, M.: Enhancing penetration testing with attack signatures and interface monitoring for the detection of injection vulnerabilities in web services. In: 2011 IEEE International Conference on Services Computing (SCC) (2011)
9. Ayewah, N., Pugh, W.: A report on a survey and study of static analysis users. In: Proceedings of the 2008 Workshop on Defects in Large Software Systems. ACM, Seattle (2008)
10. Chappell, D.A., Jewell, T.: Java Web Services. O'Reilly & Associates, Inc., Sebastopol (2002)
11. Christensen, E., et al.: Web service definition language (WSDL) 1.1. http://www.w3.org/TR/wsdl
12. Fonseca, J., Vieira, M., Madeira, H.: Testing and comparing web vulnerability scanning tools for SQL injection and XSS attacks. In: 13th Pacific Rim International Symposium on Dependable Computing (PRDC 2007). Melbourne, Australia (2007)
13. Fortify Software: Fortify 360 software security assurance. http://www.fortify.com/products/fortify-360/
14. Freedman, D.P., Weinberg, G.M.: Handbook of walkthroughs, inspections, and technical reviews: evaluating programs, projects, and products. Dorset House Publishing Co., New York (2000)
15. Howard, M., Leblanc, D.E.: Writing Secure Code. Microsoft Press, Redmond (2002)

16. HP: HP WebInspect. https://h10078.www1.hp.com/cda/hpms/display/main/hpms_content. jsp?zn=bto&cp=1-11-201-200%5E9570_4000_100
17. IBM: IBM Rational AppScan. http://www-01.ibm.com/software/awdtools/appscan/
18. JetBrains: IntelliJ IDEA. http://www.jetbrains.com/idea/free_java_ide.html
19. Jovanovic, N., Kruegel, C., Kirda, E.: Pixy: a static analysis tool for detecting web application vulnerabilities (Short Paper). In: IEEE Symposium on Security and Privacy. IEEE Computer Society, Berkeley/Oakland (2006)
20. Laranjeiro, N., Vieira, M., Madeira, H.: Experimental robustness evaluation of JMS middleware. In: IEEE International Conference on Services Computing, SCC'08. IEEE, Honolulu (2008)
21. Laranjeiro, N., Vieira, M., Madeira, H.: Improving web services robustness. In: IEEE 7th International Conference on Web Services (ICWS 2009), Los Angeles (2009)
22. Richardson, L., Ruby, S.: RESTful web services. O'Reilly Media, Inc., Sebastopol (2007)
23. Scovetta, M.: Yet another source code analyzer. www.yasca.org
24. Singhal, A., Winograd, T., Scarfone, K.: Guide to secure web services: recommendations of the national institute of standards and technology. Report, National Institute of Standards and Technology, US Department of Commerce (2007)
25. Stuttard, D., Pinto, M.: The web application hacker's handbook: discovering and exploiting security flaws. Wiley Publishing, Inc., Indianapolis (2007)
26. University of Maryland: FindBugs[TM]—find bugs in java programs. http://findbugs. sourceforge.net/
27. Vieira, M., Antunes, N., Madeira, H.: Using web security scanners to detect vulnerabilities in web services. In: IEEE/IFIP International Conference on Dependable Systems & Networks, 2009, DSN'09, Estoril (2009)
28. Wagner, S., Jürgens, J., Koller, C., Trishberger, P.: Comparing bug finding tools with reviews and tests. In: Testing of Communicating Systems (2005)
29. Williams, J., Wichers, D.: OWASP top 10. OWASP Foundation (2010)

Selected Challenges on Security and Dependability of Embedded Systems

Przemysław Osocha, João Carlos Cunha and Francesca Matarese

Abstract As embedded systems are silently spreading into every corner of our technological society and being interconnected in a world-wide network, they become invaluable to our daily lives, therefore our concern in their correct and secure behavior increases. However, improving dependability and security of embedded devices must be done with special care, since they are usually developed under severe resource- and price-constraints. In the frame of Critical Step project some FPGA-based embedded systems have been developed, with special concern for dependability and security improvement. Due to resource constraints of these devices, some particular challenges were faced, that are described in this paper: when to employ security during system lifecycle; which security threats to deal with; how to cope with computational-demanding cryptography; how to deal with security in safety-critical systems; how to increase dependability; how to assure timeliness; and how to evaluate dependability.

Keywords Security · Dependability · Embedded system · FPGA · Partial reconfiguration

P. Osocha (✉) · F. Matarese
SESM s.c.a.r.l, Via Circumvallazione Esterna di Napoli, 80014 Giugliano, Italy
e-mail: p.osocha@gmail.com

F. Matarese
e-mail: fmatarese@sesm.it

J. C. Cunha
Polytechnic Institute of Coimbra/CISUC, Pólo II—Universidade de Coimbra, Coimbra
3030-290, Portugal
e-mail: jcunha@isec.pt

D. Cotroneo (ed.), *Innovative Technologies for Dependable OTS-Based Critical Systems*, 175
DOI: 10.1007/978-88-470-2772-5_13, © Springer-Verlag Italia 2013

1 Introduction

Embedded systems are becoming available anytime and anywhere in many different forms. They may be evident and visible or hidden and integrated into equipment, devices and environment. They are: mobile devices like smartphones; household appliances like HVAC (heating, ventilation, and air conditioning); automatic equipment in the streets like traffic controls; complex airport systems like the ones for surveillance. They are seamlessly and pervasively blending into modern human environment. The constant development in embedded systems industry drives these devices to be incorporated into every product, replacing manual or mechanical solutions. The embedded electronics components share in the final products is constantly increasing, especially in ICT (information and communication technologies) and health domains.

This irrepressible spreading of embedded systems is nowadays accompanied by a new phenomenon, that is connectivity. All those small devices, often integrated into bigger products, have at their disposal wide range of possibilities to connect and exchange data. They are connecting through wired or wireless networks, utilizing numerous communication standards. This situation poses absolutely new threats for security of systems. Dependability and security cannot be considered anymore an aspect of single, separate device, but rather depending on application field, as dependability and security of system of embedded systems.

Taking advantage of researchers' mobility provided by Critical Step project [4], some research and development projects have been initiated, with the aim of exploring security and safety of embedded systems. One of these projects consisted in the definition of an architecture framework for a networked embedded node with intrinsic security, privacy and dependability capabilities [11]. An other project consisted in the development of a secure and dependable multilateration navigation system (MLAT), which provides high-performance and accurate all-weather surveillance, supporting full control of the airport surface and near-airport airspace [3].

Common to these projects was the fact that they utilized FPGA-based development boards, namely a Xilinx FPGA Virtex-5 ML507 Evaluation Platform [2], and an Altera FPGA Cyclone III 3C120 Development Board [1].

During the development of these systems, some problems that challenged the traditional approach to security and dependability, as applied to ICT systems, were faced, due to intrinsic characteristics of embedded systems, such as resource constraints and long life expectancy. These challenges are analyzed in the following sections. After defining, in Sect. 2, the scope of the studied embedded systems, in Sect. 3 some security challenges are presented, such as the need to employ security mechanisms both during the system development and its operational life, the identification of security threats, the management of computational-demanding cryptography schemes, and particularities of safety-critical systems.

Then, in Sect. 4, dependability challenges are addressed, such as how to manage space redundancy for providing system dependability, how to guarantee timeliness in fault-tolerant systems, and how to evaluate dependability in such systems. The paper concludes with summary of considered challenges.

2 Embedded Systems

Embedded systems are computer devices designed for specific functions that are incorporated into enclosed products with hardware and mechanical parts, often with real-time constraints [7]. Although this definition is generic enough, it does not reveal the huge differences that exist between embedded devices, related to capabilities, architecture or technology.

2.1 Embedded Systems Complexity

The diversity in capability requirements for embedded devices is so large that a unified architectural or technological approach is impracticable. A wireless sensor node, for example, has very simple hardware and software requirements, being very sensitive to power consumption. On the other hand, an embedded camera array with image processing requires high performance computing, large memory storage capacity, and high-speed network connection.

These different requirements lead to large variety in the assortment of technologies and architectures. Many of current low-performance embedded devices are deployed with 4- or 8-bit microcontrollers, running simple single-processing applications, or even executing discrete logic without any processor or software. These systems are very cost-sensitive, since millions of units can be built, thus functionality is often the major concern, in detriment of dependability or security.

On the other side of complexity spectrum are systems using multiple pipelined microprocessors, running real-time operating systems. If deployed in high quantities, these complex systems are usually build on top of devices with microprocessors; otherwise it could be economically advantageous to use FPGA-based systems with synthesized microprocessors (see Sect. 2.2).

In-between, there are systems that don't have any processing unit, but are high-demanding. They use discrete-logic for performing specialized operations, such as signal processing or video encoding, and are deployed on FPGAs or, if large quantities are required, in ASICs (application-specific integrated circuit) because their prices are much lower.

2.2 FPGA-Based Embedded Systems

An FPGA (field-programmable gate array) is an integrated circuit that can be easily reprogrammed during prototyping or production, giving the engineers the possibility of using different architectural hardware solutions depending on the requirements and complexity of the system. It is possible to combine different discrete-logic cores, such as video controllers, Ethernet controllers, data encryption/decryption modules, etc. and even microcontroller or microprocessors. If a microcontroller or microprocessor is present, it is possible to run on it an operating system and/or application software, turning this device into a system on a chip (SoC).

However, what is becoming really interesting, is that FPGA-based systems can be also reprogrammed after deployment, and thus it is possible to correct design errors or even upgrade it to adopt the new functionalities. The most popular FPGA devices are based on SRAM (Static Random Access Memory). They are composed of a matrix of configurable logic blocks, interconnected with routing elements, stored in a configurable memory. Every time the device is powered on, this configuration memory is programmed with a bitstream that contains the logic information describing the device. This bitstream is copied from a flash memory, usually by a microcontroller.

2.3 Characteristics of the Studied Devices

The devices studied and developed within the scope of Critical Step project were high-demanding, both in terms of computing power and processing complexity. Even if they were considered in the frame of a research project, it was decided to adopt commercial and well known FPGAs as means for further development of embedded systems, namely a Xilinx Virtex-5, and an Altera Cyclone III. These FPGAs have been successfully used with discrete logic, with soft-cores and hard-cores, and software applications written in C language.

3 Security Challenges

Many embedded systems currently available on the market completely lack of security, leaving them vulnerable to attacks. One of the main reasons for this weakness is the struggle for company's competitiveness on the market. Products have to hit the market as soon as possible, with the lowest possible cost, thus limiting physical resources to the minimum. Only key functionalities are implemented, and frequently security is not considered as one of them, but rather as an added cost with no corresponding value.

3.1 Security in System Lifecycle

Updating an embedded system after deployment is usually difficult or even impossible to implement. Systems are dimensioned with only the necessary resources, thus any change is often impossible to accommodate, or implies a thorough redesign. Therefore security usually cannot be just added later on, it must be planned and designed during development, so it can be assigned the necessary physical and time resources.

However, security provision doesn't end with system deployment; it should be addressed like a process that needs to be maintained throughout the whole product lifetime. During development it is possible to test and assure product immunity against currently existing treats, but in time new treats will appear and security can be impaired by discovery of new ways of attack. For example, cryptographic algorithms can be well accepted and considered secure in time of product design, but then are broken due to new discovered weaknesses or just by brute force attacks of more and more powerful computing units. The security of the product has to be continuously monitored and updated if necessary, to assure the required level of system security protection against attacks. Periodical evaluation of product security against new exploits and attacks should be part of the product lifecycle maintenance. It is important to remember, that embedded devices often have a much longer life than ICT systems.

One solution used by industry for long life installations is the utilization of FPGA-based embedded devices. The usage of FPGAs allows the development and installation of hardware one time only, and then, if necessary, the software and programmable part of the FPGA logic are simply upgraded. In particular, that approach is used in design of airports radar systems, where FPGA-based embedded devices operate for years, but hardware adjustments according to changes in standards are still possible thanks to the ability of the FPGA chip to reprogram its logic.

The first identified challenge consists in providing security capabilities during system development, and also reserving enough space to accommodate for latter improvements that eventually will be necessary. This means that, for FPGA-developed systems, the interfaces between the security units and the rest of the system must be carefully designed, extra space must be reserved, and time constraints must be calculated to allow for spare time that can accommodate future security enhancements.

3.2 Security Threats Identification

The attacker may gain access to the system in basically two ways [6]: physically, or remotely. If the embedded device is physically accessible to the attacker, then he has almost unlimited possibilities for tampering the product, by opening the chassis, understanding hardware design, recognition of used chips, extraction of firmware code, reverse engineering, etc. This type of attacks is particular to embedded devices, and has been studied for long time.

However, the most important security threat nowadays comes from intruders that attack remotely, have no need for special tools and equipment, and can easily hide their location by masking their own connection to the internet. As embedded devices become networked, they get vulnerable to remote attacks.

Although this is a problem that affects all systems connected to the internet, most methods used in ICT systems do not easily apply to embedded system devices. For example, due to limited resources, it is usually not possible to have strong cryptographic algorithms running; and due to a closed design it is not easy to apply patches with security updates.

Furthermore, these systems are more vulnerable to certain attacks than other ICT systems [8]: since they usually interact with the physical environment, they must act in real-time. A continuous attack on an embedded device may interfere with system timing, introducing delays that can cause missing deadlines, and the loss of control-loop stability. This kind of attacks can also provoke higher power consumption, which could drain the device's battery.

The challenge is thus to identify the possible security threats to which the embedded system can be exposed, and then address them in a proper way, by providing special capabilities to the devices. For example, a low-voltage detection circuit can physically disconnect the network access, or a tampering detection mechanism can trigger the deletion of sensitive data stored in the device, safe-guarding confidentiality.

3.3 Security and Cryptography

Strong cryptographic algorithms have high computational demands. They are usually built on software, requiring a microprocessor to be able to run. When the embedded device is based on FPGA, a soft- or hard-core microprocessor must be provided. Since synthesized models of microprocessors on FPGA run slowly, encrypting/decrypting may take a long and unpredictable time. The solution can be the choice of a simpler algorithm, with the disadvantage of being easier to break.

Another possible approach is to substitute software running on top of a microprocessor by a synthesized model of the cryptographic algorithm deployed in the FPGA. This assures that the same complex algorithm may execute much faster in a system with lower clock speed and lower power consumption. In fact, due to parallelization and low-level computation, it runs even faster than on a real microprocessor.

Some advices can be considered by developers. Elliptic curve cryptography (ECC) is an approach to public-key cryptography well accepted in embedded systems world thanks to its limited resource requirements [12]. Worth to mention is also eSTREAM project, that aims providing modern, efficient and compact stream ciphers, designed specifically for software or hardware implementations [13].

The capability of an FPGA to be reconfigured during its lifetime gives the possibility to upgrade the cryptographic scheme. For example, one of the best measures to have a password undiscovered is to change it frequently. A cryptographic key, or even the encryption/decryption algorithm itself, can be changed periodically, decreasing the chances of a successful attack.

The challenge is thus, depending on application field, to find a strong cryptographic scheme, able to process in a predictable time-bound in order to have real-time guarantee, and have it available for an FPGA. The FPGA-based device should be ready for secure upgrade, to update the cryptographic key or algorithm in case of key compromising or cipher weaknesses discovery.

3.4 Safety-Critical Systems

Security in embedded systems often implies safety issues [10], as opposite to most ICT systems. For example, if an encryption algorithm key is compromised and a malicious action is issued against a financial institution, it usually doesn't involve the loss of lives or any major environmental disaster. Furthermore, it might be possible to revert the effects of this attack. If an embedded controller is affected by a malicious attack, for example, against a train control and signaling systems, causing a railroad accident, it is not possible to *roll-back*.

When designing dependable embedded devices, the designers usually take into consideration a fault model based on physical interference, where faults have an external non-malicious origin, thus affecting the device's components in a randomly distributed way in space and time, and provoking stuck-at or bit-flip faults. When considering malicious and deliberate faults, this random and bit-flip distribution of hardware faults is no longer valid, as attackers may try, for example, to repeatedly inject faults or interfere with data communications.

The challenge here is to develop a new fault model, taking into account faults due to possible malicious remote access to device, and possible application as a part of bigger safety-critical system.

4 Dependability Challenges

Dependability is achieved through redundancy, in a combination of space, time and information. Embedded systems, having stringent resource constraints, oblige a careful utilization of space (either redundant hardware, or software or information) and, due to real-time performance constraints, also demand for a cautious utilization of time redundancy (due to repeated computation or redundant software).

In this section only transient hardware faults that may affect the FPGA configuration memory are addressed. These faults are much more common than permanent or intermittent faults. Software faults are not addressed, since the focus of this paper is mainly on FPGA related dependability issues.

4.1 Hardware Redundancy Reduction

Replication of hardware modules is a common way of implementing hardware fault tolerance. It may take the form of static redundancy, such as triple modular redundancy (TMR), where replicated modules produce results in parallel, that are voted or compared; or dynamic redundancy, such as standby spare, where the redundant modules are in standby until they are necessary to replace a failed active module. If these spare modules are executing in parallel with the active module, although their outputs are ignored, it is said they are in hot standby; if they are not executing, they are in cold standby.

The capability of an FPGA to be reprogrammed during its operational life, opens the possibility of having the spare modules in cold standby outside of the FPGA, i.e., of reprogramming the FPGA with a spare module only when it is necessary, either in a different part of the FPGA, or even substituting the failed module. This last option may simply result from a restart of the system, because during power-on the FPGA is always reprogrammed.

Concerning static redundancy, or dynamic redundancy in hot standby, it is obvious that it is not possible to avoid the existence of the replicated modules, since they must execute in parallel; however, it is possible to recover a failed replica or former active module, by reprogramming it, and thus a system with degraded fault-tolerance can fully recover its reliability (the failed replica becomes an active redundant module, or the former active module becomes a new spare module in active standby).

The main issue regarding FPGA reconfiguration relates to the introduced time overhead, which may compromise system reliability, since reconfiguration takes time. Section 4.2 will address this challenge.

The current challenge is thus to choose an adequate fault-tolerant model, considering the limitations in terms of available space and time.

4.2 Time Challenge in System Recovery

Stopping a system for repair is usually not possible in embedded systems, mainly if they are operating in real-time. For example, in a control system, if the controller stops for repair, it will probably lose control over the process.

Having static redundancy or replicas in hot standby allows the continuous operation of the system when an active module fails. However, in order to repair this module it is necessary to reprogram the FPGA. With spare modules outside the FPGA, the issue is the same. Traditional FPGA reprogramming implies that it must stop for transferring the bitstream with logical information into the SRAM configurable memory.

Some FPGA manufacturers, namely Xilinx, offer now the possibility of dynamic partial reconfiguration, meaning that it is feasible to reprogram only a part of the FPGA, while the remaining part operates uninterruptedly [9]. This opens the possibility to repair the failed replicas, while the system runs in degraded mode, but without losing control over the controlled process.

This is, however, not a solution for replacing an active module by a replica in cold standby, as it always takes time to reprogram, even partially, the FPGA. This situation may be addressed by taking advantage of the dynamics of the controlled process. Since every physical process has some inertia, it is usually possible to remain without control for some time [5]. The question is if reprogramming the FPGA is fast and predictable enough for the control system to tolerate this gap in the control-loop.

This challenge is related to the previous one: to choose an adequate fault-tolerant model for a particular application, considering space and time limitations.

4.3 Fault-Injection for Dependability Evaluation

Fault-injection is a well-known methodology for dependability evaluation of computer systems. Faults may be injected by introducing external disturbances in power supply or chip pins, or directly inside the chips by using heavy-ion radiation or laser. However, with these techniques, experiments are difficult to control and to repeat. Software implemented fault-injection (SWIFI) is, though, very popular and allows high controllability of experiments. The drawback is that software must run inside the target embedded system, which naturally interferes both with memory space and processing time.

Regarding the injection of faults into an FPGA, other options exist, such as:

1. Using a fault-injector module programmed inside the FPGA itself, that may interfere with signals, memory cells, etc.
2. Reprogramming the FPGA (partially and dynamically) with an already corrupted bitstream emulating the fault.
3. Using boundary-scan to corrupt the configuration memory (the use of boundary-scan is a technique already widespread to inject faults in functional units of a system. It is known as Scan-Chain Implemented Fault Injection—SCIFI). The first of the above described options have been used, by introducing a small module able to interfere in a predefined way with a specific signal in the device. This is a simple way to inject a fault, but with a limited scope, useful only for particular situations. Therefore more general techniques must be studied, posing a demanding challenge.

5 Conclusions

The mass deployment of networked embedded systems with critical control functions requires concentrating, more than ever, on security and dependability matters. This poses many new challenges to designers of such systems. In frame of this work, various embedded systems based on FPGA devices were developed. During this research numerous challenges, related to dependability and security implementation in resource-constrained systems, were faced.

In this paper some of those challenges were presented and discussed, together with proposals on possible solutions. In case of security of FPGA-based embedded systems, some possible solutions of the following challenges were proposed: the necessity to implement security mechanisms during design phase and maintain it throughout the whole system life; the identification of security threats; the selection of appropriate cryptography schemes; and security of safety-critical embedded systems. In case of dependability, the paper introduced the following challenges: the management of space redundancy; the issues of timeliness assurance in fault-tolerant systems; and evaluation of dependability in such systems.

It must be stressed that this list does not exhaust all the embedded systems issues related to dependability and security; it only contains those considered the most challenging during Critical Step project. Apart from the proposed possible solutions for the presented challenges, the main goal of the paper was to alert and justify their importance for future development of embedded systems.

References

1. Altera: Cyclone III 3C120 Development Board—Reference Manual. Document version 1.2, March (2009)
2. ADAM/AWAM Systems: Multilateration Solutions by SELEX Sistemi Integrati. http://www.selex-si.com/IT/Common/files/SelexSI/brochure_datasheet/2008/Data_Sheet/Adam.pdf
3. CRITICAL STEP project: The CRITICAL Software Technology for an Evolutionary Partnership. A Marie-Curie Industry-Academia Partnerships and Pathways (IAPP) project belonging to call FP7-PEOPLE-2008-IAPP. http://www.critical-step.eu/
4. Cunha, J.C., Maia, R., Rela, M.Z., Silva, J.G.: A study on failure models in feedback control systems. In: International Conference on Dependable Systems and Networks, Goteborg, Sweden (2001)
5. eSTREAM project. The ECRYPT Stream Cipher Project. http://www.ecrypt.eu.org/stream/
6. Grand, J.: Practical secure hardware design for embedded systems. In: Proceedings of the 2004 Embedded Systems Conference (2004)
7. Koopman, P.: Embedded system security. IEEE Comput. 37(7), 95–97 (2004)
8. Marwedel, P.: Embedded System Design (Embedded Systems Foundations of Cyber-Physical Systems). TU Dortmund, Informatik. Springer, Dordrecht (2011)
9. pSHIELD project co-funded by the ARTEMIS Joint Undertaking. Research of Security, Privacy and Dependability in context of Embedded Systems. http://www.pshield.eu/
10. pSHIELD project deliverables D2.3.2, D3.3, D6.2, D6.3. http://pshield.unik.no/wiki/PublicDeliverables

11. Rana, V., Santambrogio, M., Sciuto, D.: Dynamic Reconfigurability in Embedded System Design. In: IEEE International Symposium on Circuits and Systems ISCAS'2007, New Orleans (2007)
12. Schoitsch, E.: Design for safety and security of complex embedded systems: a unified approach. In: Kowalik, J.S., Gorski, J., Sachenko, A. (eds.) Cyberspace Security and Defense: Research Issues, vol. 196, NATO Science Series II—Mathematics, Physics and Chemistry (2005)
13. Xilinx: ML505/ML506/ML507 Evaluation Platform—User Guide. UG347 (v3.1.2), 16 May 2011

Part IV
Monitoring and Diagnosing

This section describes monitoring and evaluation techniques for critical complex systems. These techniques allow verifying the correctness of the system behavior and assessing its dependability properties under real workload conditions. Overall this information is crucial to engineers because it supports the design of effective error and failure mitigation means, strategies to reduce maintenance costs, or the improvement of the service provided by the system. The section includes two contributions. The former discusses monitoring approaches and tools, and proposes online diagnosis as a mean to improve software fault tolerance techniques. The latter describes well-established techniques to analyze the system failure behavior through event logs, and introduces relevant application areas and objectives of log-based failure analysis.

Antonio Pecchia

Monitoring Infrastructure for Diagnosing Complex Software

Antonio Bovenzi and Gabriella Carrozza

Abstract This work presents an overview of monitoring approaches to support the diagnosis of software faults and proposes a framework to reveal and diagnose the activation of faults in complex and Off-The Shelf (OTS) based software systems. The activation of a fault is detected by means of anomaly detection on data collected by OS-level monitors. Instead, the fault diagnosis is accomplished by means of a machine learning approach. The evaluation of the proposed framework is carried out using an industrial prototype from the Air Traffic Control domain by means of software fault injection. Results show that the monitoring and diagnosis framework is able to reveal and diagnose faults with high recall and precision with low latency and low overhead.

Keywords Kernel probes · Fault diagnosis · Machine learning · Fault tolerance

1 Introduction

Mission and safety critical software systems are expected to be reliable during operation. However, their growing complexity—which is related to the intricate interdependencies among many heterogeneous components—makes the development of fault-free systems an unaffordable task, in terms of time and cost. The

A. Bovenzi (✉)
Dipartimento di Informatica e Sistemistica (DIS), Università degi Studi
di Napoli Federico II, Via Claudio 21, 80125 Naples, Italy
e-mail: antonio.bovenzi@unina.it

G. Carrozza
Sesm S.c.a.r.l., Via Circumvallazione Esterna di Napoli, 80014 Giugliano, Italy
e-mail: gcarrozza@sesm.it

D. Cotroneo (ed.), *Innovative Technologies for Dependable OTS-Based Critical Systems*,
DOI: 10.1007/978-88-470-2772-5_14, © Springer-Verlag Italia 2013

dynamics of these systems often depends on many interdependent variables. This makes difficult both the understanding of the failure behavior and the decision process when an alert occurs.

On the other hand, quality standards impose strict requirements on the reliability attributes and measures [1, 2]. Testing and verification activities are massively used to satisfy these requirements.

Despite the efforts allocated to good development practices, thorough testing, and proper maintenance policies, a non-negligible number of faults remains during operation because of time constraints and technical limitations. Hence, fault-tolerance techniques are used to allow systems providing their service even in presence of component failures, although in a possible degraded mode.

Research effort has provided unquestionable valuable results to tolerate hardware-related faults [3, 4]. Nevertheless, the tolerance of software faults is a more difficult task due to their nature.

Recent studies [5, 6] characterize software faults by focusing on the inherent features of the activation conditions. A fault is defined as *Mandelbug* if the activation and/or the error propagation may be influenced by one or more of the following: (i) the interactions of the application with the system-internal environment (e.g., the operating system or hardware devices) (ii) the timing and the sequencing of inputs and operations (iii) the total time the system has been running. Faults that manifests consistently under a well-defined set of conditions—thus they are simple to isolate—are defined as *Bohrbugs*. In past studies the former are also known as elusive or soft faults, while the latter are also called solid or hard faults [7, 8].

For these reasons, the constant monitoring of the performance of the system at runtime is a fundamental task for verifying, online or offline, that the observed behavior meets well-defined requirements. Many probes can be placed either outside the system or inside it, with the purpose of providing information about the healthy status of the system. These probes have to collect enough information about the system to meet the goals of the activity monitoring without compromising the mission of the system. Potential applications of runtime checking include fault detection and diagnosis, performance bottleneck and/or malicious activities recognition and online fault treatment, e.g., by means of system reconfiguration and/or proper recovery actions.

In this paper the focus is on monitoring activities and online fault diagnosis. We believe that online fault diagnosis is necessary to improve software fault tolerance techniques. Indeed, starting from observed symptoms diagnosis aims to identify (i) what are the execution misbehaviors, and (ii) where these misbehaviors come from, i.e., the faulty component(s). In such a way, a precise and accurate automated diagnosis process is helpful (i) to provide information about manifested symptoms for off-line maintenance activities and also (ii) for selecting the most proper actions at runtime.

We use a lightweight and non-intrusive OS-level monitoring infrastructure to support online diagnosis activities. It consists in several monitors placed at the operating system (OS) level, which trigger alarms when the behavior of the system differs from the nominal one. The framework can infer indirectly the state of the system by monitoring different indicators such as the system call errors, the disk reads and writes, the waiting time on semaphores, the holding time into critical sections. The monitoring infrastructure has been implemented for the Linux operating system (OS) by means of dynamic probes loaded dynamically into the kernel. The approach is particularly suited when the system is the results of OTS components and legacy system integration. As a matter of fact, there is no need to modify the source code of the application and no other software modules need to be integrated in the monitored application.

As for the diagnosis module, we exploit a supervised classifier—based on a Support Vector Machine—that is trained with several features collected during a preliminary profiling phase. Other than typical application and system logs, these features encompass events collected by the OS-level monitoring infrastructure.

To show the effectiveness of the monitoring and diagnosis infrastructure we have integrated the framework in a prototype from the Air Traffic Management domain, which is based on OTS and legacy components. Then we performed fault injection experiments to accelerate the process of data collection and to evaluate the diagnosis infrastructure.

The rest of the paper is organized as follows: Section 2 provides an overview on monitoring approaches and tools that can be used for diagnosis activities; Sect. 3 describes the proposed monitoring infrastructure; Sect. 4 details the diagnosis framework; Sect. 5 concludes the paper.

2 Monitoring Approaches and Tools

The existing monitoring techniques are generally classified into direct and indirect. The former try to obtain the health of the system by directly probing and/or by receiving data that the component is able to provide (e.g., log, SNMP). The latter attempt to infer the system state by monitoring its behavior from an external point of view by recording the interactions with the environment and with other systems.

Logs represent the most common source of information to analyze and to diagnose systems behavior. This is especially true when dealing with large, complex systems, consisting of heterogeneous software components for which logs are often the only source of information about the health status of the monitored system.

Unfortunately, several studies have highlighted the inadequacy of the logs for the assessment of reliability. Logs are heterogeneous and imprecise [9, 10], and may provide ambiguous information [11]. This is a consequence of the lack of a systematic approach for the production of logs that are currently dependent on skills and competencies of developers [11]. Crucial decisions regarding the production and collection of logs are taken only in the latter stages of the life cycle of the software (e.g., during the development of the code).

For these reasons, it is reasonable to state that the current logging systems are not designed to fully support automated diagnosis process. Therefore, we also need to exploit different kind of data to better understand system's behavior.

As demonstrated by recent studies [12, 13] the information obtained indirectly is useful for understanding the possible causes of malfunction. For instance, in [12] tracing facilities provided by the OS are exploited to monitor resources such as semaphores, mutexes, processes/threads creation and termination. Then, the detection of a malfunction, such as hangs or crashes, is performed by means of thresholds violation. The Rainbow framework [14] also uses monitoring techniques to detect Quality of Service (QoS) violations by comparing the considered indicators with the predefined threshold. The approach proposed in [15] applies statistical analysis on data collected through OS-level monitors to detect anomalous behavior (e.g., due to overload conditions, faults activation or malicious attacks). Chopstix [13] exploit OS to take and store the StackTrace of a target application and then to identify faults in applications. In [16] the Authors propose a method for monitor multi-tier applications in enterprise environments. Their technique obtains performance metrics by monitoring system calls, and can identify the bottlenecks of such systems.

Monitoring OS level variables is also exploited in [17] to build a diagnosis tool by means of multi-class classifier. In [18] the combination of monitored information collected during the testing phase and during operation is exploited for the online detection of application misbehaviors. However, these approaches have a not negligible overhead because many data need to be recorded (e.g., system call parameters are recorded or application invariants). Moreover they are not well suited to detect faults that cannot be reliably reproduced, such as Mandelbugs.

Monitoring tools often combine hardware and software monitors. The work proposed in [19] exploits hardware performance counters and OS signals to monitor the system behavior and to signal possible anomalous conditions.

A similar approach is followed in [20], which provides detection facilities for large-scale distributed systems running legacy code. Authors propose to use external messages exchanged between components, which are collected at protocol level. The messages are finally used to deduce, at runtime, a state transition diagram that is exploited to detect a failure.

Network-level monitoring is also exploited in Pinpoint [21]. This tool traces client requests to obtain control paths. It takes advantage of the large number of client requests to detect performance anomalies.

In [22] Authors present Ganglia, an infrastructure for monitoring cluster and Grid resources (e.g., CPU, memory, etc.) at different time-scale. Scalability is the primary requirement of this tool because it has to do with hundreds or even thousands of nodes. To meet this requirement, it uses a hierarchical architecture and the aggregation of collected data. Another tool designed to be high scalable and flexible is Nagios, widely recognized by IT industries as the most used monitoring infrastructure (http://www.nagios.com/users/). Similar to Nagios, are the Zabbix (www.zabbix.com) and the Zenoss (www.Zenoss.com) platforms.

Comon [23] monitors the use of the resources of the nodes of PlanetLab, to understand their interactions but remaining largely agnostic about the applications running on these nodes.

Several technical problems make difficult to diagnose complex OTS systems with such kind of techniques. First, an effective diagnosis often requires a detailed analysis of the use of resources that go beyond simple measures of parameters such as average CPU load, bandwidth network, the number of activities completed (http://www03.ibm.com/autonomic/blueprInt'lshtml). Second, the overhead of the available tools is often far from negligible, making their use impractical for real systems. Third, the great diversity of systems components hampers the design of common and simple interfaces for the analysis of the behavior of the systems. Finally, the source code of the monitored components is often not available; hence more advanced techniques that insert some hooks in the executable program have to be considered [24].

In this work different sources of information, among which the classical event logs, are exploited to perform online fault diagnosis. In particular, the diagnosis relies on a monitoring infrastructure based on OS-level tracing support. This tool has been implemented to monitor the target system and indirectly identify application misbehaviors.

3 OS-Level Monitoring Infrastructure

We propose to leverage the OS tracing support to infer the health of the system by observing its behavior and interactions with the external environment.

The collection of different indicators is made by means of probes inserted dynamically without recompiling the kernel and modifying the application source code. A probe consists in a breakpoint and a handler routine. The former is a special CPU instruction that permits to suspend the execution of the kernel code. The latter collect the desired information when the breakpoint is hit, e.g., input parameters or return values of called functions. In Table 1 a detailed description of implemented probes is provided.

Monitors have been implemented using the kernel probes and they are been deployed as loadable kernel modules by means of *systemtap* (http://sourceware.org/systemtap/). This tool is integrated in 2.6 Linux kernels and allows to program breakpoint handlers by means of a high-level scripting language.

As for thread related events, e.g., time to acquire/release a lock, we used a different strategy because they are more difficult to monitor at a fine grain level. As a matter of fact, tracing kernel code does not suffice to monitor all the synchronization operations on shared resources. This is because system calls might be not invoked when dedicated multi-threading libraries are used. For this reason, we implemented a shared library to wrap the standard glibc multi-threading library PThread, which is widely used in Linux environment.

Table 1 Probes inserted in the dynamic kernel module

Probe	Trigger condition for events registration
SystemCallError	An error code is returned from systemcall
SchedulingTimeout	A timeout exceeded since the target process is preempted
Signal	A signal is received by the target process
ProcCreation	Creation of a process
ProcessEnd	Termination of a process
ThreadCreation	Creation of a thread
ThreadEnd	Termination of a thread
DiskIO	Timeout exceeded since last disk read/write
SocketIO	Timeout exceeded since last socket read/write
MutexHoldTime	Timeout exceeded for mutex possession
MutexWaitTime	Timeout exceeded for mutex acquisition
SemHoldTime	Timeout exceeded for semaphore possession
SemWaitTime	Timeout exceeded for semaphore acquisition
DiskThroughput	The bytes read/write from disk exceeds the thresholds
NetThroughput	The bytes read/write from network exceeds the thresholds

The monitoring infrastructure allows collecting the following events:

- *System call error*: numerical error codes which are returned if exceptional events occur during the execution of the system call code.
- *OS signals*: codes commonly used to notify the occurrence of a given event for coordination or information purposes. For instance, invalid memory access, process crash, loss of a socket connection, I/O data available.
- *Task scheduling timeout*: too much time (e.g., 100 ms) elapsed since the last time the process relinquishes the CPU.
- *Waiting time for critical sections timeout*: too much time elapsed (e.g., 100 ms) for a process (thread) waiting before entering a critical section.
- *Holding time in critical sections timeout*: too much time elapsed for a process (thread) holding a critical section.
- *Process and thread termination*: process/thread ends their execution.
- *network sockets timeouts*: too much time elapsed between two consecutive packets sent on a given TCP/IP socket.
- *I/O throughput:* the aggregate byte for I/O operations with respect to reads and writes on disk devices.
- *I/O throughput*: the aggregate byte for I/O operations with respect to reads and writes on network devices.

Moreover, monitors can aggregate this information to produce, per each monitored process/thread or group of process/threads, the total number of the events per unit of time, such as *#SyscallErrors/sec, #SchedulingTimeout/sec #Signals*.

It is noteworthy that similar events can be collected also in different OSs. For instance, in [25] Windows Reliability and Performance Monitor is used to monitor most of the OS-level indicators collected in Linux environments. WRPM is a monitoring tool, available on both Windows XP, 7 and Windows Server 2008. It provides several functionalities to (i) observe applications, services and hardware performance at runtime, (ii) receive alerts and reports and (iii) trigger some actions when user-defined thresholds are exceeded.

4 Automatic Online Fault Diagnosis: A Case Study in ATM

4.1 System Model and Assumptions

The target systems are complex software systems, which can be deployed on several nodes and communicate through a network.

The reference system is assumed as composed of several software components that interact each other such as the operating system processes, the middleware, the database, the support libraries and the user applications. These components are usually non self-protecting, i.e., an error occurred in the component A can be propagated to component B, eventually causing a system failure. Since our focus is on software faults the underlying hardware faults are not encompassed in the system model and cannot be diagnosed.

We define the components as the diagnosable units, i.e., the atomic software entities that can become faulty. When a fault is activated we need to be properly diagnose the faulty component in order to trigger the most proper countermeasure.

4.2 Approach

The diagnosis engine has been realized using a machine learning classifier. This approach has been used in other works focused on document classification [26] or on failure diagnosis in software programs [27].

The proposed classifier is based on a supervised multi-class support vector machines (SVM), which extends the classical SVM framework [28] to distinguish between more than two classes.

We used a simple strategy based on software fault injection to accelerate the failure data collection; we exploit an automatic tool presented in [30]. Then, we build the base fault knowledge, i.e., the training set, to train the classifier.

The basic idea to train the classifier is to associate to each injected fault some features that include the indicators collected by means of the OS-level monitoring infrastructure and the application and systems log files. The training procedure is depicted in Fig. 1.

Monitored indicators and event logs have been translated into a feature vector that needs to be classified by the multi-class SVM classifier. These features

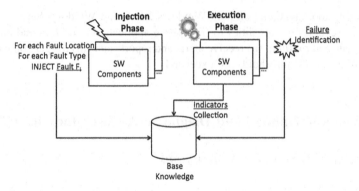

Fig. 1 The training process of the diagnoser

Table 2 Feature extracted from system execution

Indicator	Features	Description
Event logs	#Error event	Binary feature: 1 if the an error entries is logged
System calls	1141	For each pair (system call, error code), there is a binary feature (it is 1 if the pair occurred, 0 otherwise)
Signals	32	For each signal, there is a binary feature (it is 1 if the signal occurred, 0 otherwise)
Task scheduling timeout	4	The mean, the standard deviation, the minimum, and the maximum waiting time for scheduling of DU's tasks
Waiting time on semaphores	4	The mean, the standard deviation, the minimum, and the maximum waiting time for a semaphore of DU's tasks
Holding time in critical sections	4	The mean, the standard deviation, the minimum, and the maximum holding time for a semaphore of DU's tasks
Task lifecycle	2	Binary features representing the occurrence of tasks newly allocated or deallocated, respectively
I/O Throughput	1	Binary feature (it is 1 if the throughput exceeded a bound, 0 otherwise)
Send/receive timeout on a socket	2*4*# Socket	The mean, the standard deviation, the minimum, and the maximum time since last packet sent over the socket to that node, both in input and in output

represent the symptoms that the engine has to classify. Examples of selected features are in Table 2.

The output of the classification process consists into the diagnosis label. The label uniquely identifies the *type* of occurred component failure, e.g., a hang that eventually causes a system failure, and the *location*, i.e., the software components in which the fault was activated.

A probabilistic SVM variant has been developed to provide also an estimation of the classification confidence. More details about the design and the implementation of the classifier are in [29]. The confidence C is a probability that measures the extent to which a set of observations, i.e., the collected features, belongs to a given class. As a matter of fact, the classifier output is an array of probabilities whose length is equal to the total number of classes that the engine has been trained to identify. A diagnosed fault consists into the label associated to the bigger confidence level of the array given in output by the classifier. When C is less or equal than a given threshold t, it means that the experienced failure does not match any of the failure behavior "learned" by the engine. For this reason, we also provided the *UNKNOWN* class. The engine gives the *UNKNOWN* output when a failure is diagnosed but it cannot identify the type and/or the location of the fault.

On the contrary, to reveal the occurrence of false alarms coming from OS-level monitors, the *NOFAULT* class has been introduced. When the classifier is confident that a given set of observations belongs to the *NOFAULT* class, the monitors that were responsible to trigger the alarm can be retrained. After the retraining procedure the probability that the indicators, which are related to the collected observations, will be considered normal behavior (and not erroneously anomalies) in future decisions is increased. It is noteworthy that the choice of threshold t impacts on the diagnosis performance. For this reason, the impact of this parameter on the diagnose performance has to be evaluated.

The overall monitoring and diagnosis infrastructure is depicted in Fig. 2.

4.3 Case Study

To evaluate the proposed monitoring and diagnosis infrastructure we have used a prototype from the Air Traffic Control (ATC). This case study consists of a complex distributed application for Flight Data Plan (FDP) processing. The system

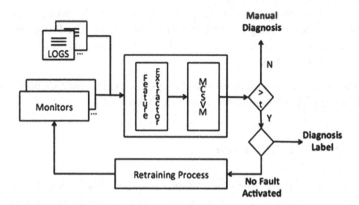

Fig. 2 The overall monitoring and diagnosis infrastructure

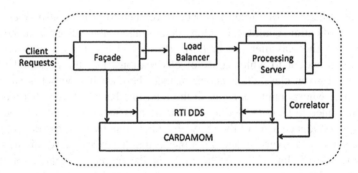

Fig. 3 The architecture of the prototype used in the case study

is in charge of processing flight plans and radar tracks by updating the contents of Flight Data Object and distributing them to controllers. A simplified overview of the architecture is depicted in Fig. 3.

The prototype was the result of the integration of Off-The-Shelf components and other software modules that were developed from scratch, among which:

- *CARDAMOM*, i.e., an open-source CORBA middleware used in mission and safety critical applications, which is compliant with OMG FT CORBA specifications (OMG 2001).
- the *RTI* middleware (http://www.rti.com) that implements the Data Distribution Service (DDS) standard for publish-subscribe communication.
- the *Facade* is the interface between the clients (e.g., the flight controller console) and the rest of the system. It provides a remote object API for the atomic operations such as addition, removal, and update of FDPs. This component is replicated according to the warm-passive replication schema.
- the *Correlator* component collects flight tracks generated by radars, and associates them to FDPs.
- the *Load Balancer* is in charge of routing the client requests to the proper server by means of a Round Robin policy.
- the *Processing Server* is in charge of processing FDPs by taking into account other information coming from Correlation component. The Processing Server is replicated on three different nodes, and operations are assigned to a server by means of the Load Balancer.

According to our assumptions and the system model some examples of the output of the diagnosis engine are shown in Table 3.

4.4 Performance Evaluation

The evaluation of the performance of the proposed monitoring and diagnosis infrastructure has been conducted by injecting different faults with respect to the ones used during the training phase. These new faults constitute the *test set*.

Table 3 Examples of the output of the diagnosis engine

Diagnosis label	Failure type	Location
0	None	–
1	Crash	Façade
2	Passive hang	Façade
3	Active hang	Façade
4	Crash	Server
5	Passive hang	Server
6	Active hang	Server
7	Crash	DDS
8	Passive hang	DDS
9	Active hang	DDS
10	Crash	CARDAMOM
11	Passive hang	CARDAMOM
12	Active hang	CARDAMOM
13	Crash	LOAD BALANCER
14	Passive hang	LOAD BALANCER
15	Active hang	LOAD BALANCER
16	Crash	Correlator
17	Passive hang	Correlator
18	Active hang	Correlator

It is noteworthy that the evaluation has been performed using different confidence thresholds t. In all the cases, the diagnoser has been able to identify the fault type. Moreover, the diagnoser has identified *false alarms* produced by the monitoring infrastructure, i.e., the detected anomalies that are not related to the activation of a fault.

The following metrics have been used to evaluate the classifier engine:

- *Precision* represents the conditional probability that, if a fault is classified as belonging to class A, the classification is correct. It can be expressed as $P = TP/(TP + FP)$.
- *Recall* represents the conditional probability that, if a fault belongs to class A, the classifier decides for A. $R = TP/(TP + FN)$.

Where TP are True Positives, i.e., the faults that are correctly classified; FP are the False Positives, i.e., normal events that are erroneously classified as faults; FN are the faults that are not correctly diagnosed.

We also evaluated the diagnosis *latency* and the *overhead*. The former accounts for the time between the activation of the injected fault and the diagnosis output. The latter represents the average percentage of the extra execution time required by the system to reply to a client request when the infrastructure is enabled.

Results with the respect to difference confidence thresholds are shown in Table 4. We can notice that a confidence level t = 0.995 or t = 0.999 provides good performance on both the training and the testing set.

Table 4 Precision and recall on the training set and testing set

	Training set		Testing set		Average	
t	P (%)	R (%)	P (%)	R (%)	P (%)	R (%)
0.9	59.1	100	100	5.2	80	53
0.99	70.2	100	100	42.1	85	71
0.995	73.5	96.1	90.9	52.6	82	74
0.999	80	76.9	70	73.6	75	75

Fig. 4 Cumulative number of false alarms while performing the retraining process

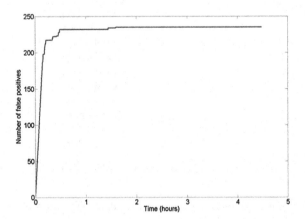

As for the diagnosis latency we measured the average mean times for detection and classification that are 84 and 917 ms, respectively. Hence, the average amount of time required to diagnose a fault, which is the sum of the time for detection and classification, is about 1 s. As for the overhead, the whole infrastructure impacts for about 10 %, in the worst case, on the considered testbed.

Finally, we also evaluated the retraining process of the anomaly-based detector. Figure 4 shows the cumulative number of false alarms (false positives) produced by the anomaly detection during about 5 h. The retraining process has been tuned to retrain the monitors each time an erroneous alarm is triggered.

5 Conclusions

Fault tolerant software systems need to be continuously monitored to effectively manage the system at runtime. This paper presents an overview of monitoring techniques that enable the diagnosis of complex systems and proposes an integrated framework to reveal and diagnose software faults by combining several information sources. Apart from the classical event logs, OS-level monitors provide data such as the system call errors, the bytes read (written) from (to) disk/network, the waiting time on semaphores, the holding time into critical sections.

This information is exploited to detect the activation of the fault and to perform the diagnosis.

We analyze the framework performance by means on an experimental campaign using a prototype from the Air Traffic Control domain. We inject several faults to evaluate the framework recall and precision and latency and its overhead. At the price of about 10 % overhead, in the worst case, the framework can reveal and correctly diagnose about 75 % of the injected faults with a precision of about 85 % in average, with a very low diagnosis latency of about 1 s.

References

1. IEC 61508: Functional safety of electrical/electronic/programmable electronic safety-related systems. In: 1st IEE Automotive Electronics Conference (2005)
2. RTCA SC-167, EUROCAE WG-12. Software considerations in airborne systems and equipment certification. DO-178B (1992)
3. Serafini, M., Bondavalli, A., Suri, N.: On-line diagnosis and recovery: on the choice and impact of tuning parameters. IEEE Trans. Dependable Secure Comput. 4(4), 295–312 (2007)
4. Bondavalli, A., Chiaradonna, S., Cotroneo, D., Romano, L.: Effective fault treatment for improving the dependability of COTS and legacy-based applications. IEEE Trans. Dependable Secure Comput. 1(4), 223–237 (2004)
5. Grottke, M., Trivedi, K.: Fighting bugs: remove, retry, replicate, and rejuvenate. Computer 40(2), 107–109 (2007)
6. Trivedi, K., Mansharamani, R., Kim, D.S., Grottke, M., Nambiar, M.: Recovery from failures due to Mandelbugs in IT Systems. In: 17th IEEE Pacific Rim International Symposium on Dependable Computing, pp. 224–233 (2011)
7. Avizienis, A., Laprie, J.C., Randell, B., Landwehr, C.: Basic concepts and taxonomy of dependable and secure computing. IEEE Trans. Dependable Secure Comput. 1(1), 11–13 (2004)
8. Gray, J.: Why do Computer Stop and What Can be About it? Büroautomation (1985)
9. Buckley, M.F., Siewiorek, D.P.: VAX/VMS event monitoring and analysis. In: Fault Tolerant Computer Systems (FTCS), pp. 414–423 (1995)
10. Simache, C., Kaaniche, M.: Availability assessment of sunOS/solaris unix systems based on syslogd and wtmpx log files: a case study. In: IEEE Pacific Rim International Symposium on Dependable Computing, pp. 49–56 (2005)
11. Kalyanakrishnam, M., Kalbarczyk, Z., Iyer, R.K.: Failure data analysis of a LAN of windows NT based computers. In: Proceedings of Symposium on Reliable and Distributed Systems (SRDS '99), pp. 178–187 (1999)
12. Carrozza, G., Cinque, M., Cotroneo, D., Natella, R.: Operating system support to detect application hangs. In: Proceedings of International Workshop on Verification and Evaluation of Computer and Communication Systems, pp. 117–127 (2008)
13. Bhatia, S., Kumar, A., Fiuczynski, M.E., Peterson, L.L.: Lightweight, high resolution monitoring for troubleshooting production systems. In: Proceedings of OSDI (2008)
14. Garlan, D., Cheng, D.S. W., Huang, A.C., Schmerl, B., Steenkistz, P.: Rainbow: architecture-based self-adaptation with reusable infrastructure. Computer 37(10), 46–54 (2004)
15. Bovenzi, A., Brancati, F., Russo, S., Bondavalli, A.: A statistical anomaly-based algorithm for on-line fault detection in complex software critical systems. In: Computer safety, reliability, and security, Lecture Notes in Computer Science, vol. 6894 (2011)
16. Agarwala, S., Schwan, K.: Sysprof: Online distributed behavior diagnosis through fine-grain system monitoring. In: Proceedings of ICDCS (2006)

17. Podgurski, A., Leon, D., Francis, P., Masri, W., Minch, M., Sun, J., Wang, B.: Automated support for classifying software failure reports. In: Proceedings of the 25th International Conference on Software Engineering, pp. 465–475 (2003)
18. Bovenzi, A., Carrozza, G., Cotroneo, D., Pietrantuono, R.: Error detection framework for complex software systems. In: Proceedings of the 13th European Workshop on Dependable Computing, pp. 61–66 (2011)
19. Wang, L., Kalbarczyk, Z., Weining, G., Iyer, R.K.: Reliability microkernel: providing application-aware reliability in the OS. IEEE Trans. Reliab. **56**(4), 597–614 (2007)
20. Khanna, G., Varadharajan, P., Bagchi, S.: Automated online monitoring of distributed applications through external monitors. IEEE Trans. Dependable Secure Comput. **3**(2), 115–129 (2006)
21. Kiciman, E., Fox, A.: Detecting application-level failures in component-based internet services. IEEE Trans. Neural Netw. **16**(5), 1027–1044 (2005)
22. Massie, M.L., Chun, B.N., Culler, D.E. The ganglia distributed monitoring system: design, implementation, and experience. Parallel Comput. **30**(7), 817–840 (2004)
23. Park, K., Pai, V.S.: CoMon: a mostly-scalable monitoring system for PlanetLab. SIGOPS OSR **40**(1), 75–88 (2006)
24. Lenglet, R., Coupaye, T., Bruneton, E.: Composing transformations of compiled Java programs with Jabyce. ComSIS **1**(2), 83–125 (2004)
25. Bovenzi, A., Brancati, F., Russo, S., Bondavalli, A.: Towards identifying OS-level anomalies to detect application software failures. In: Proceedings of IEEE International Workshop on Measurements and Networking, pp. 71–76 (2011)
26. Manevitz, L.M., Yousef, M.: One-class SVMs for document classification. J Mach. Learn. Res. **2**, 139–154 (2002)
27. Jagadeesh, R.P., Bose, C., Srinivasan, S.H.: Data mining approaches to software fault diagnosis. In: 15th International Workshop on Research Issues in Data Engineering: Stream Data Mining and Applications, pp. 45–52 (2005)
28. Vapnik, V.N.: The Nature of Statistical Learning Theory. Springer, New York (1995)
29. Carrozza., G., Natella, N.: A recovery-oriented approach for software fault diagnosis in complex critical systems. Int. J. Adapt. Resilient Autonomic Syst. (IJARAS) **2**(1), 77–104 (2011)
30. Natella, R., Cotroneo, D., Duraes, J., Madeira, H.: On fault representativeness of software fault injection. IEEE Trans. Softw. Eng. (TSE) (2011)

Log-Based Failure Analysis of Complex Systems: Methodology and Relevant Applications

Antonio Pecchia and Marcello Cinque

Abstract Failure analysis is valuable to dependability engineers because it supports designing effective mitigation means, defining strategies to reduce maintenance costs, and improving system service. Event logs, which contain textual information about regular and anomalous events detected by the system under real workload conditions, represent a key source of data to conduct failure analysis. So far, event logs have been successfully used in a variety of domains. This chapter describes methodology and well-established techniques underlying log-based failure analysis. Description introduces the workflow leading to analysis results starting from the raw data in the log. Moreover, the chapter surveys relevant works in the area with the aim of highlighting main objectives and applications of log-based failure analysis. Discussion reveals benefits and limitations of logs for evaluating complex systems.

Keywords Event logs · Filtering · Coalescence · Failure analysis · Dependability evaluation

A. Pecchia (✉) · M. Cinque
Dipartimento di Informatica e Sistemistica (DIS), Università degli Studi di Napoli Federico II, Via Claudio 21, 80125 Naples, Italy
e-mail: antonio.pecchia@unina.it

M. Cinque
e-mail: macinque@unina.it

D. Cotroneo (ed.), *Innovative Technologies for Dependable OTS-Based Critical Systems*,   203
DOI: 10.1007/978-88-470-2772-5_15, © Springer-Verlag Italia 2013

1 Introduction

Failure analysis consists in characterizing the dependability behavior of computer systems by observing *naturally* occurring failures under real workload conditions, i.e., failures not induced or forced by means of fault/error injection. This approach is recognized to be among the most accurate ways to evaluate dependability properties, and it is usually based on the analysis of failure data collected during system operations. **Event logs**, or simply *logs*, represent a key source of failure data [1, 2] because they store textual information about regular and anomalous events detected by a system during execution. Logs have been successfully used by industry and academia for failure analysis in a variety of application domains. A non-exhaustive list includes, for example, operating systems [3, 4], control systems and mobile devices [5, 6], supercomputers [7, 8], and large-scale applications [9, 10].

Accuracy of log-based failure analysis is affected by the ability of inferring meaningful information from available logs, which is a challenging task [11]. Logs usually report large volumes of data consisting of sequences of **text entries**, i.e., lines, produced by a variety of computing entities (e.g., operating system modules and daemons, middleware supports, application components). Figure 1 reports an example of entries taken from a real event log. Entries provide a *timestamp*, i.e., the time the event has been logged, and a text *message* describing the event. Entries may contain further data, such as the *source* (e.g., the generating process) and the *severity* (i.e., the criticality of the notification). Example shows that logs have a subjective [12] and unstructured [13] nature. Even of more relevance, logs contain many entries that are not useful for failure analysis, redundant notifications caused by error propagation phenomena [14]. Overall these issues make log analysis a hard process.

Log-based failure analysis usually encompasses three steps, i.e., *collection*, *manipulation*, and *analysis*. Each step is critical to the objective of obtaining accurate dependability characterization [15, 16]. Figure 2 shows the analysis process. Text entries in the logs are manipulated to infer failure data points, which are then analyzed to assess dependability properties of a given system.

This chapter describes well-established techniques supporting each of the mentioned steps, and it discusses main applications of log-based failure analysis (e.g., error/failure classification, evaluation of dependability attributes, failure

```
1  [May−12−2011  09:30:11]  get manager reference from local daemon
2  [May−12−2011  09:30:11]  supervision property change event notifier
3  [May−12−2011  09:30:12]  event notifier is running
4  ... omissis ...
5  [May−12−2011  09:35:22]  exception raised by process 'P1', PID 2264
6  [May−12−2011  09:35:23]  error: managed process 'P1', PID 2264 aborted
7  ... omissis ...
8  [May−12−2011  09:38:46]  created DS Sys_Converter
9  [May−12−2011  09:38:46]  created SystemAccessor
```

Fig. 1 Example of entries in the event log

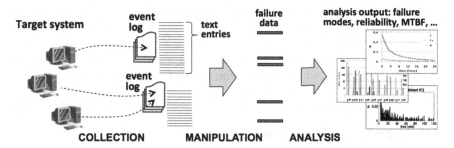

Fig. 2 Log-based failure analysis: overview

prediction) by surveying relevant works in the area. Discussion reveals benefits and potential of logs for the quantitative evaluation of complex systems. Moreover, it provides system engineers and dependability analysts with a concrete workflow to conduct log-based failure analysis campaigns.

The rest of the chapter is organized as follows. Section 2 describes main logging APIs and collection protocols. Section 3 presents manipulation strategies that are commonly adopted to infer the failure data from the log. Section 4 discusses analysis and relevant applications of event logs, whereas Sect. 5 concludes the work with final remarks and discussion of log analysis limitations.

2 Protocols and Tools to Collect Logs

System components usually adopt a logging API to produce text entries, such as the ones reported in Fig. 1. Entries are either stored in a file available at the node hosting the component, or forwarded to a remote location to ease centralization of logs. A variety of logging protocols and supports have been developed to ease collection. Main efforts are described in the following.

UNIX syslog [17] defines a log format and collection protocol that has become a *de facto* standard over the years. A syslog entry is characterized by *severity* and *facility* (i.e., the indication of the source of the event, such as kernel or the security subsystem.) that can be combined to define the priority of the message. Severity varies in the interval $\{0, ..., 7\}$, with 0 representing an *emergency*-level entry, down to 7, reporting a *debug* entry. **Microsoft Event Log** protocol is another example of log-collection system [18]. Each Windows machine runs an Event Log provider that is accessible by means of system calls. Once an entry is logged, it can be stored in a log file and forwarded to a remote machine. Another popular framework is Apache Software Foundation's **log4x** [19]. The framework is available for C++, PHP, Java and .NET applications, and it can be configured in terms of syntax of log messages, e.g., to support automatic parsing of the entries, and destination.

A variety of ad-hoc logging and monitoring subsystems have been developed to supplement described frameworks. For example, Analyze NOW [20] consists of a set of tools to support log-based failure analysis of networks of workstations, whose monitoring is challenging because of the frequent addition and removal of components. Authors in [21] discuss the design of a logger application to collect failure data of mobile phones. Another proposal is IBM Common Event Infrastructure [22], introduced to save the time needed for root cause analysis.

3 Manipulation Techniques

A crucial step for each log-based measurement study is inferring the failure data from collected logs. Manipulation allows (i) *filtering* non useful entries from the log, and, even more important, (ii) *coalescing*, i.e., grouping, entries that are related to the same failure manifestation.

3.1 Filtering

Logs report many non-error entries (such as lines 1, 2 in Fig. 1) that can be excluded from the log before the analysis [14]. Several techniques are adopted to identify and remove non useful entries. For example, analysts might select entries of interest based on the *severity* field or focus on the entries containing error-specific keywords (e.g., pinpointed by means of regular expressions [23]). At a finer grain, filtering can be conducted with **de-parameterization**, which allows replacing variable fields in the text entries (e.g., usernames, IP and memory addresses, folders) with generic tokens. For example, the entries "new con-nection from 192.168.0.184" and "new connection from 221.145.31.27" would appear the same once the IP addresses are replaced with a generic "IP-ADDR" token. De-parameterization significantly reduces the number of distinct messages to scrutinize with the aim of identifying entries of interest. For examples, authors in [8] show that around 200 million entries in the log of a supercomputing system were generated by only 1,124 distinct messages. De-parameterization can be supplemented by statistical approaches to faster the identification of the subset of entries that are useful to the analysis. Authors in [13] apply the Leveinshtein distance to cluster similar log messages. The work [24] presents a clustering algorithm and a tool for mining line patterns from the log.

3.2 Coalescence

In practice, faults generate multiple errors (because of error propagation phenomena and the workload, which may trigger the same fault many times) and, consequently, multiple notifications in the log [14]. Entries representing the

```
1  1167657137 n−238 +START HARDWARE ERROR STATE AT CPE
2  1167657137 n−238 +END HARDWARE ERROR STATE AT CPE
3  1167657137 n−238 +PCI Component Error Info Section
4  1167657140 n−238 +START HARDWARE ERROR STATE AT CPE
5  +214 omitted entries
```

Fig. 3 Example of failure notification in the log

manifestation of the same problem have to be **coalesced** into the same failure point. Example reported in Fig. 3 shows that a single PCI card failure in a supercomputer log produced 218 entries. Coalescing related error entries is crucial to obtain realistic measurements [15, 16]. One of the most adopted coalescence strategies is the **tuple heuristic**. The intuition underlying the approach is that two entries in the log, if related to the same fault activation, are likely to occur close in time. Consequently, if the time distance of the entries is smaller than a predetermined threshold, i.e., the *coalescence window* (W), they are placed in the same group (called *tuple*). Figure 4a clarifies the concept. The value of the coalescence window is critical, because the number of tuples provides an approximation of the actual number of failures occurred at runtime. When W is too small, the risk is to put entries related to same problem into different tuples (truncation); viceversa, if W is too large, entries related to different problem might be placed in the same tuple (collision). A sensitivity analysis is conducted to investigate how the number of tuples (tuple count) varies when W varies. Figure 4b reports a generic plot to clarifying the output of such an analysis. Experimental studies assume that a good choice for the coalescence window is the value right after the "knee" of the curve, where the tuple count sharply flattens [14].

Several techniques have been proposed to improve the results of the tuple heuristic, i.e., to reduce the number of accidental collisions and truncations. For instance, in [25] two coalescence windows are adopted to improve grouping. A recent solution adopts spherical covariance estimates for the grouping of events in coalitions of clusters [26]. According to this scheme, two events of the same type are grouped if they fall within the typical *time to recover*. A different methodological improvement of the tuple heuristic is represented by the concept of *spatial coalescence* [2, 7]: errors can propagate among the nodes of the system, and

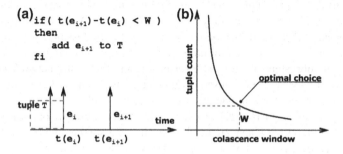

Fig. 4 Tuple heuristic: grouping condition (**a**); sensitivity analysis (**b**)

notifications related to the same fault manifestation might be spatially distributed as a result. Authors in [8] combine the temporal information of the entries with a statistical indicator to identify independent errors that occur close in time, reducing the incidence of accidental collisions. A rather different approach is *content-based coalescence*: in this case, events in the log are grouped based on the content of the text entries. For example, authors in [4] use a `perl` algorithm to identify OS reboots based on the sequential parsing of the log.

4 Analysis and Relevant Applications

The analysis of manipulated failure data pursues a variety of objectives, ranging from error/failure classification to dependability modeling and assessment. Despite analysis usually relies on ad-hoc algorithms and techniques, several **software packages** have been made available by academia to supplement analysis. For example, MEADEP [27] implements an analyzer module for graphical data-presentation and parameter estimation along with a modeling interface for building block diagrams and Markov reward chains. Analyze NOW [20] provides a monitor of the state of the machines belonging to the network, and dependency-table generator to pinpoint correlated failures among machines. In [23] it is presented the Simple Event Correlator (SEC), i.e., a tool for on-line log analysis based on rules to model and to correlate log events at runtime. In the following we discuss relevant applications and reference works in the area of log-based failure analysis. Works are grouped based on the main **analysis objectives** they aim to pursue.

4.1 Error and Failure Classification

Classifying error and failures modes based on the collected data is a primary analysis task. For examples, classification allows determining the predominant failure classes, pinpointing failure-prone components, and assessing improvements between subsequent releases of the same product. Overall this information is valuable to drive quantitative evaluation and to supplement measurements.

Authors in [28] present a study of a UNIX system. Analysis is based on an event log spanning around 11 months. Data in the log is classified and categorized to identify error trends preceding failures. For example, the study shows that the input-output subsystem is the most error-prone, and that many network problems observed in the log were not caused by the system under study. The cause of some failures, i.e., around 9 %, remained unknown in the study.

The study proposed by [29] provides a characterization of operating system reboots of Windows NT and 2K machines. The data source adopted in the study was collected over a period of 36 months. The study focuses on unplanned reboots, representing the occurrence of a failure. The classification of identified reboots demonstrates that the number of failures caused by the operating system itself is smaller in Windows 2K when compared to NT machines; however, the number of failures caused by application code is larger in Windows 2K. This result is justified by the introduction of kernel memory isolation in Windows 2K, improving the robustness of the kernel. A similar classification study is conducted in [30], which analyzes crash and usage data from Windows XP SP1 machines. The study confirms that many failures observed during operations are not caused by the operating system itself, but by applications and third-party components. According to the data, web browsers are the most failure-prone application. Authors conduct a detailed classification to pinpoint .dll and executable files causing crashes.

Authors in [31] face a rather different application domain. In particular, they analyze failure data collected from Online, Content, and ReadMostly, i.e., three large-scale Internet services. Results indicate that operator errors and network-related problems are the major failure contributors. Furthermore, authors show that the percentage of failures caused by the software running in the front-end nodes is significant.

4.2 Evaluation and Modeling of Dependability Attributes

Adoption of statistical distributions. Measurement works usually aim at determining the statistical distribution of the *time to failure* variable. This allows refining the failure model of a given system and understanding the failure phenomenology. To this aim, failure points and related timestamps are fitted with continuous time distributions.

For instance, authors in [32] model the *time to failure* by adopting a hyper-exponential distribution, i.e., $\sum_{i=1}^{N} \lambda_i e^{-\lambda_i t} p_i$. This distribution is used to model failures that represent the manifestation of independent and alternate underlying causes. Distribution used in the study allowed inferring the existence of two separate recovery paths selected in a fixed ratio, resulting from two different classes of software failures.

Another relevant distribution is the lognormal. In [33] the author hypothesizes that the failure rate of a complex system can be tough as a multiplicative process of independent factors, e.g., activations of faults. The lognormal distribution can be used when the value of a variable can be determined by the multiplication of many random factors: for this reason, it is adopted to model software failure rates. The lognormal distribution has been also used in the context of high-performance computing systems [10].

The Weibull distribution, i.e., $e^{-(\lambda t)^{\alpha}}$ [34], is the most adopted to model the failure data. The value of the shape parameter α allows modeling decreasing ($\alpha < 1$), increasing ($\alpha > 1$), and constant ($\alpha = 1$), failure distribution rates. For this reason, Weibull distributions have been used in many application domains, e.g., [12, 32, 34].

Modeling approaches. Failure data can be used to develop dependability models. Examples are discussed in the following. Authors in [35] address the analysis of the MVS operating system by developing a semi-markov model based on both the regular and error behavior. Analysis of the failure distribution highlighted a significant incidence of software-induced failures, i.e., 36 %. Other relevant causes of failures were CPU, memory and I/O errors.

In [12] authors use log data to propose a finite state machine to model the error behavior and the availability of a LAN of Windows NT machines. The adoption of the model showed that, even if the measured system availability was around 99 %, the user-perceived availability was significantly smaller, i.e., 92 %: in some cases, even if a machine of the LAN was up, it was not able to provide correct service to the user.

Analysis of the data in the log is also valuable to validate assumptions made in system models. Authors in [36] analyze the data collected from five VAXcluster systems to validate availability Markov models previously derived for those machines. Surprisingly, the analysis revealed that some modeling assumptions were not supported by the real data. For example, the model did not take into account dependent failure behaviors across the devices of the system; furthermore, data demonstrated that failures were non-exponentially distributed, as opposite to the model assumption.

4.3 Diagnosis and Correlation of Failures

Several studies demonstrated that log-based analysis allows understanding causes and correlation phenomena of system failures. Works in the area, dating back to the 1980s, prove the existence of a relationship between the failure behavior and the **workload** run by a system. A performance study of a DEC system conducted in [37, 38], showed that the failure rate is not constant; nevertheless, many models adopted at that time relied on such an assumption. A doubly stochastic Poisson model was developed to highlight the relationship between the instantaneous failure rate of a resource and its usage. A similar finding has been confirmed by authors in [39], by evaluating the relationship between system load and failures by means of empirical data.

Several works suggest that failures observed in different system components are correlated. For example, [40] applies factor and cluster analysis to pinpoint halts dependencies among components and halt patterns from the log. Although the number of errors observed during the system operations was relatively small, authors demonstrated that multiple processes were affected by the same problem, because of the presence of shared resources.

Authors in [41] perform a measurement study to assess the dependability of seven DEC VAX machines. Analysis aimed to estimate the distributions of the Time Between Errors and Time Between Failures and to analyze dependencies between errors and failures. Again, shared resources turned out to be a relevant dependability bottleneck. Evaluation proposed by [42] uses statistical techniques to quantify the strength of the relationship among entries in the log. The approach aimed to discriminate transient, permanent and intermittent failure manifestations by assessing the correlation between failure events.

4.4 Failure Prediction

Failure prediction has gained increasing popularity over the years. Predicting failures based on patterns observed in the log is challenging; however, it is valuable to apply failure avoidance strategies, to trigger corrective and recovery actions, and to improve system dependability.

Authors in [34] present the Dispersion Frame Technique (DFT), implemented as part of a distributed on-line monitoring system. They analyzed the data collected from 13 file servers running the VICE file system over a 22-month period. The principle underlying the technique is recognizing recurring error trends leading to failures. DFT achieved 93.7 % success rate in failure prediction by using a smaller number of data points.

The approach proposed by [43] focuses on the use of event-driven data sources, such as error notifications in the log, to develop prediction models. In particular, authors develop a Hidden Semi-Markov Models (HSMMs) and validate the effectiveness of such models by analyzing the field data produced by a telecommunication system. For example, the proposed model achieves precision of 0.85 and recall of 0.66 that, according to the data available in the study, was a better result when compared to other prediction techniques.

Authors in [44] analyze event logs from a 350-node cluster system. Logs encompass reliability, availability and serviceability (RAS) events, and system activity reports collected over one year. Authors observed that data in the log were highly redundant: for this reason, they apply filtering techniques to model the data into a set of primary and derived variables. The prediction approach, based on a classification algorithm, was able to identify the occurrence of critical events with up to 70 % accuracy.

Prediction methods have been proposed for IBM BlueGene/L [7]. The approach proposed in the paper was able to predict around 80 % of memory and network failures and 47 % of I/O failures.

4.5 Further Applications

Event logs collected during the progression of malicious activities and security attacks have been recently used to perform **security analysis**. Data are collected either with *honeypots* (i.e., monitored computer environments placed on the Internet with the deliberate purpose of being attacked) or during naturally-occurring incidents. Authors in [45] use honeypots to validate vulnerability assumptions adopted in the design of intrusion-tolerant systems. The work [46] investigate the features that support recognizing ongoing attacks. Authors in [47] use real attack data to understand progression of attacks. The work [48] uses real incident data to design an automated approach for detecting attacks.

Authors in [49] characterize the dependability of 13 mobile robots based on the analysis of the failure data collected during 673 h of operations. Another interesting application is the one proposed [5], where authors analyze the data of around 11 years experience on safety critical software for nuclear reactors. The Java Virtual Machine has been recently analyzed by means of failure data [50]. The work [6, 51] analyze the failure data of Bluetooth Personal Area networks.

5 Conclusions and Final Remarks

Log-based failure analysis is a powerful methodology to evaluate operational systems. The variety of concrete applications discussed in this chapter shows that logs are extremely valuable to dependability engineers. Notwithstanding its practical usefulness, it must be noted that analysis is limited to manifested failures, that is, the ones reported by the log. Several types of failures, such as application crash or hangs, can escape logging mechanisms and go unreported [52]. Further research is needed to devise novel logging strategies dealing with above types of failures and to avoid missing failure data in the logs [53].

Furthermore, the specific conditions under which the system is observed can vary from an installation to another. Doubts can be raised on the validity of obtained results across different installations of the same system. Log-based failure analysis is particularly useful for stable installations, such as critical embedded systems, signal processing equipments, long running server systems. In these systems, dependability needs to be analyzed in order to be continuously improved. On this last point, it is worth noting that log analysis is partially beneficial to current system installations, while it provides crucial guidelines to improve successive releases.

References

1. Iyer, R.K., Kalbarczyk, Z., Kalyanakrishnan, M.: Measurement-based analysis of networked system availability. In: Haring, G., et al. (eds.) Performance Evaluation: Origins and Directions. Springer, Berlin (2000)
2. Oliner, A.J., Stearley, J.: What supercomputers say: a study of five system logs. In: Proceedings of the International Conference on Dependable Systems and Networks, IEEE Computer Society (DSN) (2007)
3. Murphy, B., Levidow, B.: Windows 2000 dependability. MSR-TR-2000-56 Technical Report, Redmond, WA (2000)

4. Simache, C., Kaâniche, M.: Availability assessment of sunOS/solaris unix systems based on syslogd and wtmpx log files: a case study. In: Pacific Rim International Symposium on Dependable Computing (PRDC), IEEE Computer Society (2005)
5. Laplace, J., Brun, M.: Critical software for nuclear reactors: 11 years of field experience analysis. In: Proceedings of the International Symposium on Software Reliability Engineering (ISSRE), IEEE Computer Society (1999)
6. Cinque, M., Cotroneo, D., Russo, S.: Collecting and analyzing failure data of bluetooth personal area networks. In: Proceedings of the International Conference on Dependable Systems and Networks (DSN), IEEE Computer Society (2006)
7. Liang, Y., Zhang, Y., Sivasubramaniam, A., Jette, M., Sahoo, R.K.: BlueGene/L failure analysis and prediction models. In: Proceedings of the International Conference on Dependable Systems and Networks (DSN), IEEE Computer Society (2006)
8. Pecchia, A., Cotroneo, D., Kalbarczyk, Z., Iyer, R.K.: Improving log-based field failure data analysis of multi-node computing systems. In: Proceedings of the International Conference on Dependable Systems and Networks (DSN), IEEE Computer Society (2011)
9. Oppenheimer, D.L., Ganapathi, A., Patterson, D.A.: Why do internet services fail, and what can be done about it? In: USENIX Symposium on Internet Technologies and Systems (2003)
10. Schroeder, B., Gibson, G.A.: A large-scale study of failures in high-performance computing systems. In: Proceedings of the International Conference on Dependable Systems and Networks (DSN), IEEE Computer Society (2006)
11. Chillarege, R., Biyani, S., Rosenthal, J.: Measurement of failure rate in widely distributed software. In: Proceedings of the International Symposium on Fault-Tolerant Computing (FTCS), IEEE Computer Society (1995)
12. Kalyanakrishnam, M., Kalbarczyk, Z., Iyer, R.K.: Failure data analysis of a LAN of windows NT based computers. In: Proceedings of the International Symposium on Reliable Distributed Systems (SRDS), IEEE Computer Society (1999)
13. Lim, C., Singh, N., Yajnik, S.: A log mining approach to failure analysis of enterprise telephony systems. In: Proceedings of the International Conference on Dependable Systems and Networks (DSN), IEEE Computer Society (2008)
14. Hansen, J.P., Siewiorek, D.P.: Models for time coalescence in event logs. In: Proceedings of the International Symposium on Fault-Tolerant Computing (FTCS), IEEE Computer Society (1992)
15. Iyer, R.K., Young, L.T., Sridhar, V.: Recognition of error symptoms in large systems. In: Proceedings of 1986 ACM Fall Joint Computer Conference. ACM '86 (1986)
16. Buckley, M., Siewiorek, D.: A comparative analysis of event tupling schemes. In: Proceedings of the International Symposium on Fault-Tolerant Computing (FTCS) IEEE Computer Society (1996)
17. Lonvick, C.: The BSD Syslog Protocol. Request for Comments 3164, The Internet Society, Network Working Group, RFC3164 (2001)
18. Microsoft: Windows Event Log. http://msdn.microsoft.com/en-us/library/aa385780 (v=VS.85).aspx
19. Apache: Software Foundation, Logging Services. http://logging.apache.org/
20. Thakur, A., Iyer, R.K.: Analyze-NOW—an environment for collection and analysis of failures in a networked of workstations. IEEE Trans. Reliab. **4**, 561–570 (1996)
21. Ascione, P., Cinque, M., Cotroneo, D.: Automated logging of mobile phones failures data. International Symposium on Object-Oriented Real-Time, Distributed Computing (ISORC) (2006)
22. IBM: Common Event Infrastructure. http://www-01.ibm.com/software/tivoli/features/cei
23. Vaarandi, R.: SEC—a lightweight event correlation tool. In: Proceedings of 2002 IEEE Workshop on IP Operations and Management (IPOM) (2002)
24. Vaarandi, R.: A data clustering algorithm for mining patterns from event logs. In: Proceedings of 2003 IEEE Workshop on IP Operations and Management (IPOM) (2003)
25. Tsao, M.M., Siewiorek, D.P.: Trend analysis on system error files. In: Thirteenth Annual International Symposium on Fault-Tolerant Computing (1983)

26. Fu, S., Xu, C.: Exploring event correlation for failure prediction in coalitions of clusters. In: Proceedings of the 2007 ACM/IEEE conference on Supercomputing. SC '07 (2007)
27. Tang, D., Hecht, M., Miller, M., Handal, J.: MEADEP: A dependability evaluation tool for engineers. IEEE Trans. Reliab. (1998)
28. Lal, R., Choi, G.: Error and failure analysis of a UNIX server. In: IEEE International Symposium on High-Assurance Systems Engineering (1998)
29. Simache, C., Kaaniche, M., Saidane, A.: Event log based dependability analysis of windows NT and 2K systems. In: Pacific Rim International Symposium on Dependable Computing (PRDC), IEEE Computer Society(2002)
30. Ganapathi, A., Patterson, D.A.: Crash data collection: a windows case study. In: Proceedings of the International Conference on Dependable Systems and Networks (DSN), IEEE Computer Society (2005)
31. Oppenheimer, D., Patterson, D.A.: Studying and using failure data from large-scale internet services. In: Proceedings of the 10th Workshop on ACM SIGOPS European Workshop (2002)
32. Matz, S., Votta, L., Makawi, M.: Analysis of failure recovery rates in a wireless telecommunication system. In: Proceedings of the International Conference on Dependable Systems and Networks (DSN), IEEE Computer Society (2002)
33. Mullen, R.: The lognormal distribution of software failure rates: origin and evidence. In: Proceedings of the International Symposium on Software Reliability Engineering (ISSRE), IEEE Computer Society (1998)
34. Lin, T.T., Siewiorek, D.: Error log analysis: statistical modeling and heuristic trend analysis. IEEE Trans. Reliab. 39, 238–249 (1990)
35. Hsueh, M.C., Iyer, R.K., Trivedi, K.S.: Performance modeling based on real data: a case study. IEEE Trans. Comput. c-37, 478–484 (1988)
36. Wein, A., Sathaye, A.: Validating complex computer system availability models. IEEE Trans. Reliab. 39(4), 468–479 (1990)
37. Castillo, X., Siewiorek, D.: A performance-reliability model for computing systems. In: Proceeding of the International Symposium on Fault-Tolerant Computing (FTCS), IEEE Computer Society (1980)
38. Castillo, X., Siewiorek, D.: Workload, performance, and reliability of digital computing systems. In: Proceedings of the International Symposium on Fault-Tolerant Computing (FTCS), IEEE Computer Society (1981)
39. Iyer, R.K., Rossetti, D.J., Hsueh, M.C.: Measurement and modeling of computer reliability as affected by system activity. ACM Trans. Comput. Syst. 4, 187–213 (1986)
40. Lee, I., Iyer, R., Tang, D.: Error/failure analysis using event logs from fault tolerant systems. In: Proceedings of the International Symposium on Fault-Tolerant Computing (FTCS), IEEE Computer Society (1991)
41. D., T., Iyer, R.K.: Dependability measurement and modeling of a multicomputer system. IEEE Trans. Comput. 42(1), 62–75 (1993)
42. Iyer, R., Young, L., Iyer, P.: Automatic recognition of intermittent failures: an experimental study of field data. IEEE Trans. Comput. 39(4), 525–537 (1990)
43. Salfner, F., Malek, M.: Using hidden semi-markov models for effective online failure prediction. In: Proceedings of the International Symposium on Reliable Distributed Systems (SRDS), IEEE Computer Society (2007)
44. Sahoo, R.K., Oliner, A.J., Rish, I., Gupta, M., Moreira, J.E., Ma, S., Vilalta, R., Sivasubramaniam, A.: Critical event prediction for proactive management in large-scale computer clusters. In: Proceedings of the International Conference on Knowledge Discovery and Data Mining (2003)
45. Dacier, M., Pouget, F., Debar, H.: Honeypots: practical means to validate malicious fault assumptions. In: Pacific Rim International Symposium on Dependable Computing (PRDC), IEEE Computer Society (2004)

46. Cukier, M., Berthier, R., Panjwani, S., Tan, S.: A statistical analysis of attack data to separate attacks. In: Proceedings of International Conference on Dependable Systems and Networks (DSN), IEEE Computer Society (2006)
47. Sharma, A., Kalbarczyk, Z., Barlow, J., Iyer, R.: Analysis of security data from a large-scale organization. In: Proceedings of the International Conference on Dependable Systems and Networks (DSN), IEEE Computer Society (2011)
48. Pecchia, A., Sharma, A., Kalbarczyk, Z., Cotroneo, D., Iyer, R.K.: Identifying compromised users in shared computing infrastructures: a data-driven bayesian network approach. In: Proceedings of International Symposium on Reliable Distributed Systems (SRDS), IEEE Computer Society (2011)
49. Carlson, J., Murphy, R.: Reliability analysis of mobile robots. In: Proceedings of IEEE International Conference on Robotics and Automation (ICRA) (2003)
50. Cotroneo, D., Orlando, S., Russo, S.: Failure classification and analysis of the java virtual machine. In: Proceedings of 26th International Conference on Distributed Computing Systems (ICDCS) (2006)
51. Carrozza, G., Cinque, M., Cotroneo, D., Russo, S.: Dependability evaluation and modeling of the bluetooth data communication channel. In: Proceedings of the 16th Euromicro Conference on Parallel, Distributed and Network-Based Processing (PDP) (2008)
52. Cinque, M., Cotroneo, D., Natella, R., Pecchia, A.: Assessing and improving the effectiveness of logs for the analysis of software faults. In: Proceedings of the International Conference on Dependable Systems and Networks (DSN), IEEE Computer Society (2010)
53. Cinque, M., Cotroneo, D., Pecchia, A.: A logging approach for effective dependability evaluation of complex systems. In: Proceedings of the International Conference on Dependability (DEPEND), IEEE Computer Society (2009)